I0800469

Postcard History Series

Kendallville & Noble County

in Vintage Postcards

POSTCARD HISTORY SERIES

Kendallville & Noble County

IN VINTAGE POSTCARDS

John Martin Smith

ARCADIA PUBLISHING

ISBN 978-0-7385-1920-3

Published by Arcadia Publishing
Charleston, South Carolina

Printed in the United States of America

Library of Congress Catalog Card Number: 2001093321

For all general information contact Arcadia Publishing at:
Telephone 843-853-2070
Fax 843-853-0044
E-mail sales@arcadiapublishing.com
For customer service and orders:
Toll-Free 1-888-313-2665

Visit us on the Internet at www.arcadiapublishing.com

Contents

ACKNOWLEDGMENTS

The author is indebted to several people who have contributed to

this production of this book:

My wife, Barbara Clark Smith, has participated in the collection of these postcards for nearly 40 years. I thank her for her patient search through thousands of postcards at antique shows and antique malls to find those relevant to Northeastern Indiana.

My son and lawyer partner, Thompson Smith, has made law office facilities available to assist in the production of this book. His paralegal, Tricia Hertsel, has done the computer input and organization. My secretary of 32 years, Sharon George, has also assisted.

Arcadia editor, Ann Fugman, has been of great assistance in getting the book into print in accordance with the high standards of Arcadia. The quiet behind-the-scenes efforts of a good editor always makes an author look good!

Lastly, I am indebted to those photographers and merchants who had the foresight and vision to create and distribute the original postcards. While postcards have a fleeting, ephemeral quality to them, those "packrats" who have collected and saved them have provided us a legacy of our towns that would have otherwise been lost after the click of the camera and the thunk of the postmark!

John Martin Smith

Introduction

After my grandfather died in 1961, we found a box of old postcards which were exchanged between my grandmother, Viola Smith, and her sister, Iona. They both lived in Butler, Indiana, but several blocks apart. I arranged them in chronological order and scanned the messages. Some were post marked the same day.

With a little research and questions to my father, Walter M. Smith, who served as postmaster in Butler from 1950 to 1976, I found that beginning in 1907, there was mail delivery twice each day in the town. Therefore, the sisters could exchange messages the same day—i.e. "Can you and Carl come for supper at 6PM? Iona" "Yes, I will bring an apple pie, Viola"

Some of the cards had floral and holiday scenes on the front and others had real photographs of buildings located in Butler. Postage was 1¢. I later sorted out the scenes of buildings and started looking for others. At antique shops, flea markets, antique malls, and auctions I found more postcards from Butler. This search then expanded to all of Northeastern Indiana. Over a period of about 30 years, I have accumulated hundreds of postcards. One of the best sources now is ebay on the Internet. Since most of the postcards were sent away from their place of origin, many are listed for sale from places far from Northeast Indiana. This source has enabled me to augment the collection presented here.

The history of the use of postcards centers around United States Postal Laws and Regulations. The printed format of postcards also enables one to generally date postcards. The sequence is as follows:

1893–1898 Pioneer Cards

These cards are quite rare and are sometimes labeled as "Souvenir Postcards."

1898–1901 Private Mailing Cards

These cards are labeled "Private Mailing Card" on the address side and usually also state "Authorized by Act of Congress of May 19, 1898."

1901–1907 Undivided Backs

Postal regulations did not permit a message on the back—just the address. This was also true of the Pioneer and Private Mailing Cards.

1907–1915 Divided Backs

On March 1, 1907, the United States Postal Service approved the divided back card which permitted the address on the right side and a message on the left side of the back. This change made the use of postcards much more prevalent as a means of communication.

1915–1930s White Borders

A change in printing techniques resulted in a printed image with a narrow white border.

1935–1955 Linens

These cards were printed on cardboard stock with a "linen" like surface. The publisher started with a photograph but modified it to make an idyllic image that was also colorized.

1945–Present Chromes

These cards are printed in color on a slick stock.

The foregoing date categories overlap considerably. Sometimes the same basic photographs were used for several postcard versions. Pre-linen cards were frequently colorized in various ways. For example, a black and white image would be overprinted with a brick color on a brick building. The Auburn Postcard Company was known for its "Blue Sky" cards which were a black and white image with the sky overprinted in light blue.

From about 1900–1915, many cards were "Real Photo" cards. That term is used to describe a photograph printed by the photographer directly onto postcard stock. Sometimes only a single postcard was made. Usually, the number of cards printed was limited. Real photo cards are sought by collectors due to their relative rarity and sharp, clear image. Real photo cards were also issued in the 1940s and 1950s. A real photo card and a printed card can be distinguished quite easily by magnifying the image—a printed card will have a pattern of small dots to create the contrast, whereas a real photo card will have a solid image.

The bulk of the images in this book date from 1910-1915, which was the golden era of postcard production. It is likely that the local use of postcards waned after the telephone came into general use. As automobile travel increased, postcards were used by tourists to send a photograph and message back home. Many persons also collected postcards which led to friends and relatives sending them postcards for their collection.

There were several local postcard companies in Bryan, Ohio; Fort Wayne, Indiana; and Auburn, Indiana. The Auburn Postcard Company was a major international publisher of postcards. The Whitten-Dennison Post Card Company moved to Auburn from Maine in 1910. They built a small factory on East Seventh Street adjacent to Cedar Creek which employed five women. The name of the company was changed to Auburn Post Card Manufacturing Company in 1913, and to Auburn Greeting Card Company in 1929. In 1933, D.E. Messenger acquired the company and changed the name to Messenger Corporation, which is still in operation at 318 E. Seventh Street and is a major printer of religious calendars and printed materials for the funeral home industry.

How were the subjects of postcards chosen? Generally, they were chosen by local merchants on the basis of what would sell in their drugstore, restaurant, or bookstore. In some cases the scenes selected were designed to show off the town. The most common are scenes of the courthouses and principle streets. They were ordered in quantities of 500-1,000, so the merchant wanted to make sure that they would sell.

The images selected for this book are designed to present a representative selection of images for Steuben County. The space and format of the book did not permit the use of all cards in our collection for this county. In some cases, the messages on the back are as interesting as the image on the front. I have incorporated some of these in my interpretations. The bold type in my captions repeats the caption of the card. If the date is not contained in the caption and the card is postmarked, the postmarked date is stated "*c.* 19—." If the card is not postmarked, or if the postmark is not readable, no date is stated. I then supplement the caption with other information when appropriate. Some images simply speak for themselves, so I refrain from any further comment.

While not originally intended to document a town or place historically, I find that they are a great source of local history and images that is otherwise unavailable. As persons restore buildings to their original design, a postcard may be the only source of a period image of that particular building.

I sincerely hope that my readers enjoy and use the image and captions contained herein to appreciate their heritage and sense of place.

John Martin Smith

One

Kendallville

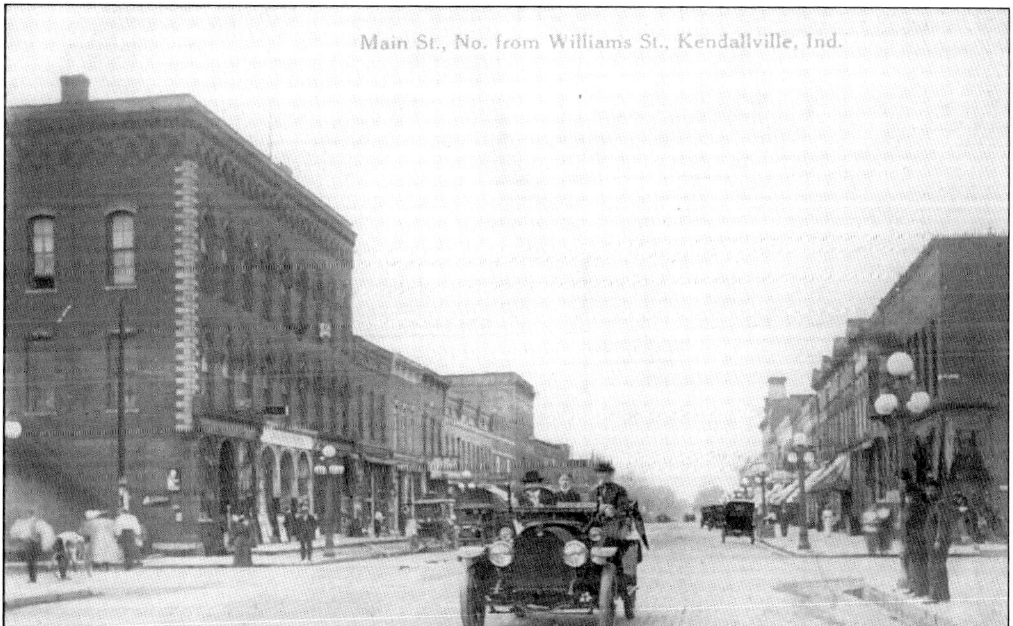

Main Street, North from Williams Street, Kendallville, Indiana, *c*. 1920. Traffic was light in this era.

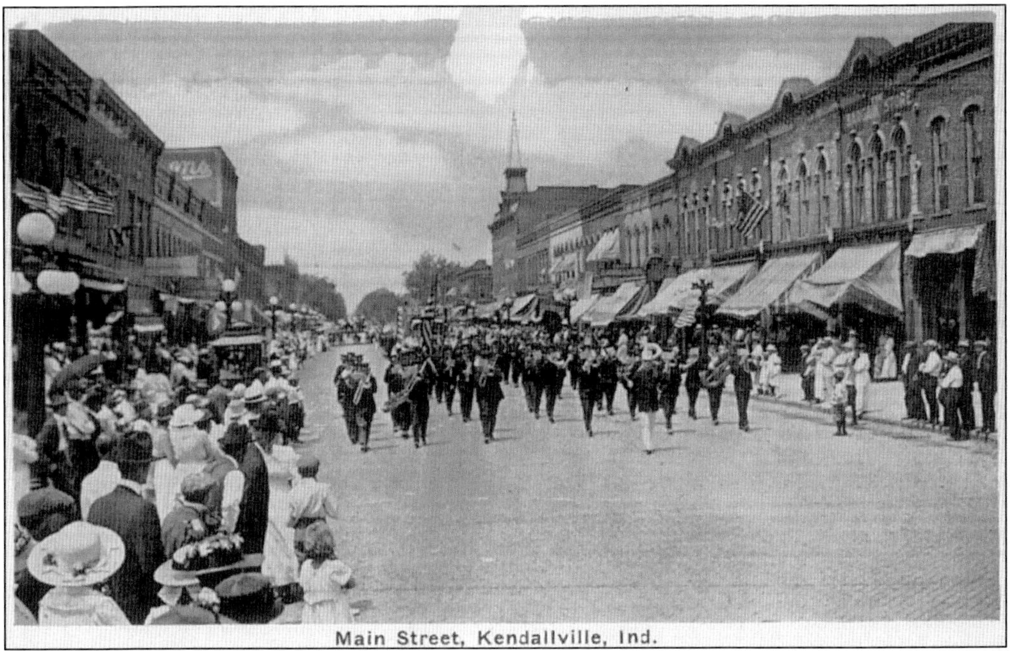

Main Street, Kendallville, Indiana. A parade has always drawn a crowd.

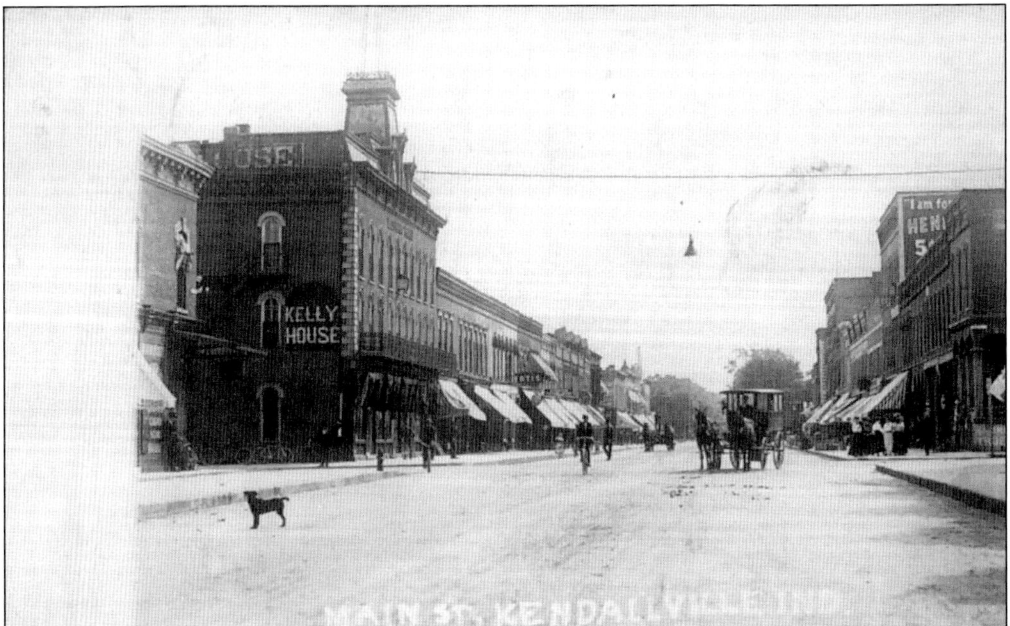

Main Street, Kendallville, Indiana. Kelly House Hotel is on the left.

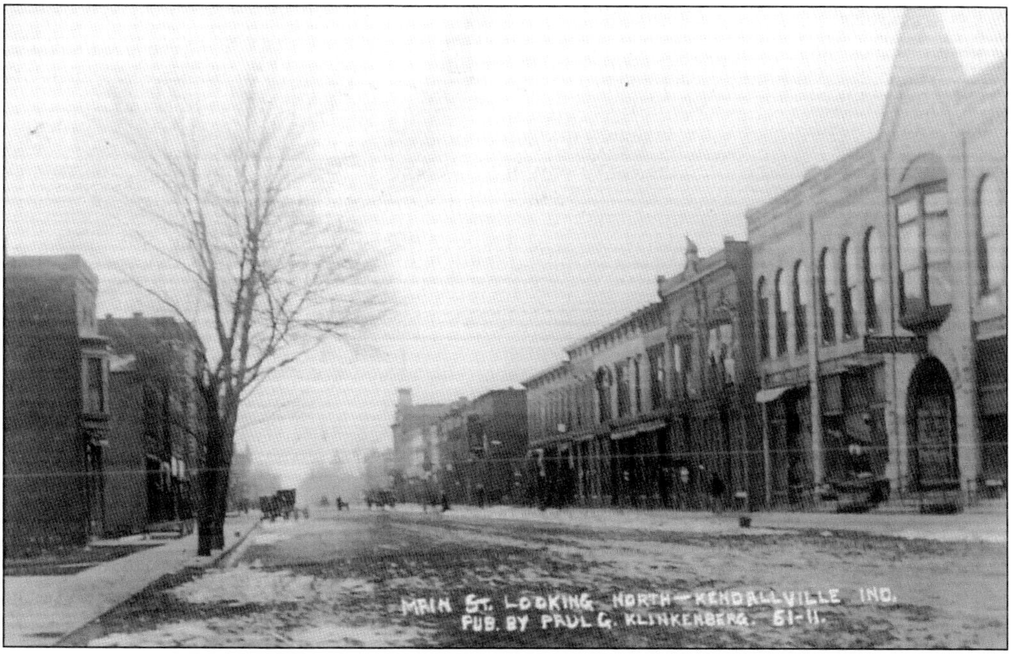

MAIN STREET LOOKING NORTH, KENDALLVILLE, INDIANA, *c.* 1910. This card was published by Paul C. Klinkenberg. Dirt streets were common.

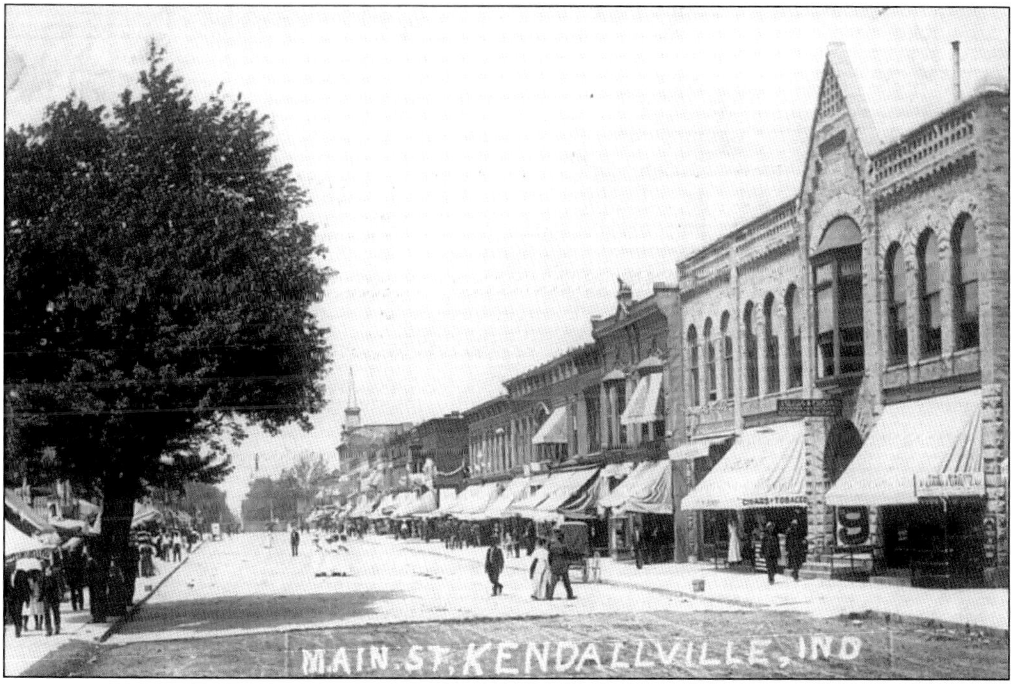

SOUTH MAIN STREET, KENDALLVILLE, INDIANA, *c.* 1908. The signs read Berhalter Bros., The Bacon Furniture Co., and Cigars-Tobacco.

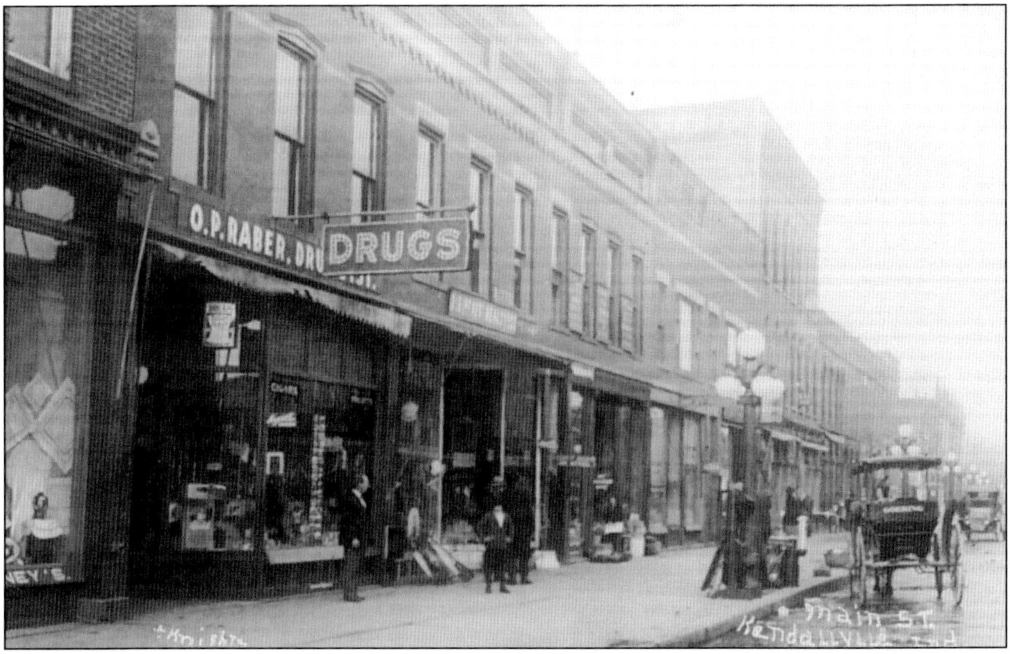

MAIN STREET, KENDALLVILLE, INDIANA, *c.* 1910. The store in foreground is O.P. Raber, Druggist. Next is U.S. Pfaff Realty Co. The name on the back of the horsedrawn hack on the right is "Goering."

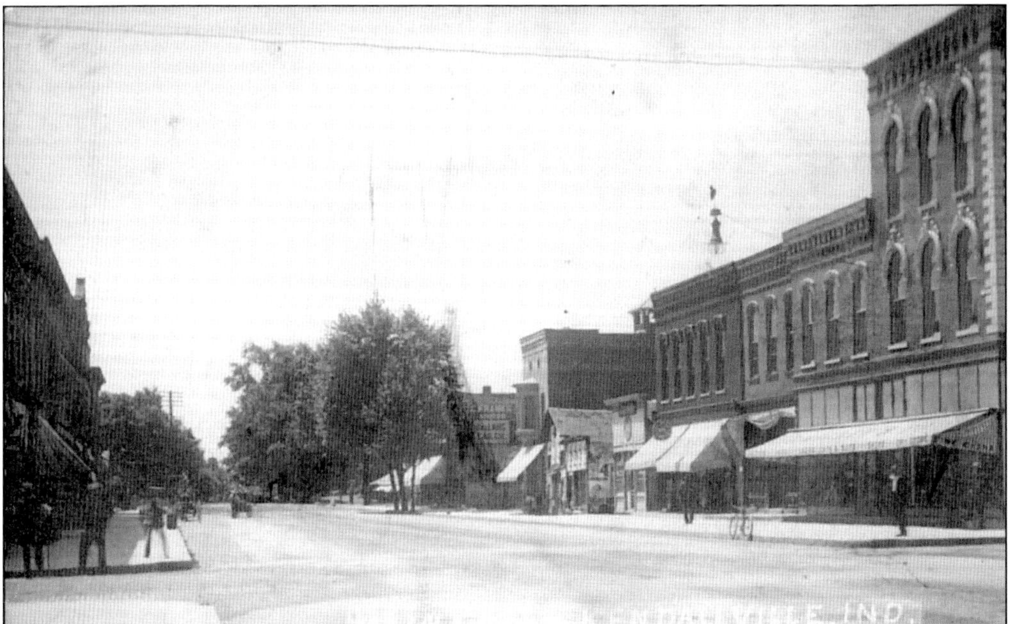

MAIN STREET, KENDALLVILLE, INDIANA, *c.* 1907. Awnings on the store fronts were necessary to protect the merchandise displayed in store windows from the rays of the sun.

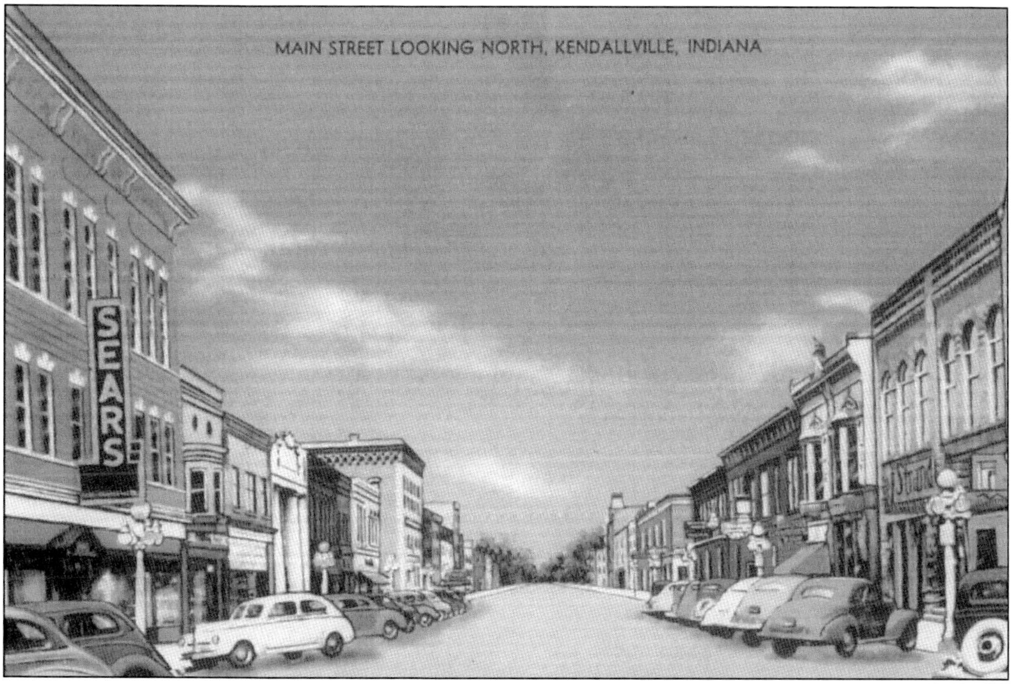

Main Street Looking North, Kendallville, Indiana, *c.* 1948. This is a linen postcard. The Sears Store is on the left and the Strand Theatre is on the right.

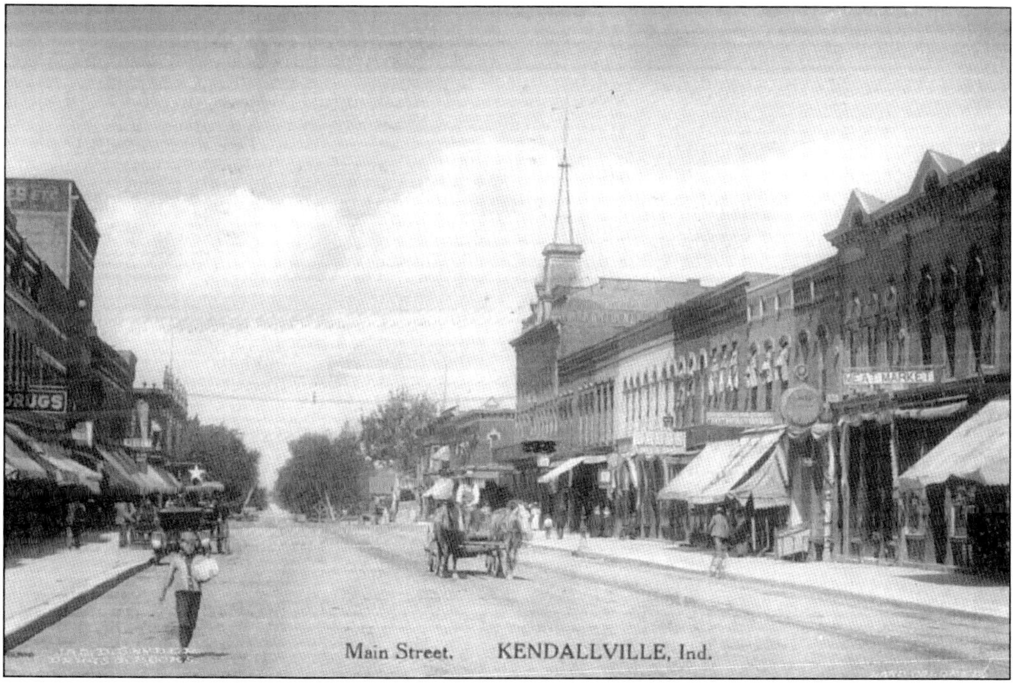

Main Street, Kendallville, Indiana, *c.* 1910. This card looks north toward the railroad tracks. Note the railroad gates and warning sign. Horses were used long after the advent of the automobile.

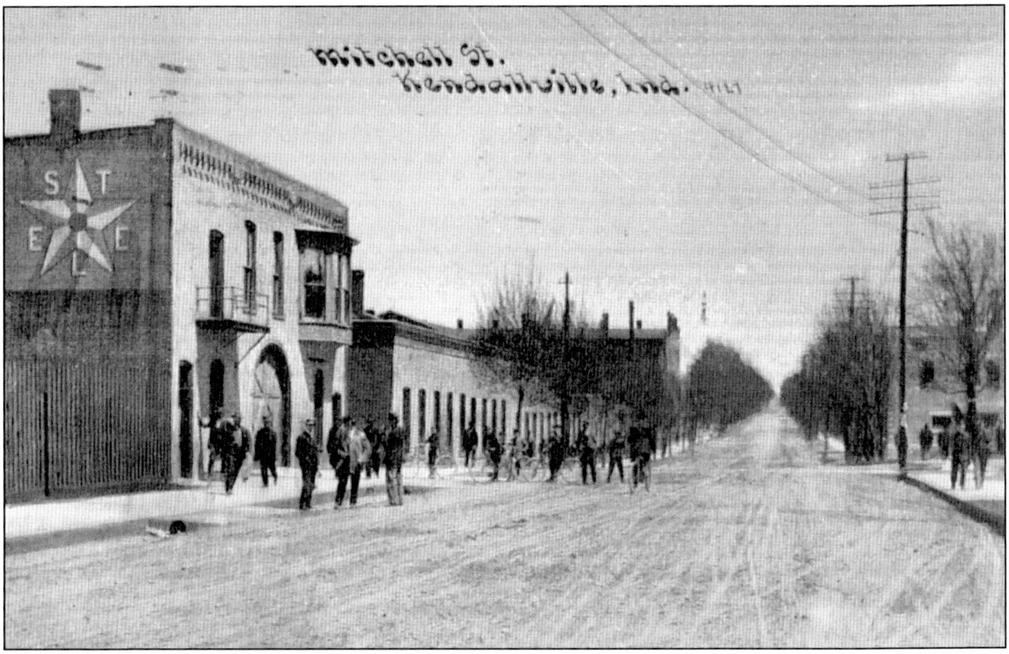

MITCHELL ST., KENDALLVILLE, INDIANA. This card is dated December 29, 1910. The message reads: "Rec'd your card, told Hallibaugh, and I will be watching for you Jan 2nd. Think I will have the band out to the big Union Depot on your arrival. 'Ha,' 'Ha.' Wishing you happy New Year. Yours. Ross."

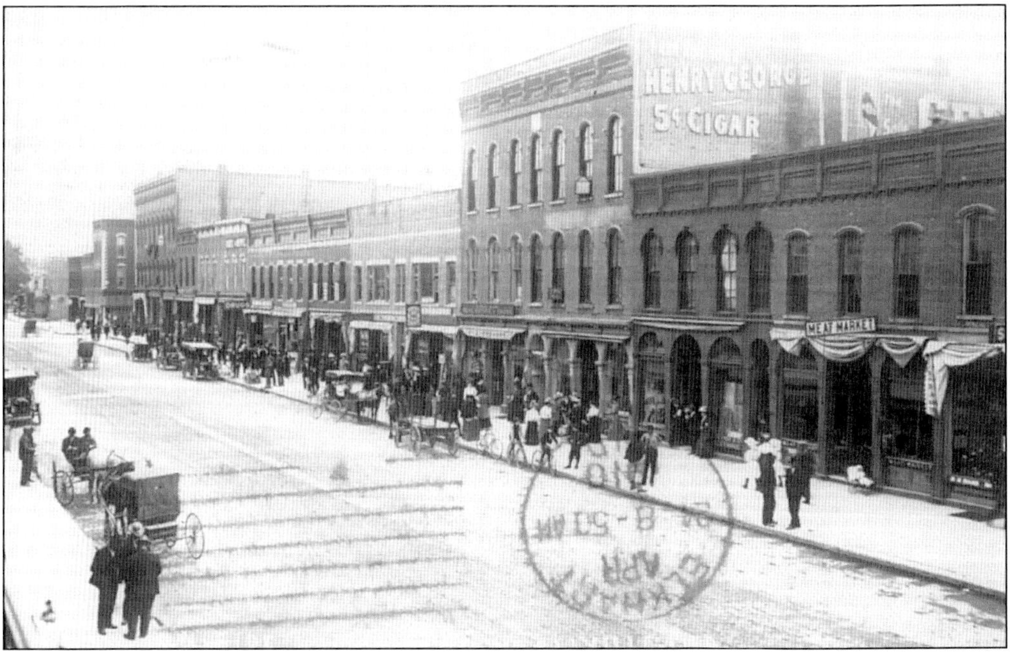

WEST SIDE OF MAIN STREET, KENDALLVILLE, INDIANA, *C.* 1910. Several automobiles are visible in background. Any visible wall was used for signs. The sign on the brick wall on the right states, "I am for men—Henry George 5 cent cigar."

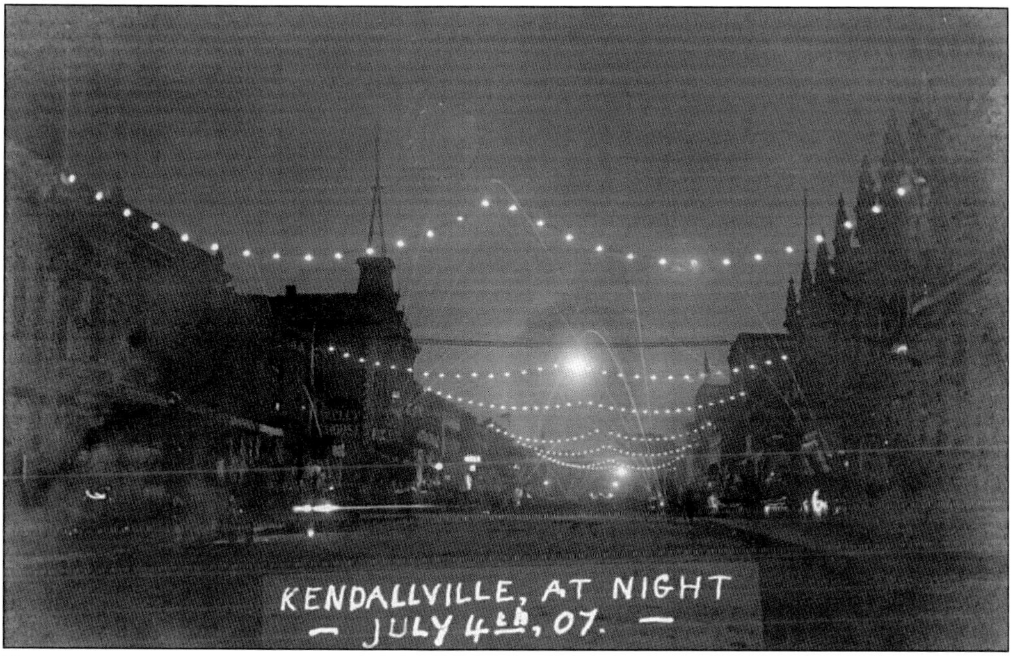

KENDALLVILLE, AT NIGHT—JULY 4TH, 1907. Seen here is a gala celebration, complete with fireworks and electric lights! Addressed to Zoe in Rome City: "I was at Rome City, Wed. eve; called on you at the office but you had gone to the dance. Please exchange soon. Frank." "Exchange soon" means to send him a card.

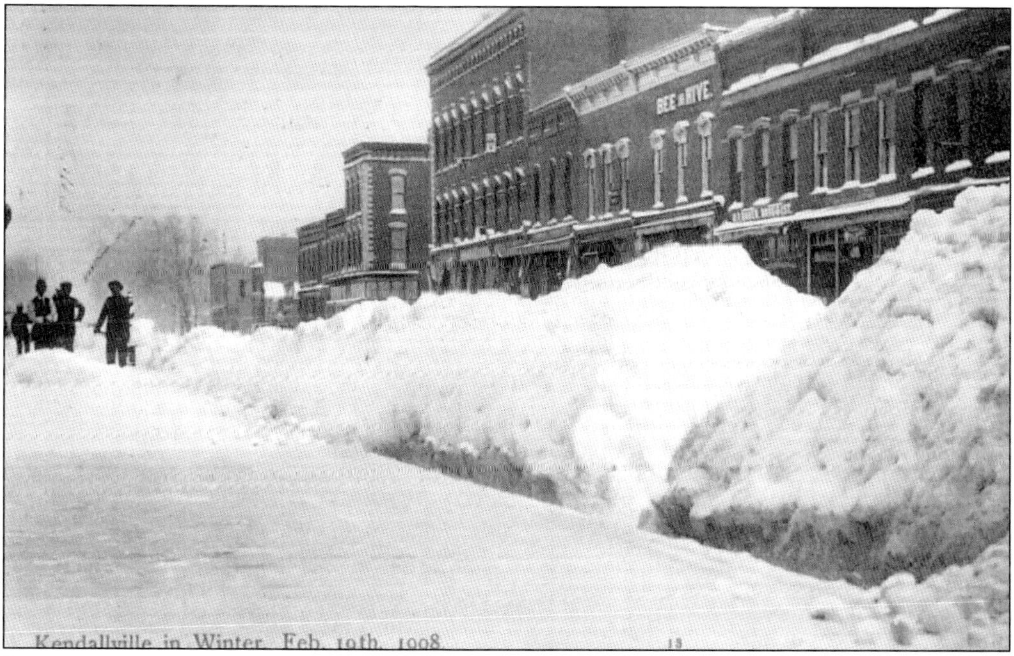

KENDALLVILLE IN WINTER, FEBRUARY 19TH, 1908. This card was mailed the following winter on January 6, 1909. Signs visible are "Bee Hive" and "O.P. Raber, Druggist."

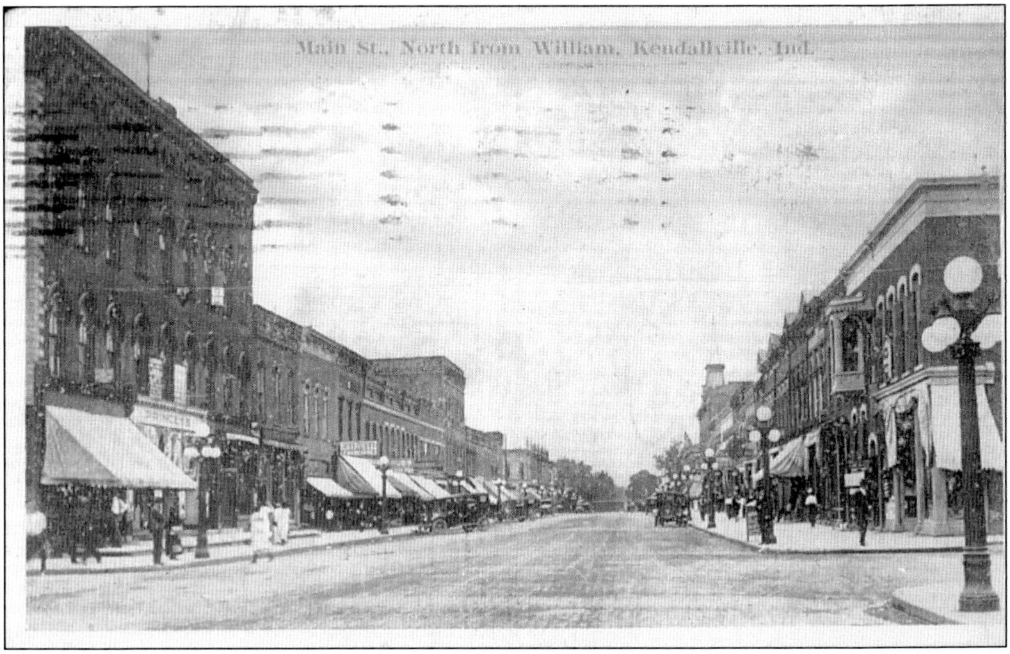

MAIN STREET, NORTH FROM WILLIAM, KENDALLVILLE, INDIANA. The cast iron street lights with cluster lights are an attractive addition to Main Street.

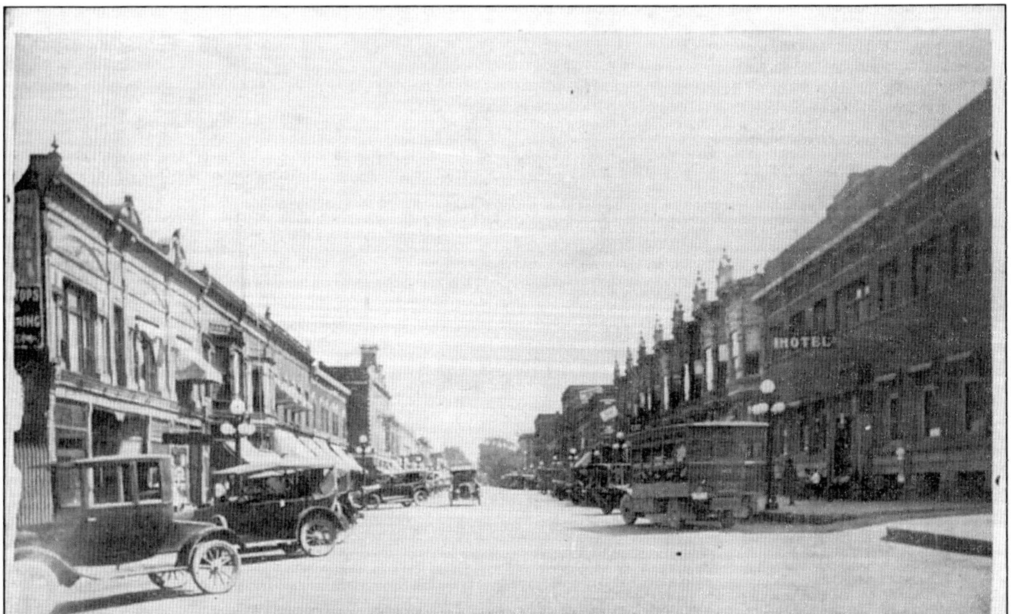

Main Street Looking South, Kendallville, Ind.

MAIN STREET LOOKING SOUTH, KENDALLVILLE, INDIANA. The "Seven Sisters" buildings are on the right. A bus is in front of the hotel.

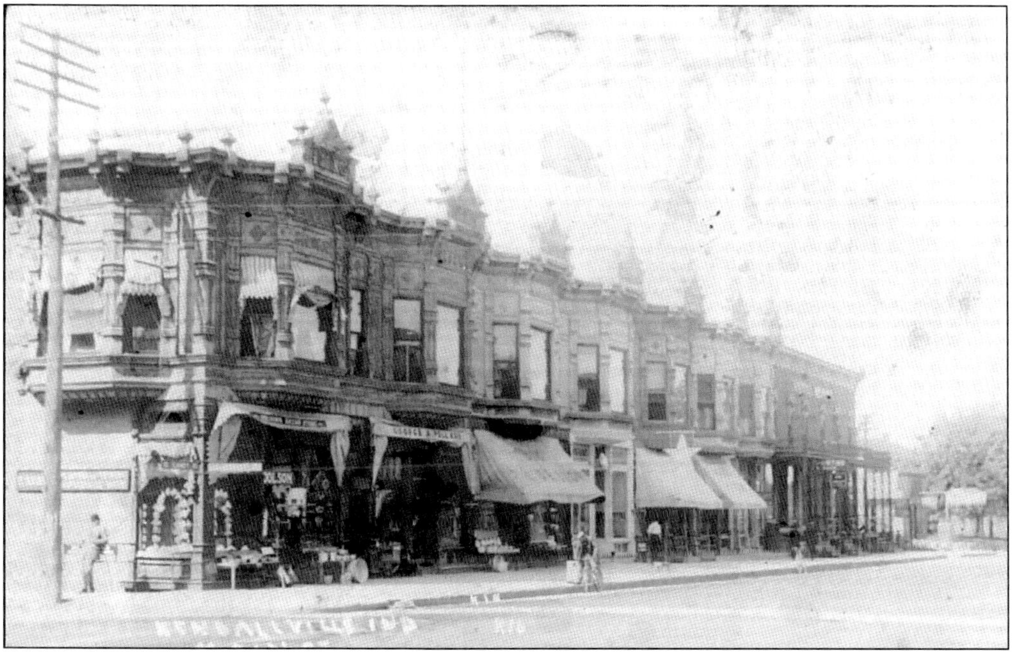

KENDALLVILLE, INDIANA, MAIN STREET. Stores are Dolson's Bazaar Store and George A. Pollard. These buildings are fine examples of cast iron architecture.

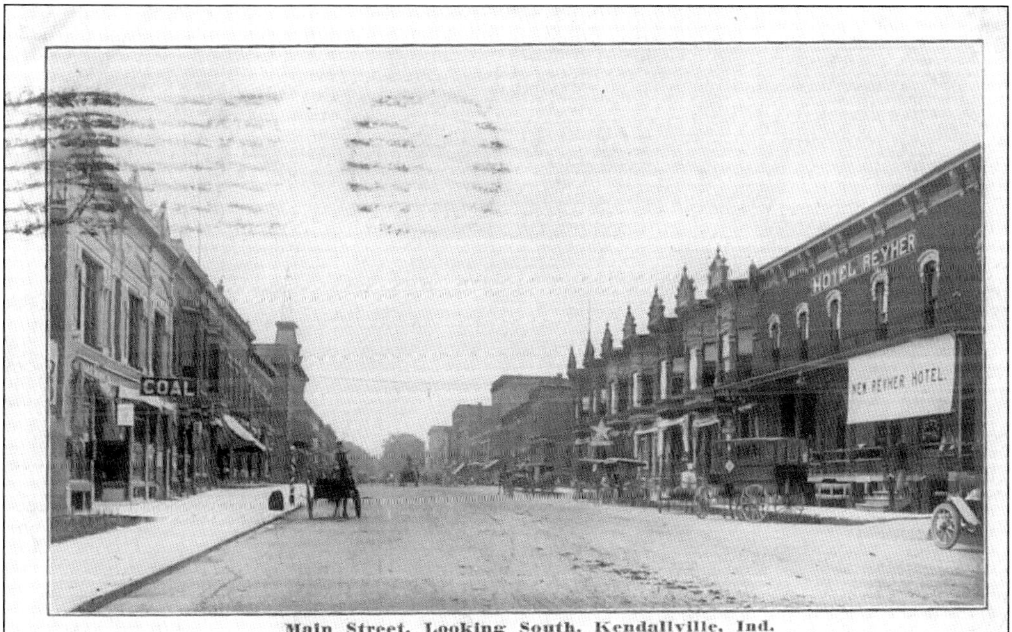

MAIN STREET, LOOKING SOUTH, KENDALLVILLE, INDIANA. The "New Reyner Hotel" is seen on the right along with the "Seven Sisters" buildings. A horsedrawn hack in front of the hotel probably brought travelers from the railroad depot. A coal dealer's office is on the left.

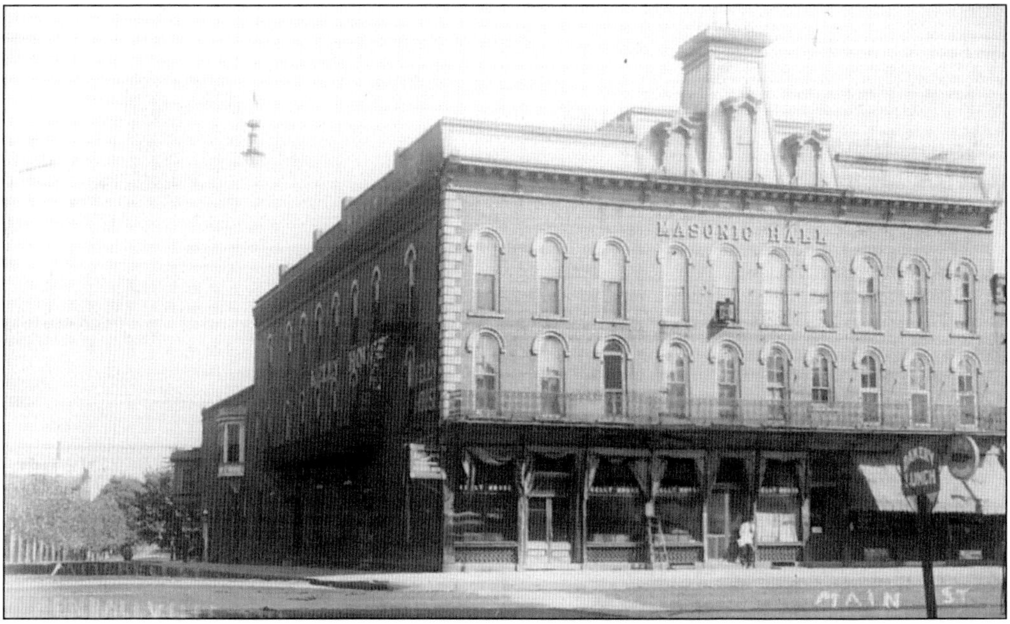

Main Street, Kendallville, Indiana. With its tower, the Masonic Hall was a major landmark. Lodges frequently built grand buildings with store fronts on the street level which they rented. The upper floors were used as lodge rooms. The Kelly House Hotel was located in the building.

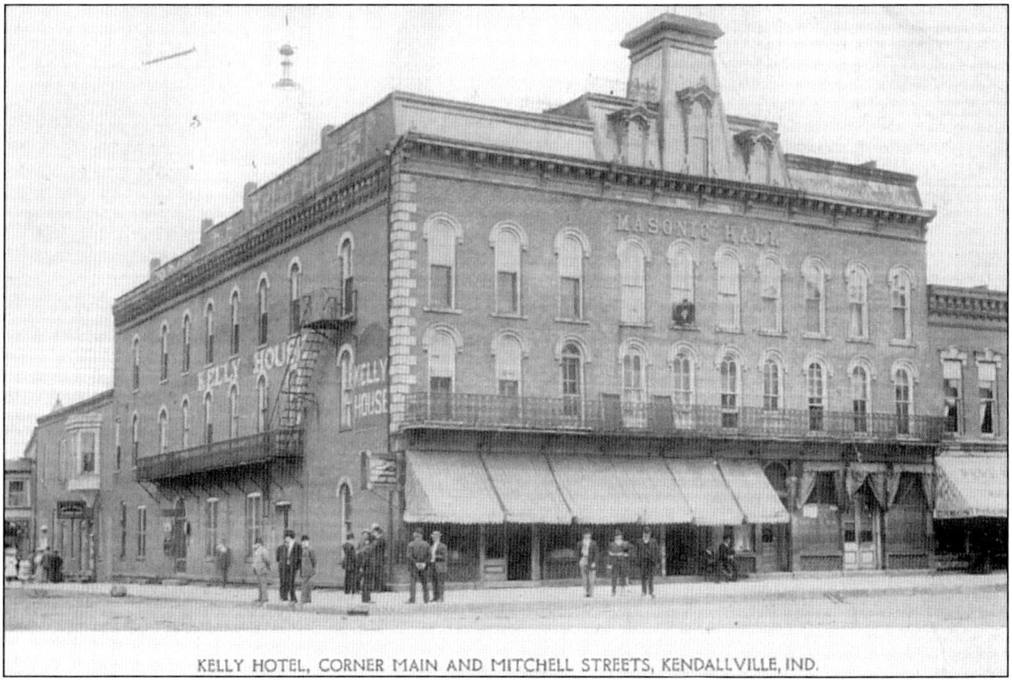

KELLY HOTEL, CORNER MAIN AND MITCHELL STREETS, KENDALLVILLE, IND.

Kelly Hotel, Corner Main and Mitchell Streets, Kendallville, Indiana, *c.* 1910. This was a beautiful building in its day. Three story buildings were a status symbol in this era. The awnings were common. They were opened and closed with a crank.

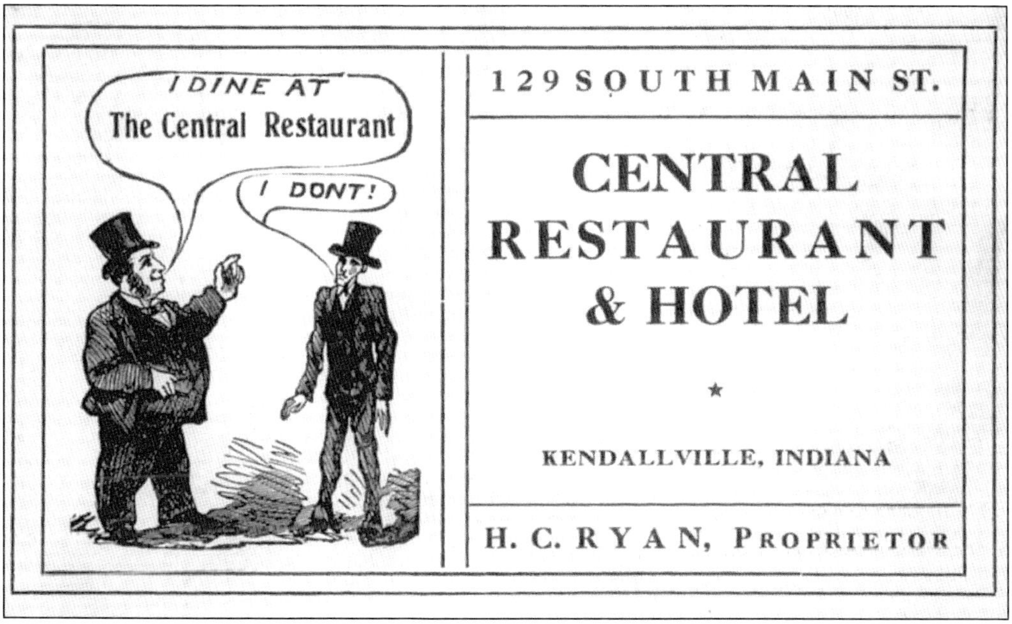

RESTAURANT & HOTEL, KENDALLVILLE, INDIANA. Trade cards were a popular form of advertising.

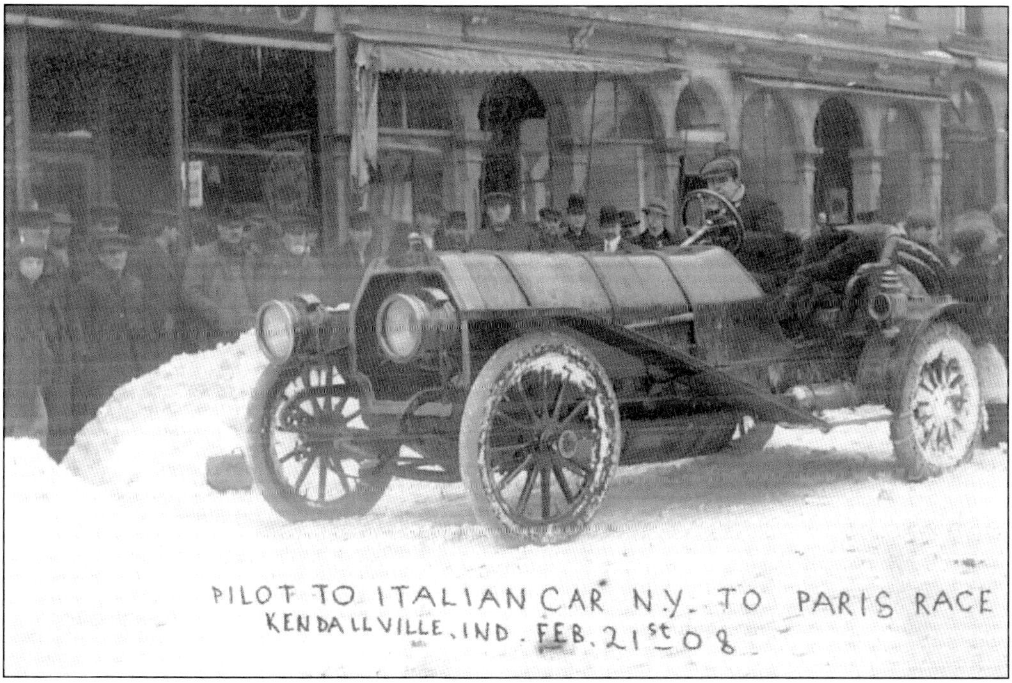

PILOT TO ITALIAN CAR, N.Y. TO PARIS RACE, KENDALLVILLE, INDIANA, FEBRUARY 21, 1908. The first International Automobile Race traversed Noble County in the winter of 1908. The cars had a great deal of difficulty with the heavy snow at the time.

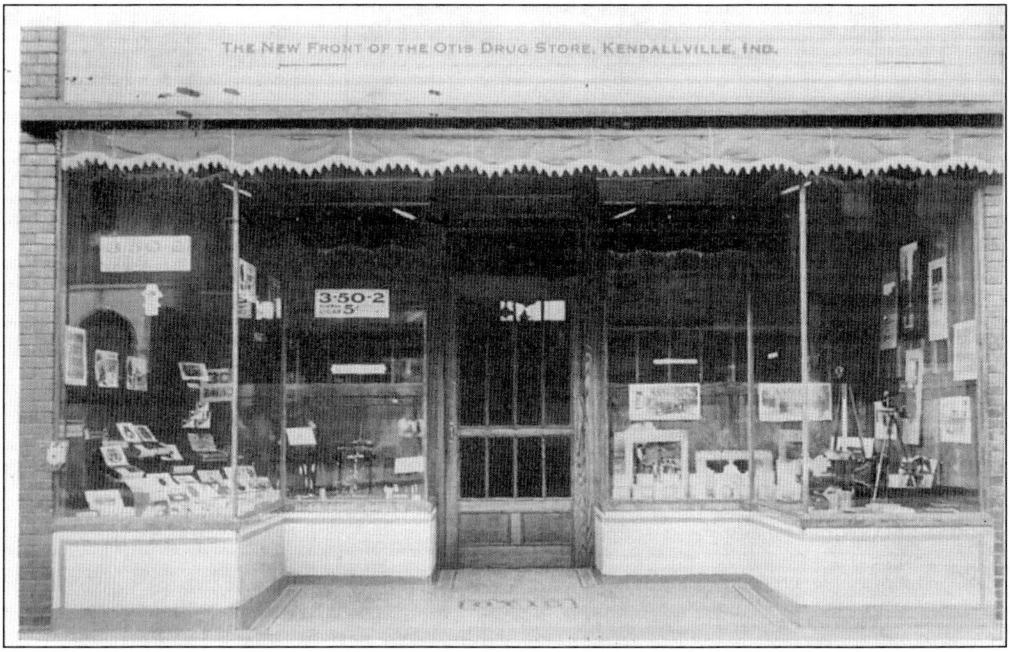

THE NEW FRONT OF THE OTIS DRUG STORE, KENDALLVILLE, INDIANA. Elaborate displays of merchandise enticed pedestrians to enter the store.

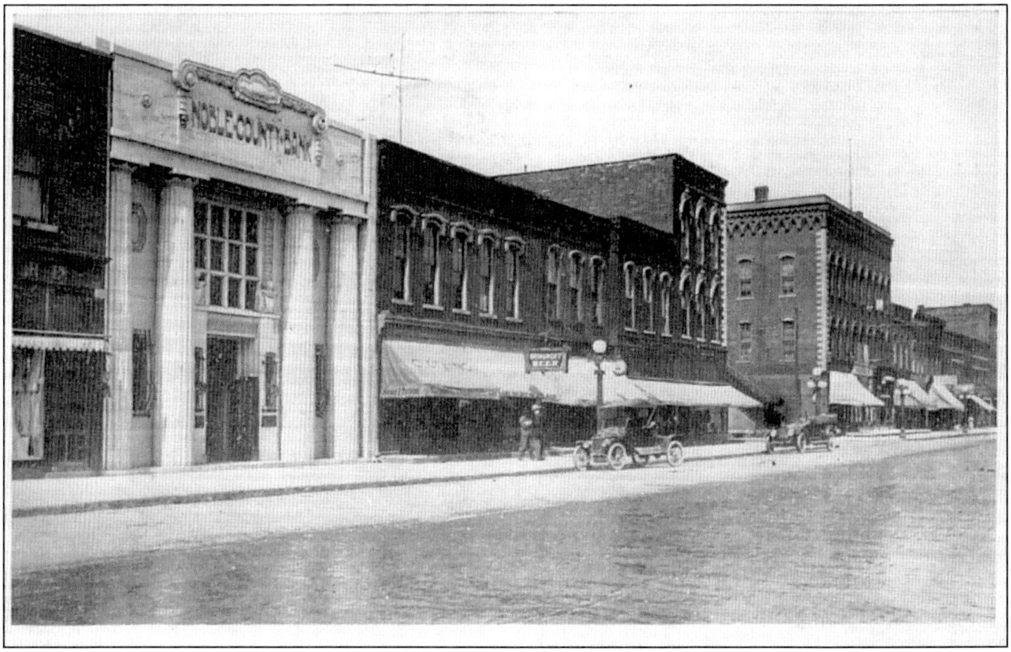

NOBLE COUNTY BANK, KENDALLVILLE, INDIANA. Classic bank architecture indicated solidarity and permanence of the financial institution.

Noble County Bank, Exterior, Kendallville, Indiana, *c.* 1940. The close up view of the bank shows the heavy bronze doors and the cast iron bars on the windows.

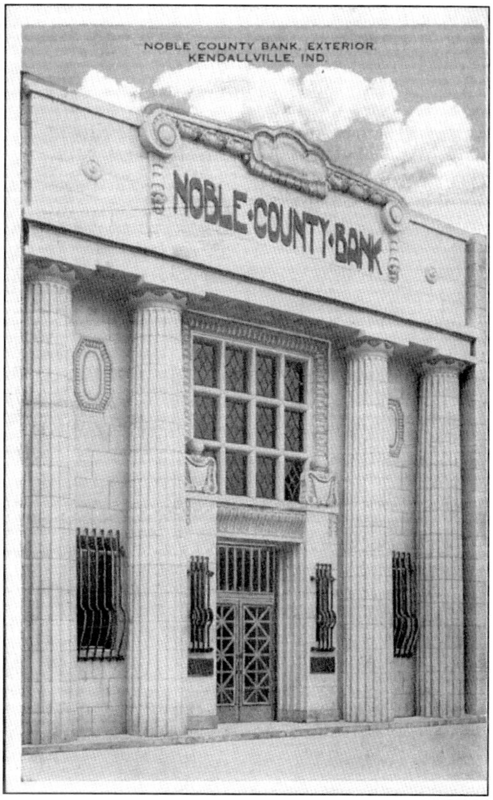

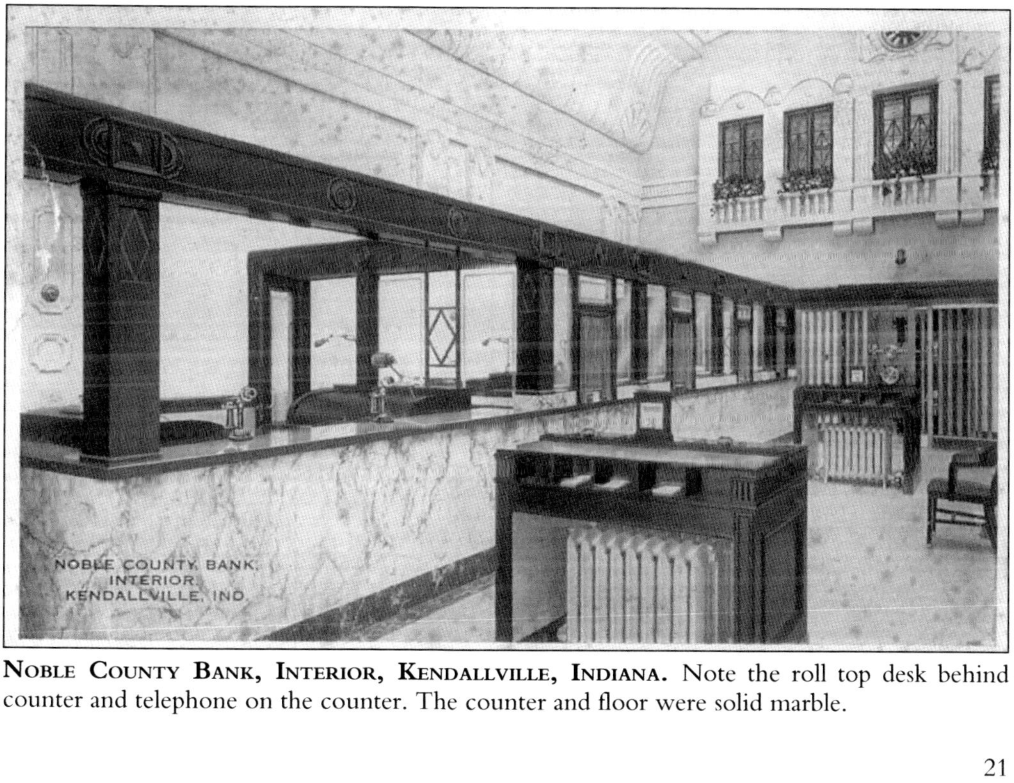

Noble County Bank, Interior, Kendallville, Indiana. Note the roll top desk behind counter and telephone on the counter. The counter and floor were solid marble.

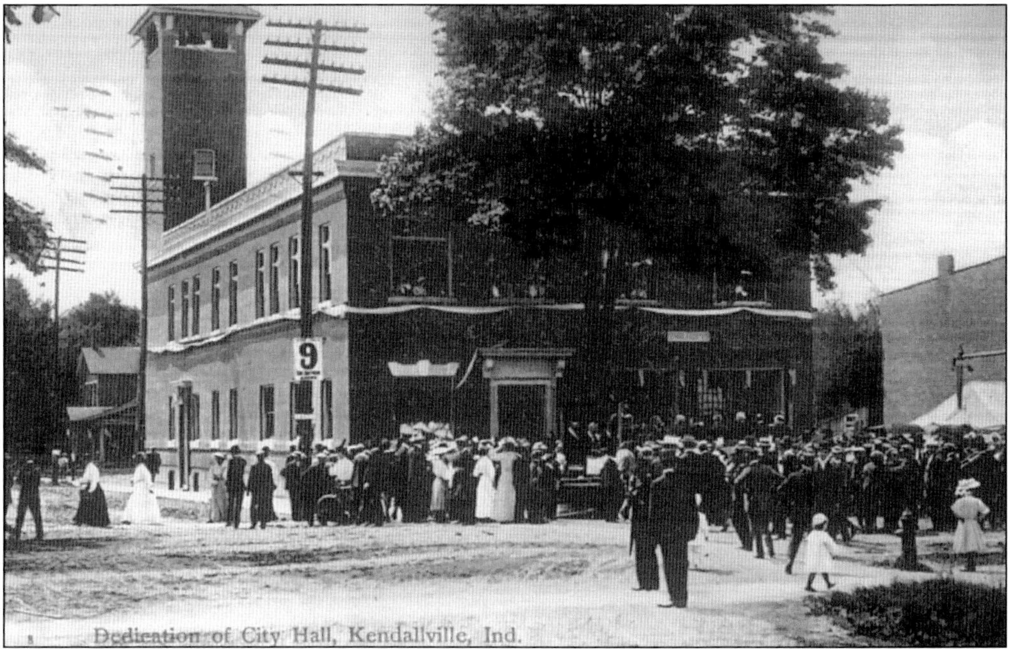

Dedication of City Hall, Kendallville, Indiana, *c.* 1913. It seems that the long dresses would have been a hazard on the dirt streets.

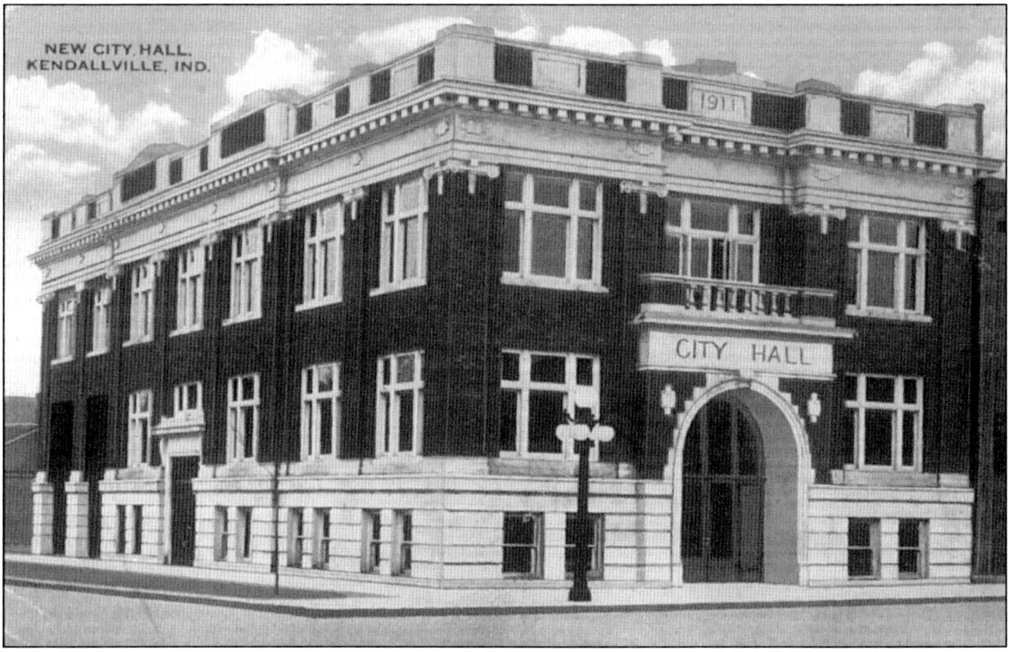

New City Hall, Kendallville, Indiana *c.* 1915. The building is dated 1911. This view is "sanitized."

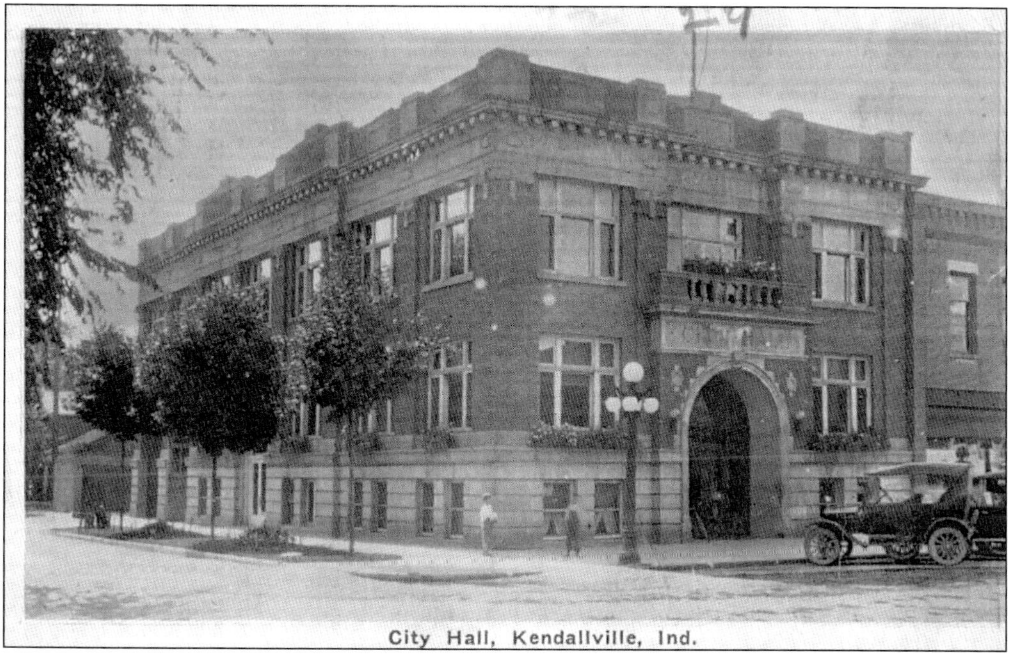

City Hall, Kendallville, Indiana, c. 1925. Note the flowers in the window boxes on the first and second floors.

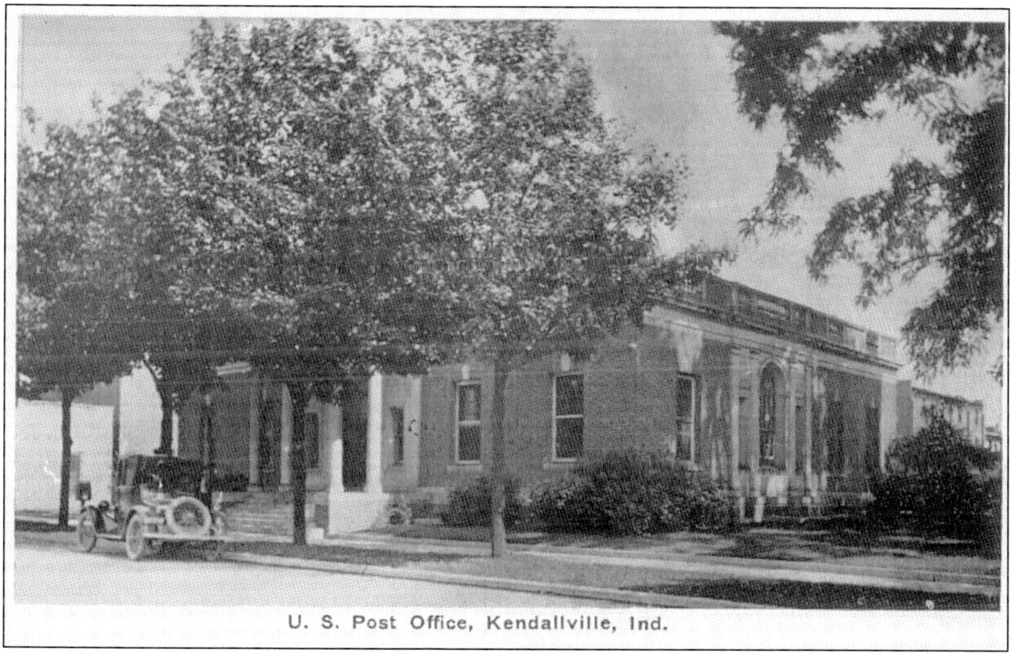

United States Post Office, Kendallville, Indiana, c. 1928. This card was published by the Auburn Post Card Manufacturing Co., Auburn, Indiana.

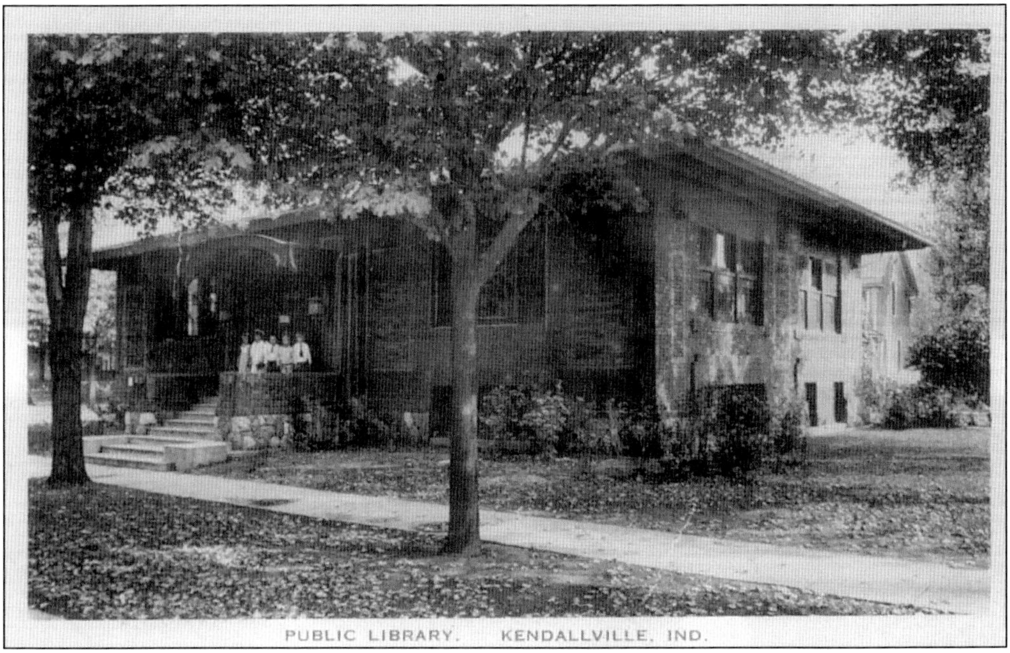

PUBLIC LIBRARY, KENDALLVILLE, INDIANA. The librarians are standing on the steps.

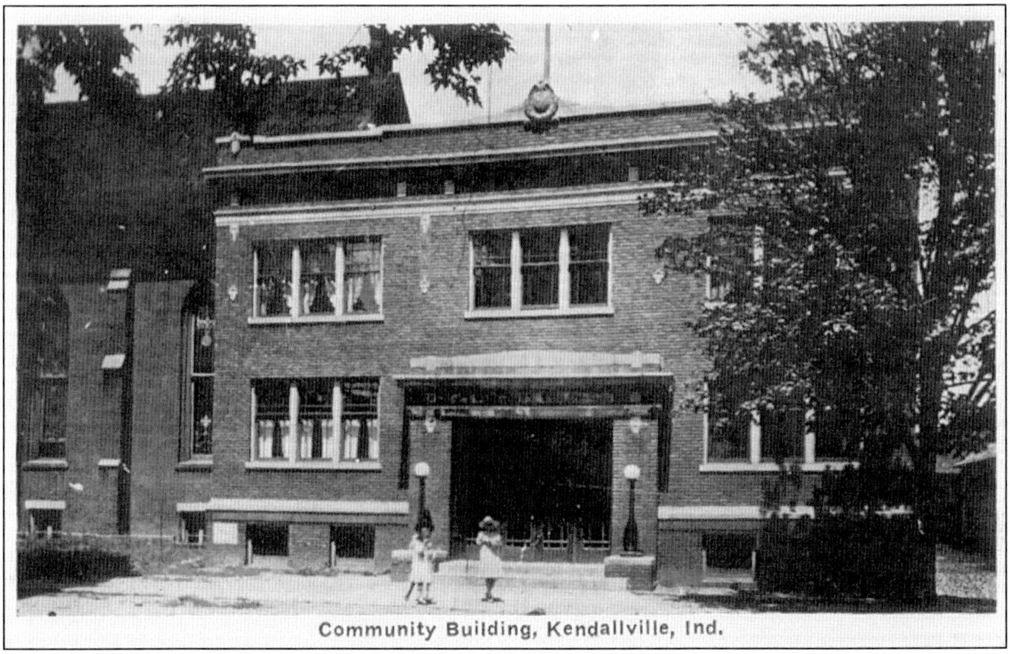

COMMUNITY BUILDING, KENDALLVILLE, INDIANA, *c.* 1940. Note the young girls in the foreground.

WATER WORKS STATION, KENDALLVILLE, INDIANA, *c.* 1909. The message states, "Dear friend: Will meet the 8:10 car Monday night & will try & help you enjoy the 2 hours you'll have here. Don't say anything to anyone as I don't want the folks to know it. C? Will explain later. You'd better not fail me this time. E"

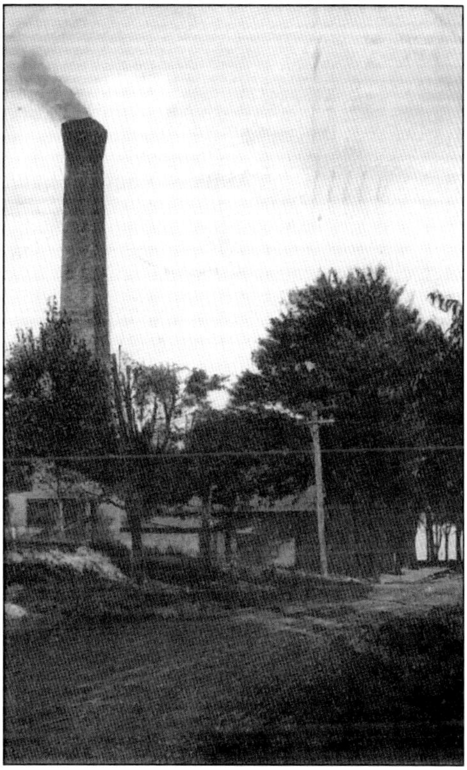

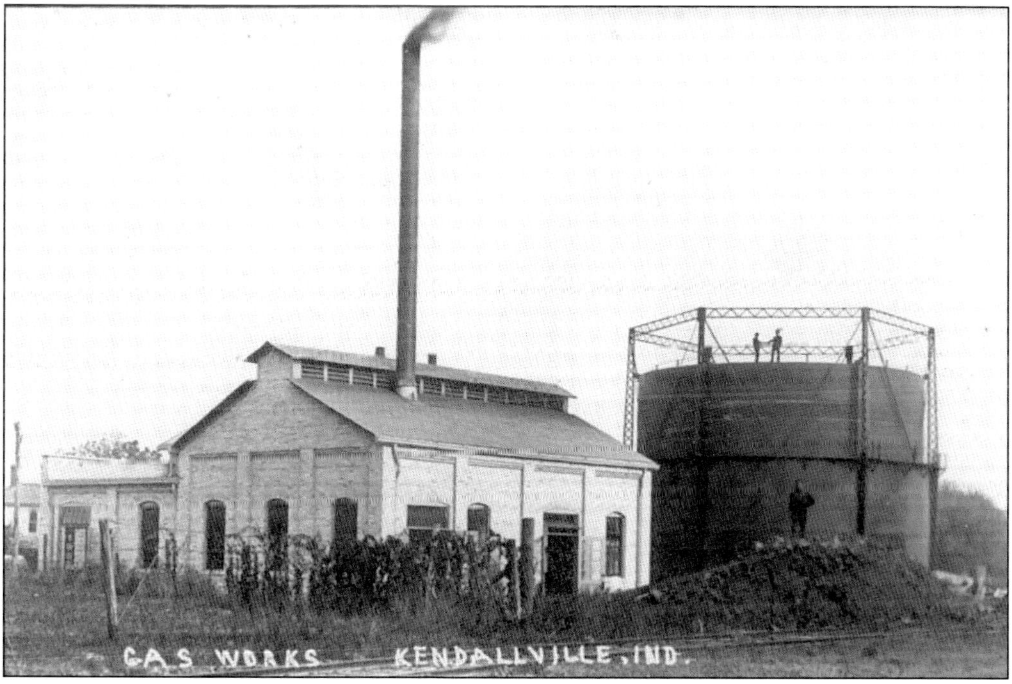

GAS WORKS, KENDALLVILLE, INDIANA, *c.* 1908. The men on top of the tank are shaking hands as if they had just finished the construction.

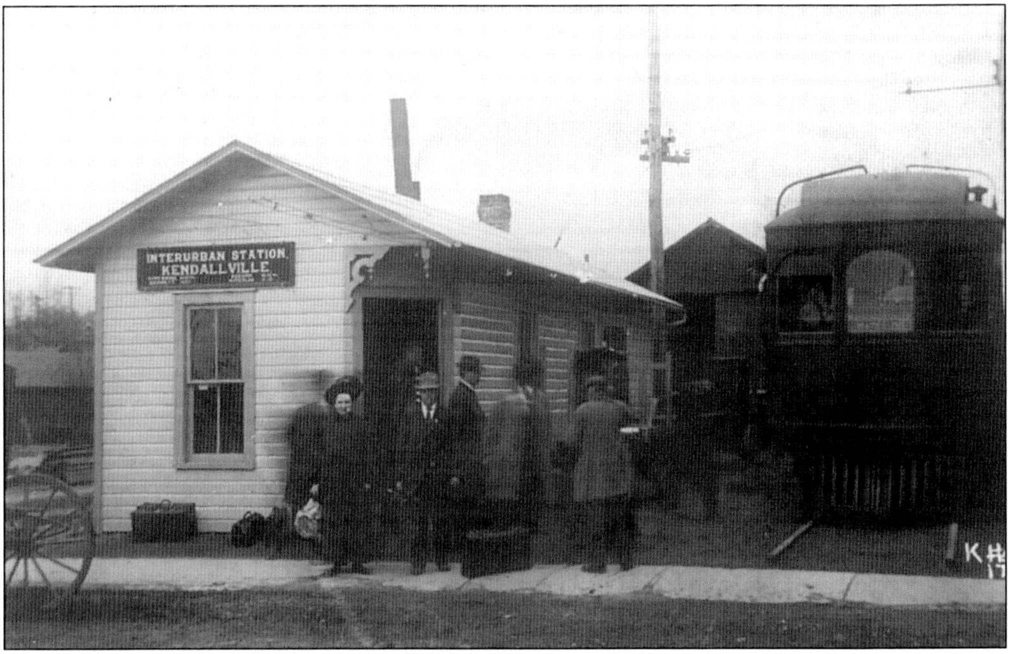

Interurban Station, Kendallville, Indiana. This was the northwest terminus of the line which connected Kendallville with Garrett and Fort Wayne.

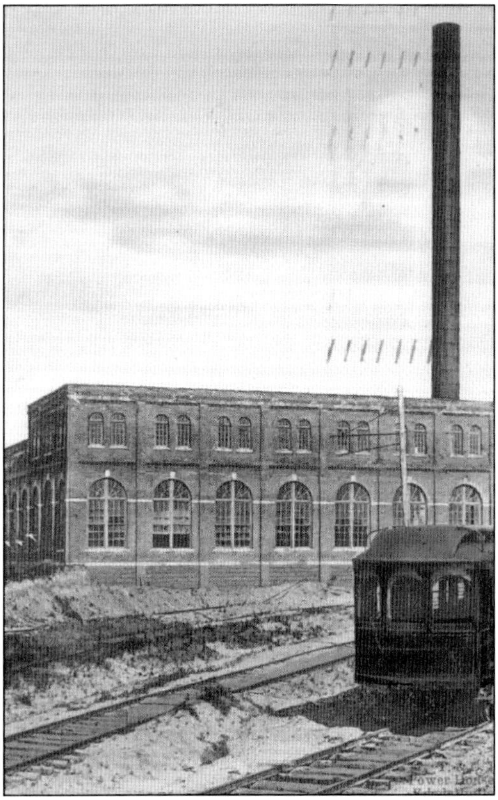

T. & C.I. Power House, Kendallville, Indiana, *c.* 1913. Seen here is the powerhouse where electric current was generated for the interurban lines. T. & C.I. Stood for "Toledo and Chicago Interurban." Despite the name, the lines never got near Chicago nor Toledo. It connected Waterloo, Auburn, Garrett, and Kendallville to Fort Wayne.

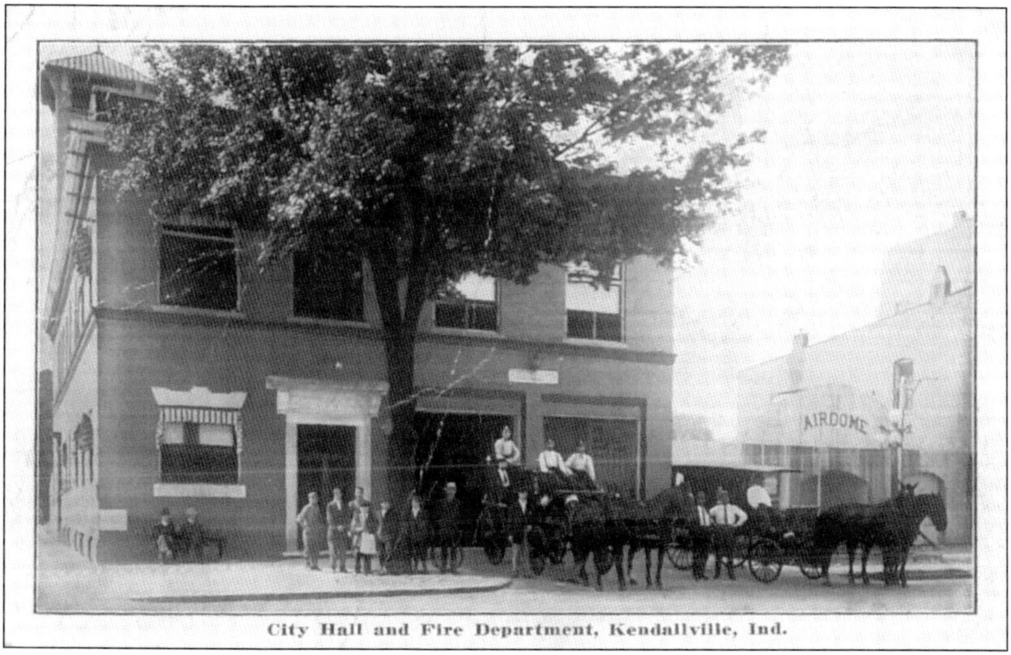

CITY HALL AND FIRE DEPARTMENT, KENDALLVILLE, INDIANA, c. 1912. Firemen are in uniform and manning horsedrawn file apparatus. The steam powered pump was taken to the site of a fire and used to pump water from cisterns or other bodies of water nearby. Note the "Airdome" on the right.

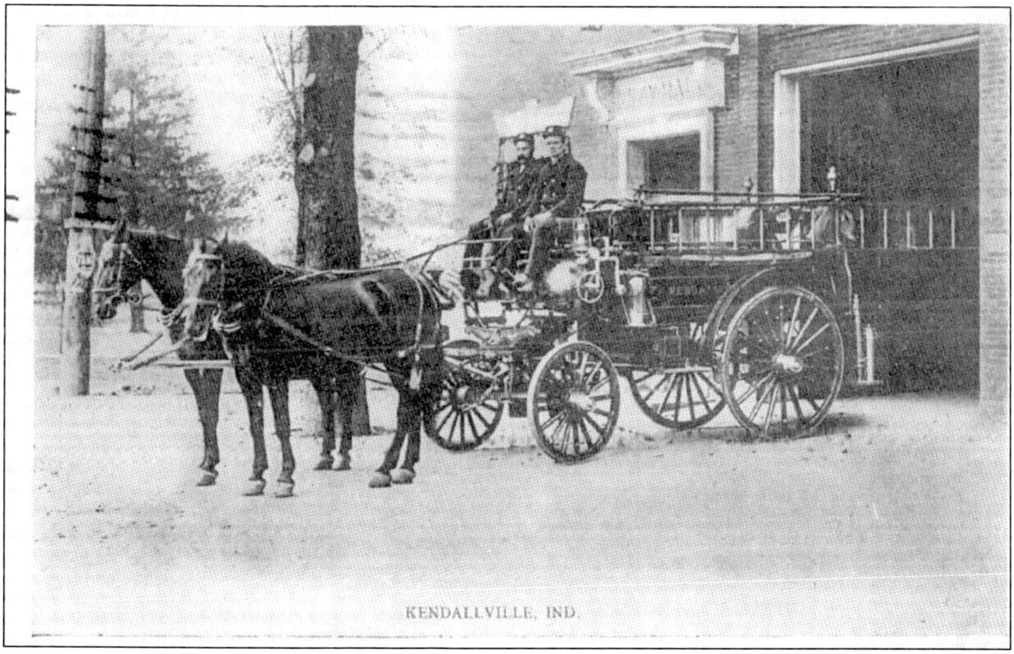

KENDALLVILLE, INDIANA. Seen here are horsedrawn fire wagon with ladders, hose, and buckets.

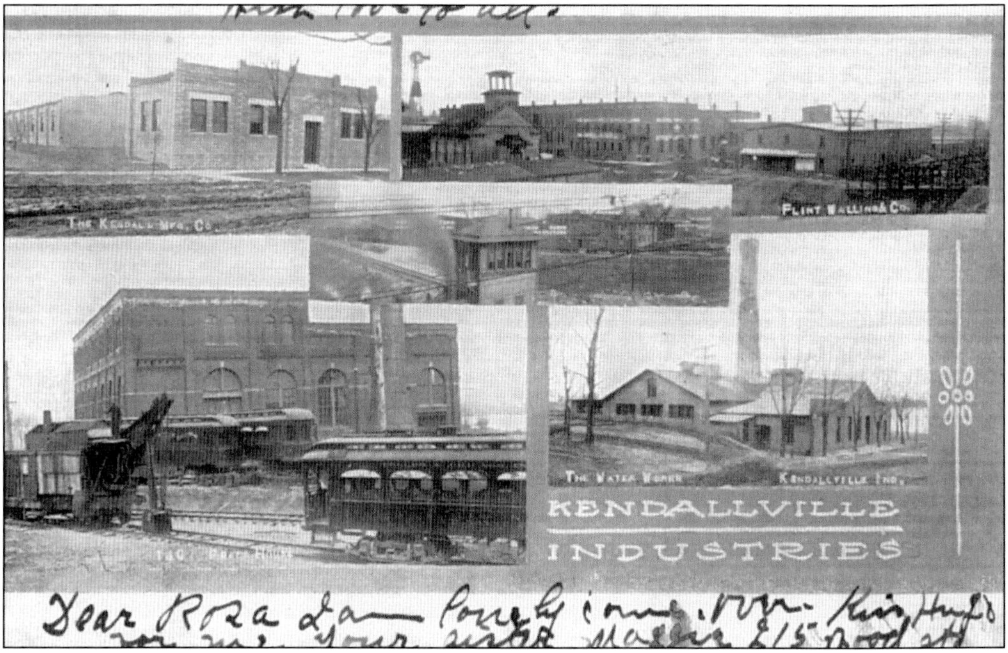

KENDALLVILLE INDUSTRIES, *c.* 1907. The Kendallville Manufacturing Co., Flint Walling & Co., The Water Works, and T & C Power House. Communities were proud of their industries.

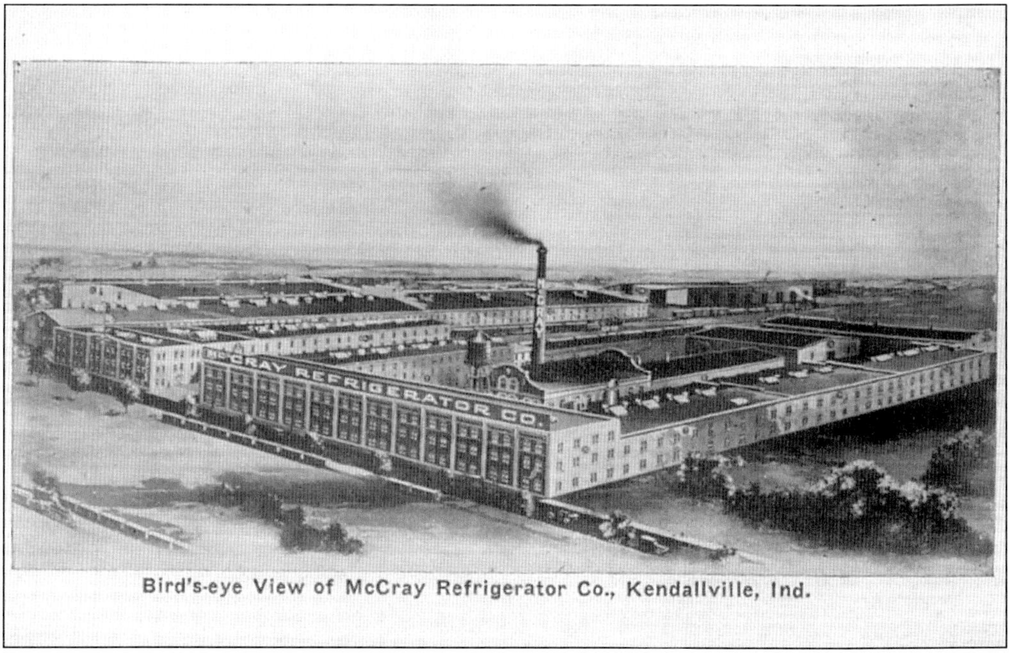

BIRD'S-EYE VIEW OF MCCRAY REFRIGERATOR CO., KENDALLVILLE, INDIANA, *c.* 1920. McCray was a major manufacturer of residential and commercial refrigeration equipment. Smoke from the chimneys was a symbol of activity and progress.

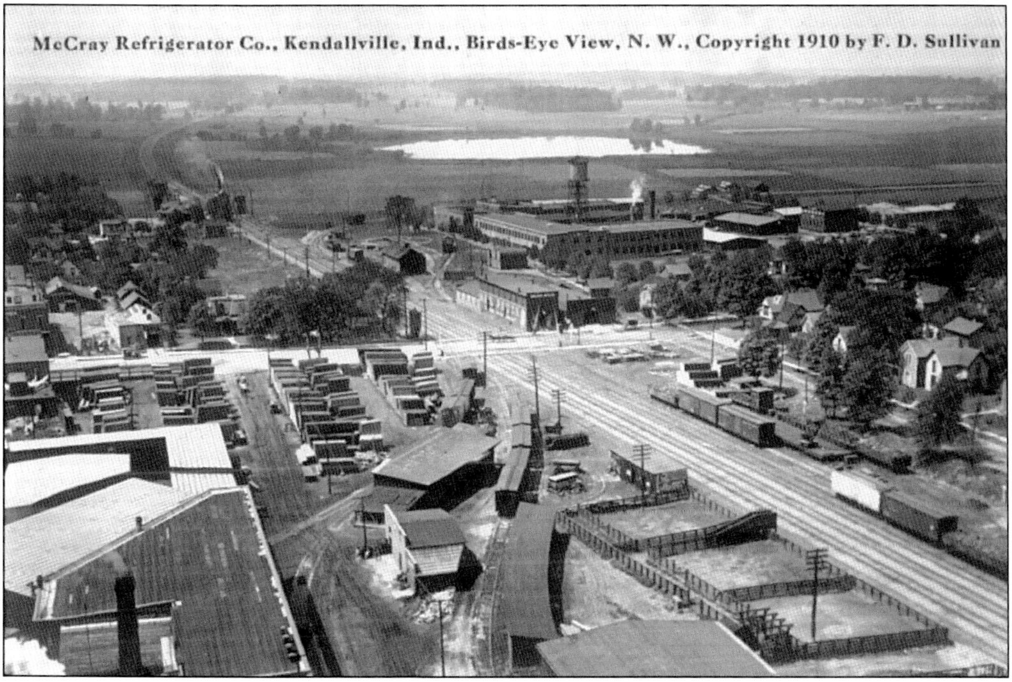

McCray Refrigerator Co., Kendallville, Indiana, Bird's Eye View, *c.* 1910. The McCray Refrigerator Co. was served by the New York Central Railroad. The fenced enclosures in the lower right were used to hold livestock pending shipping via railroad.

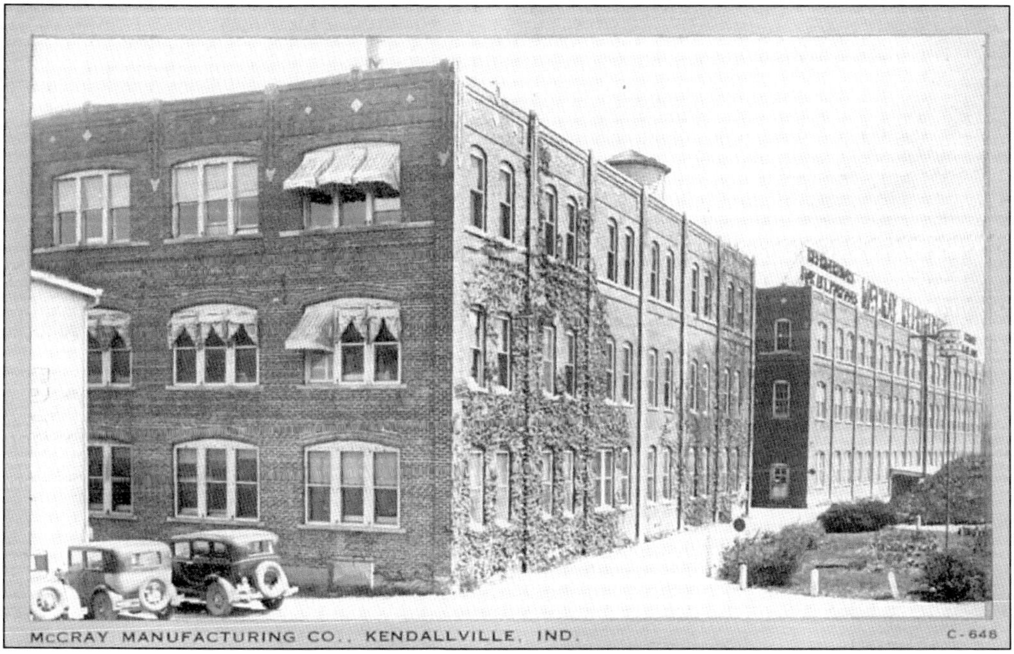

McCray Manufacturing Co., Kendallville, Indiana, *c.* 1940. The buildings are ivy covered. Striped awnings kept out the bright sun.

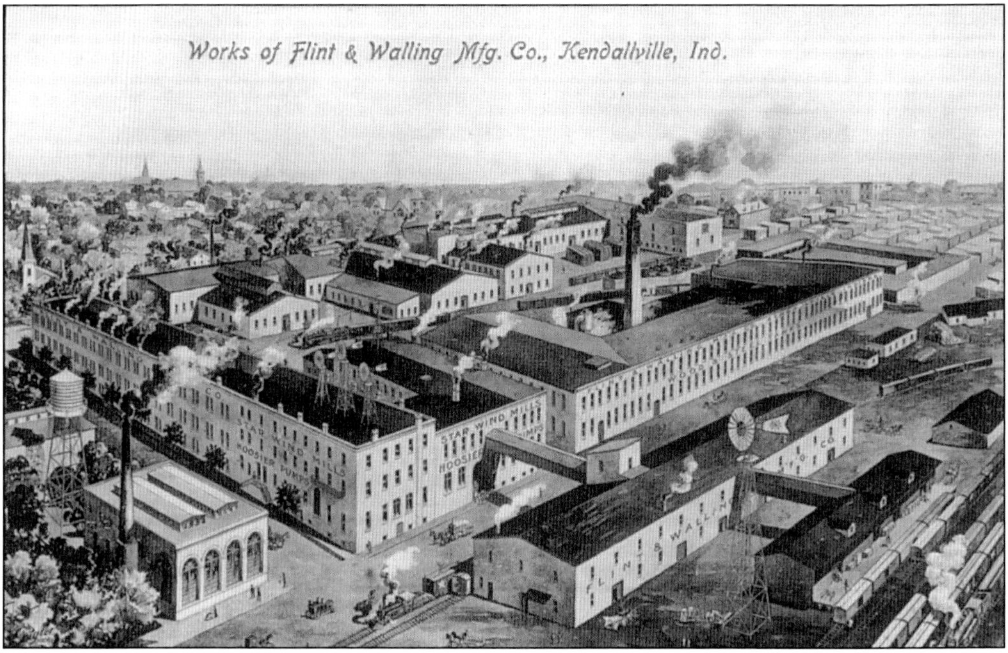

WORKS OF FLINT & WALLING MANUFACTURING CO., KENDALLVILLE, INDIANA, *c.* 1910. Seen here is an artist's conception of a bird's eye view of the company, manufacturer of Star Wind Mills and Hoosier Pumps. In this era, smoke belching from stacks was a sign of progress and great industry.

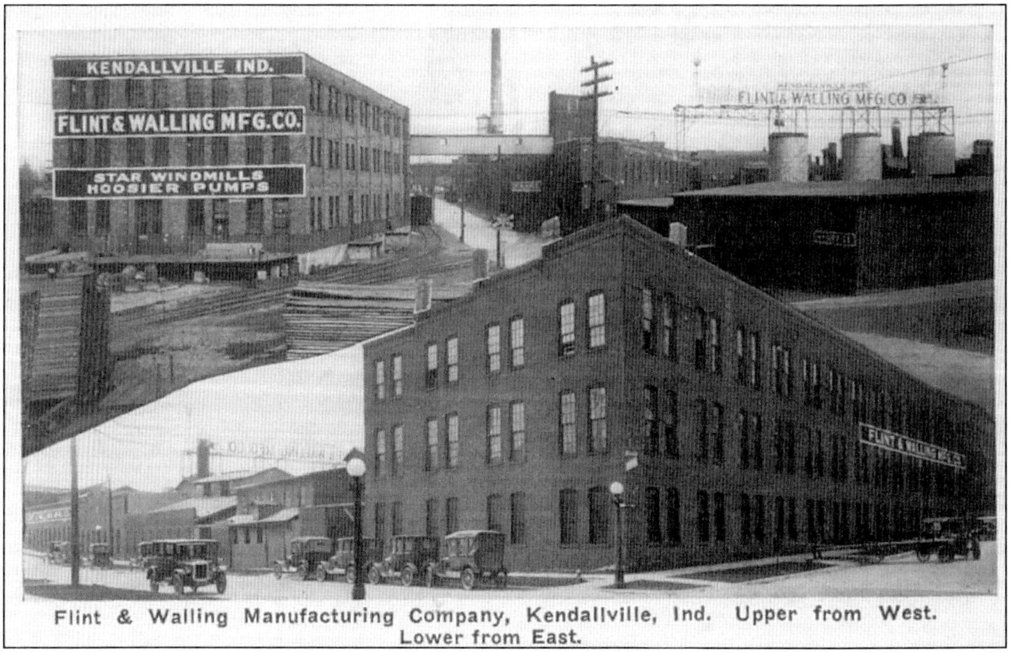

FLINT & WALLING MANUFACTURING COMPANY, KENDALLVILLE, INDIANA, *c.* 1925. Star Windmills were seen in many states. The company's "Hoosier Pumps" were leaders in pressurized water systems.

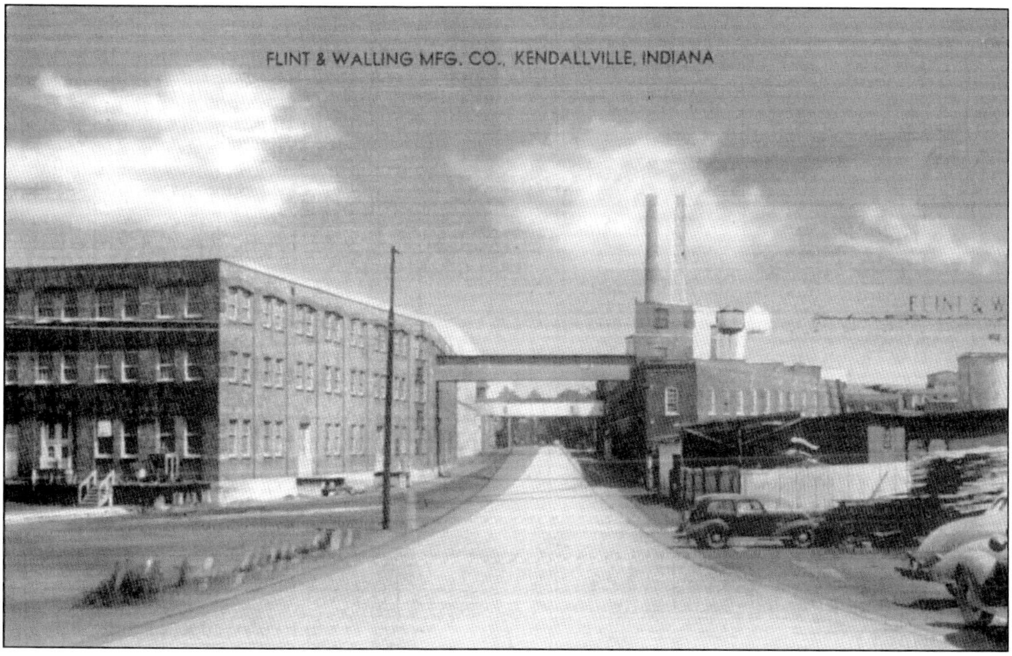

FLINT & WALLING MANUFACTURING CO., KENDALLVILLE, INDIANA, *c.* 1940. This linen postcard shows how the buildings were connected by bridges at the third floor level.

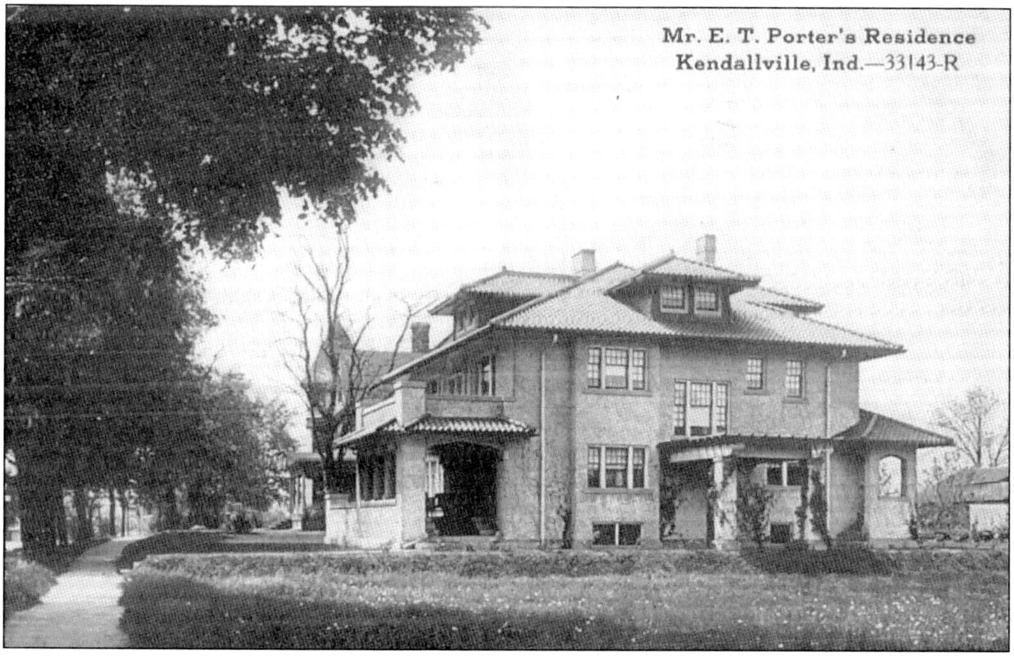

MR. E.T. PORTER'S RESIDENCE, KENDALLVILLE, INDIANA, *c.* 1912. E.T. Porter was the principal stockholder of Flint & Walling Manufacturing Company and built a mansion appropriate for his status and wealth.

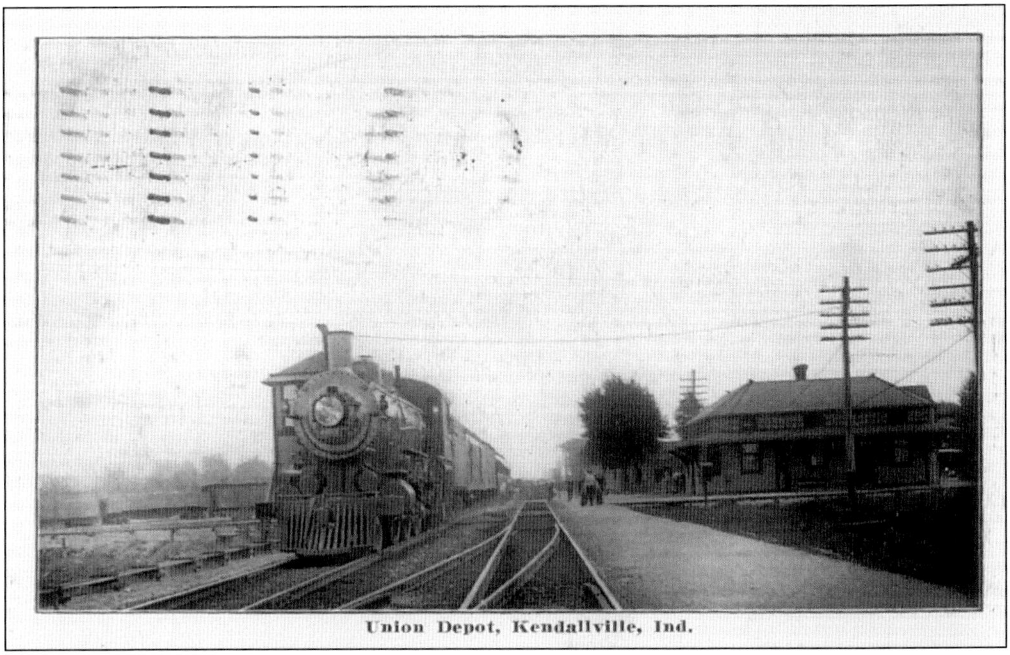

UNION DEPOT, KENDALLVILLE, INDIANA. This card is postmarked January 5, 1914. The message states, "It is good sleighing here now." The New York Central Railroad was the connecting link of Kendallville to the outside world. Most freight in and out of a town was shipped by rail.

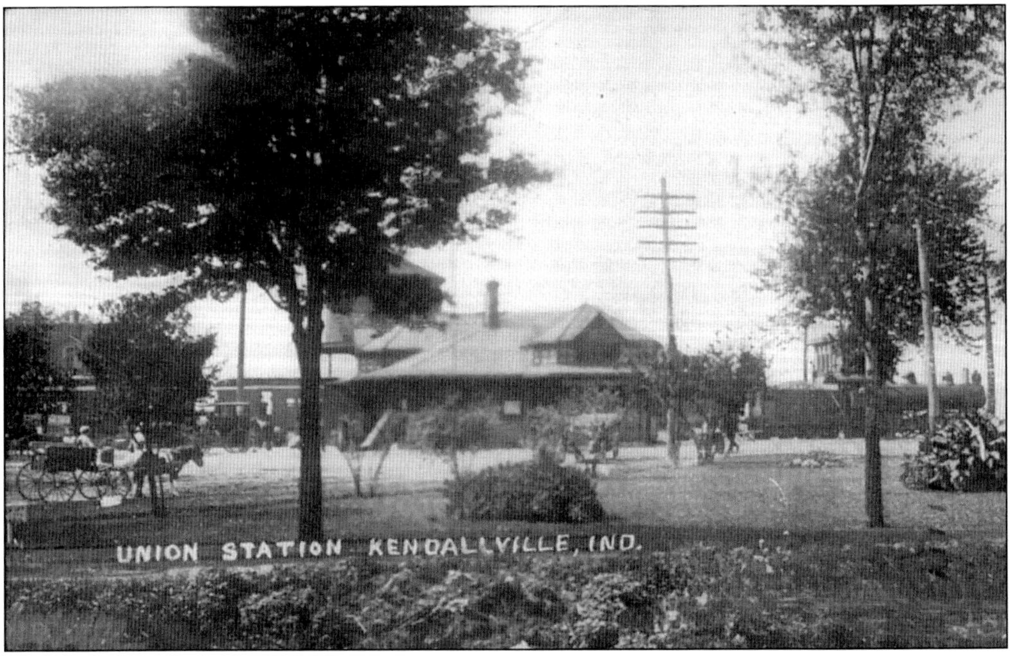

UNION STATION, KENDALLVILLE, INDIANA, C. 1912. In this era, nearly every station, regardless of size, was known as the "Union Station."

German Lutheran Church and School, Kendallville, Indiana. This card was published for Gutelin & Miller, Kendallville, Indiana. Northeastern Indiana was populated by many German immigrants. Services were commonly held in the German language until the 1930s.

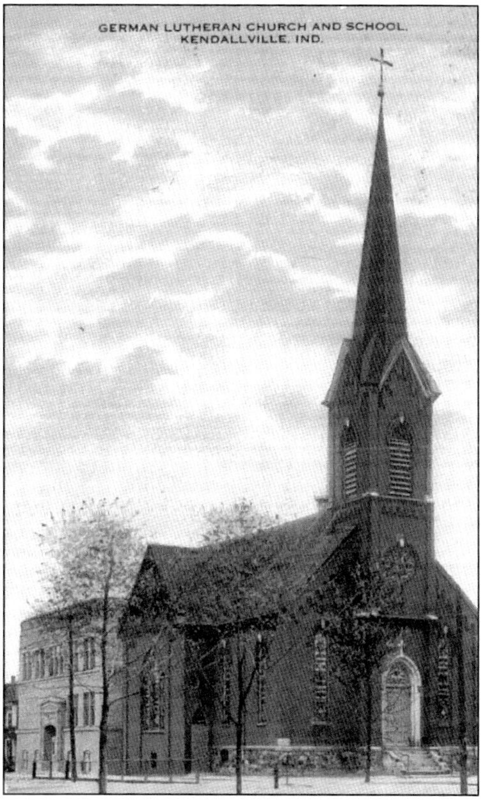

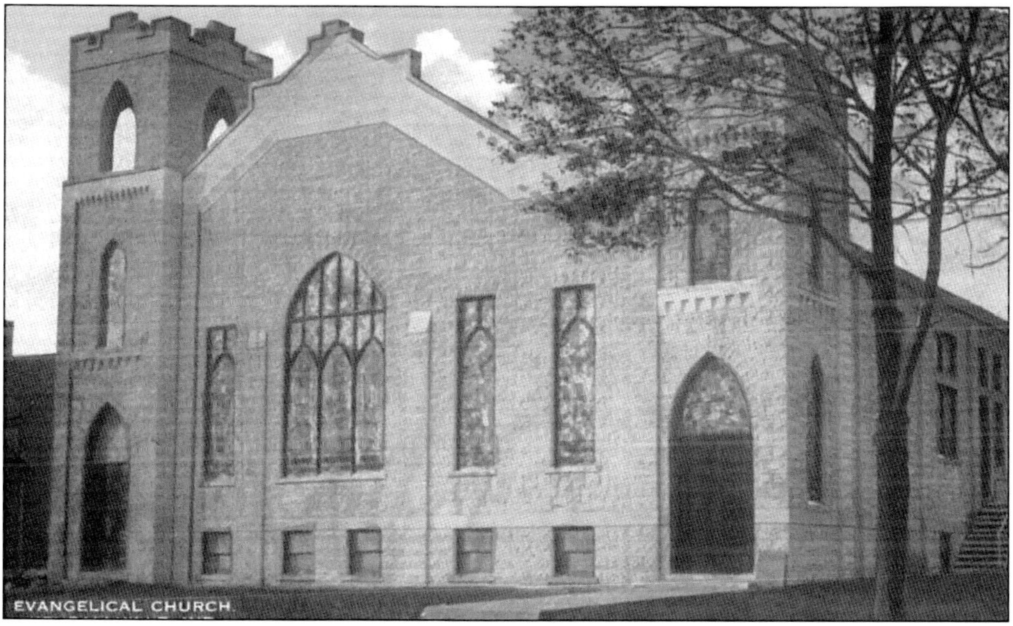

Evangelical Church, Kendallville, Indiana. Seen here is a handsome building with elaborate stained glass windows.

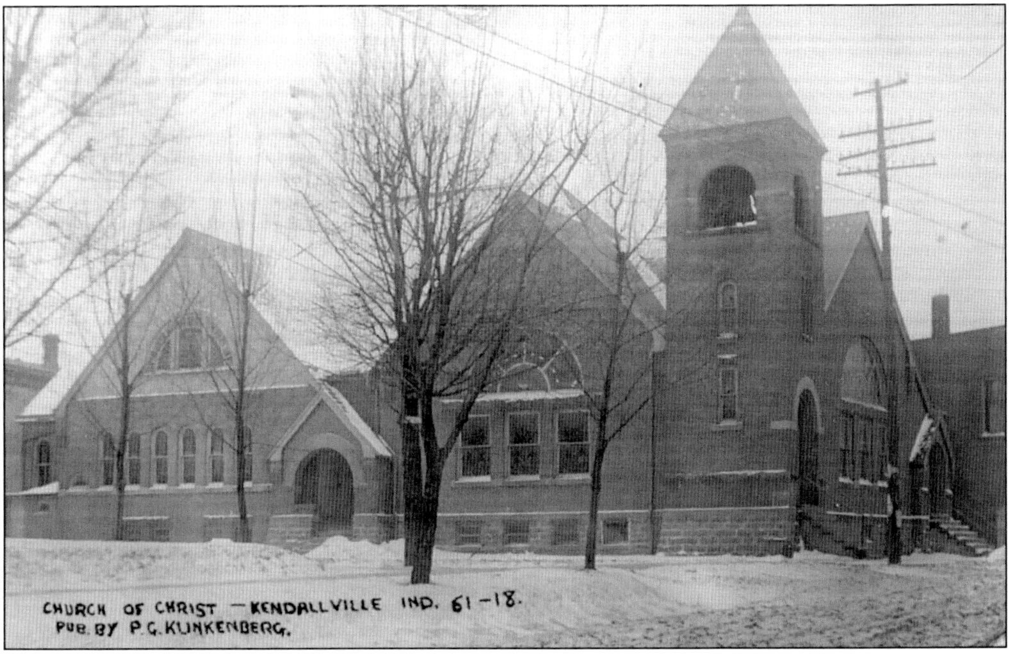

CHURCH OF CHRIST, KENDALLVILLE, INDIANA. This card was published by P.C. Klinkenberg. It was postmarked July 20, 1909. P.C. Klinkenberg was the proprietor of a popular drugstore.

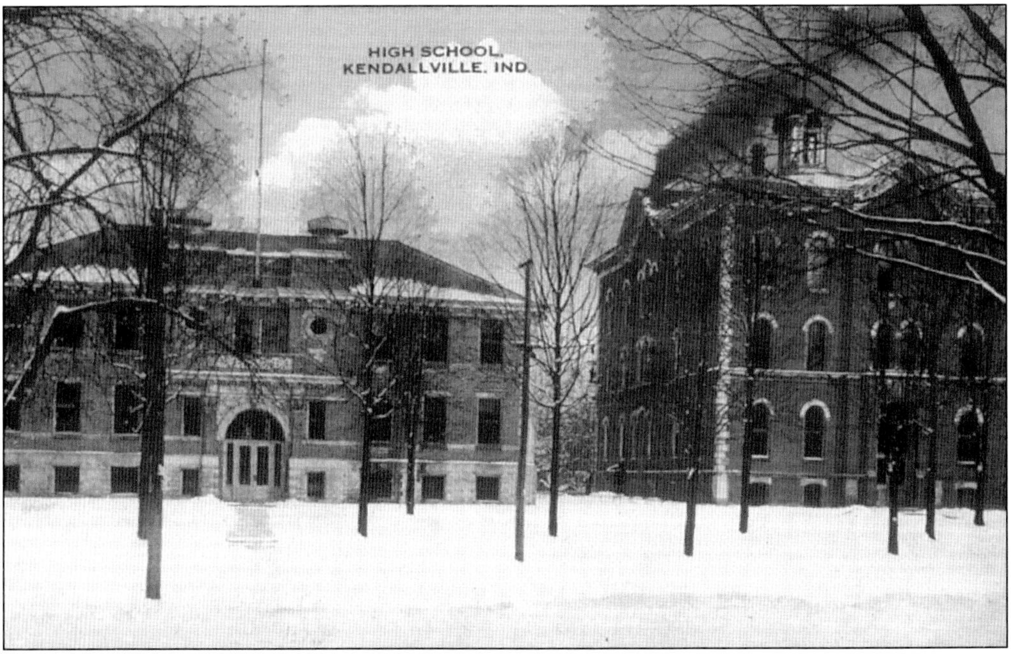

HIGH SCHOOL, KENDALLVILLE, INDIANA. Buildings were photographed in the winter due to the foliage on the trees.

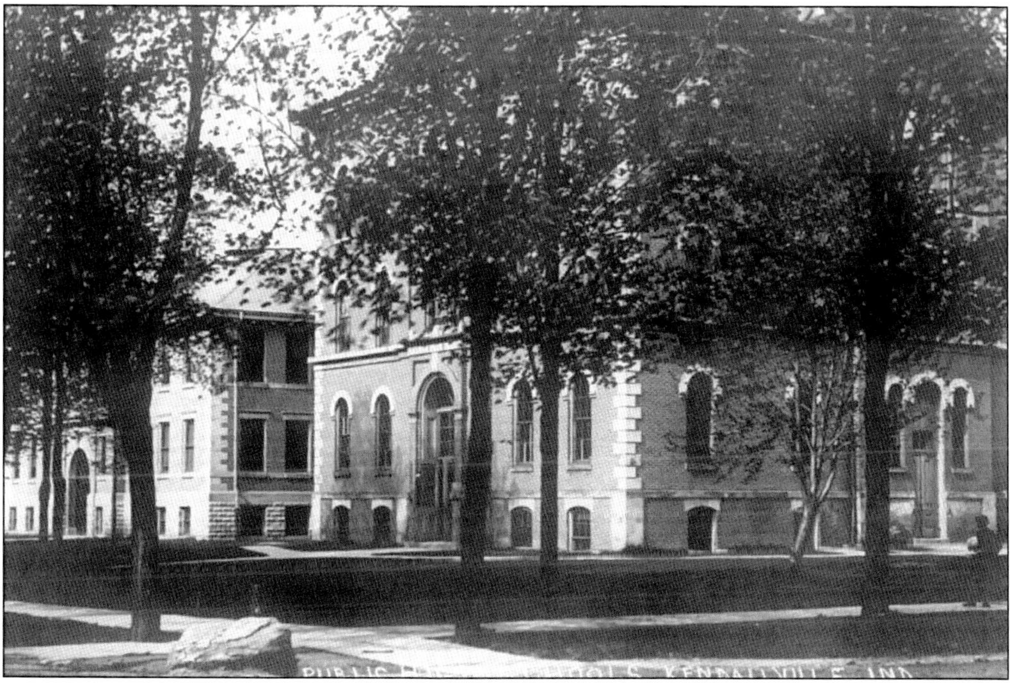

PUBLIC HIGH SCHOOLS, KENDALLVILLE, INDIANA, *c.* 1908. Seen here is a spring view.

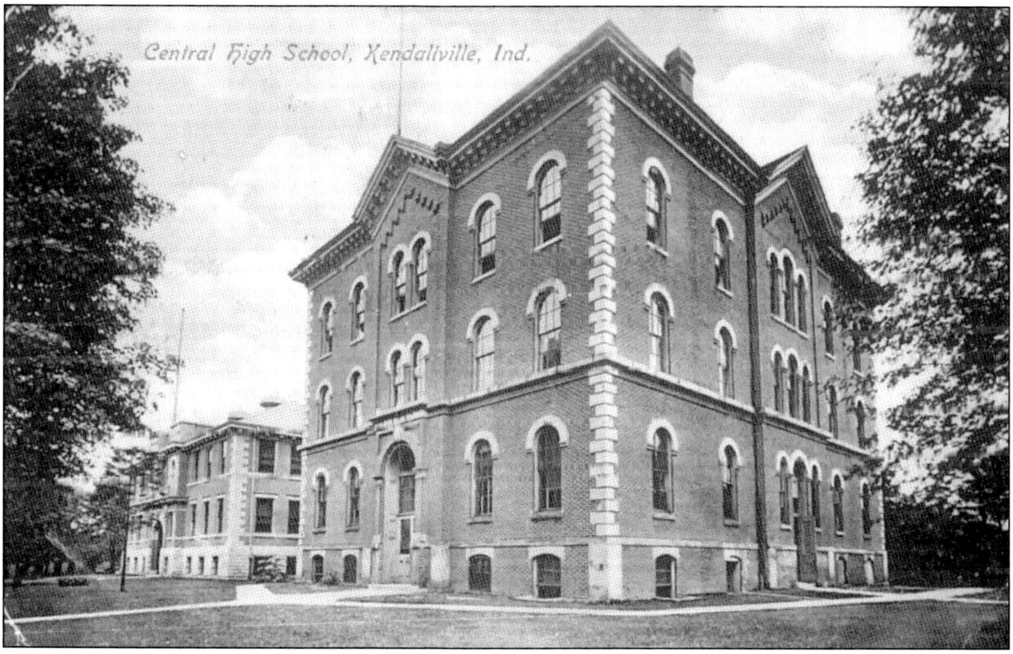

CENTRAL HIGH SCHOOL, KENDALLVILLE, INDIANA. Seen here is another view showing the handsome brick/stone construction.

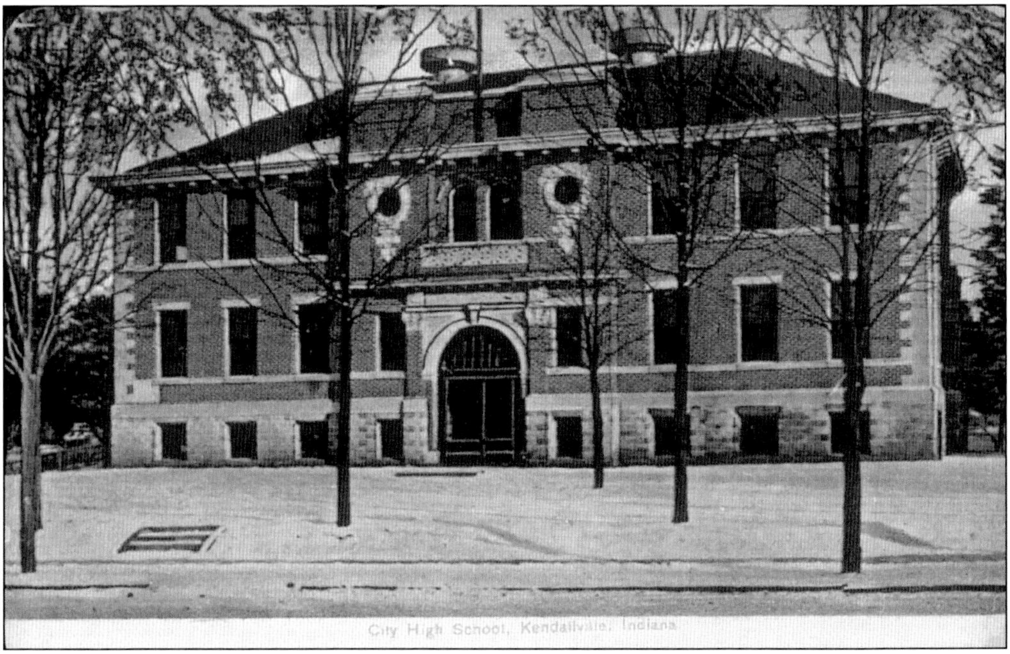

City High School, Kendallville, Indiana. Arched entrances were a common architectural device of the era.

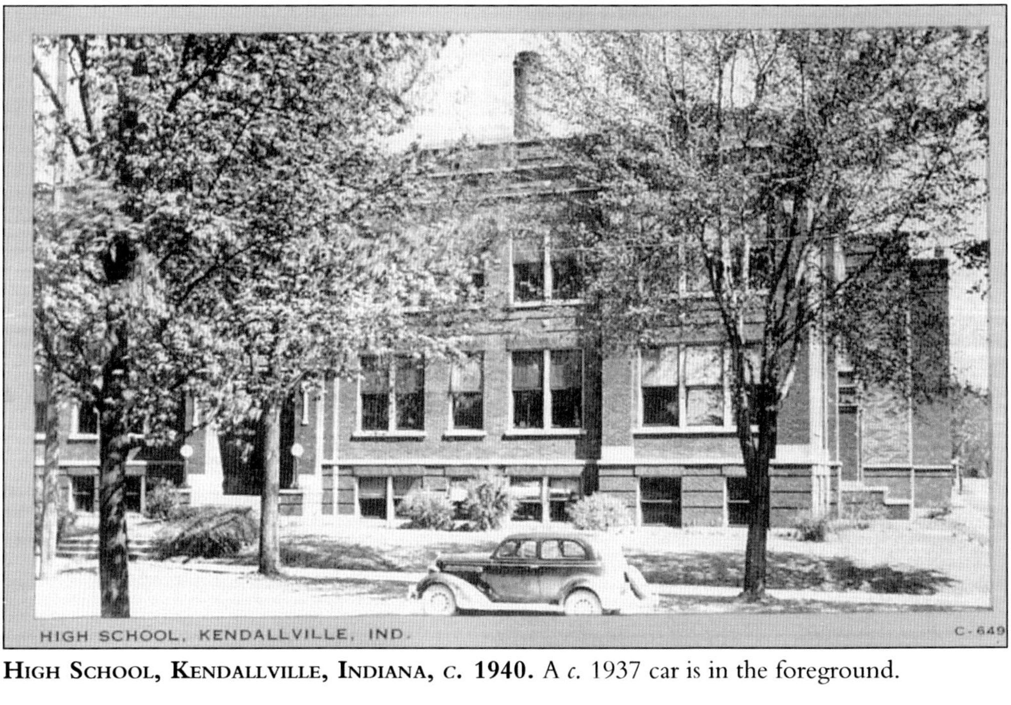

High School, Kendallville, Indiana, *c.* 1940. A *c.* 1937 car is in the foreground.

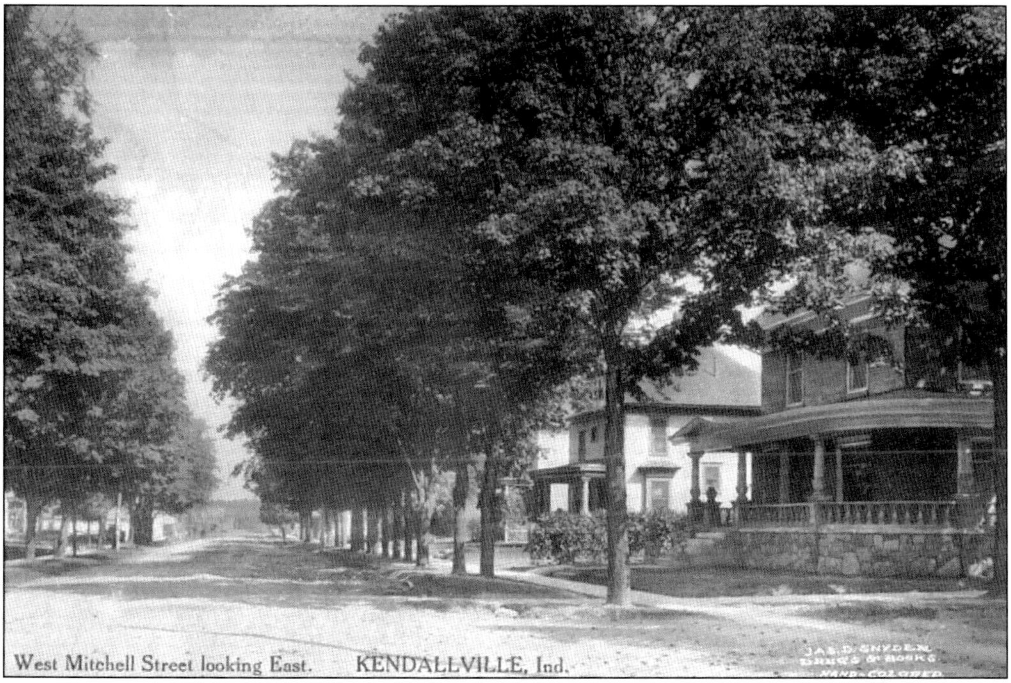

WEST MITCHELL STREET LOOKING EAST, KENDALLVILLE, INDIANA, *C.* 1917. This card was published by Jas. D. Snyder—Drugs & Books. Broad front porches provided the "air conditioning."

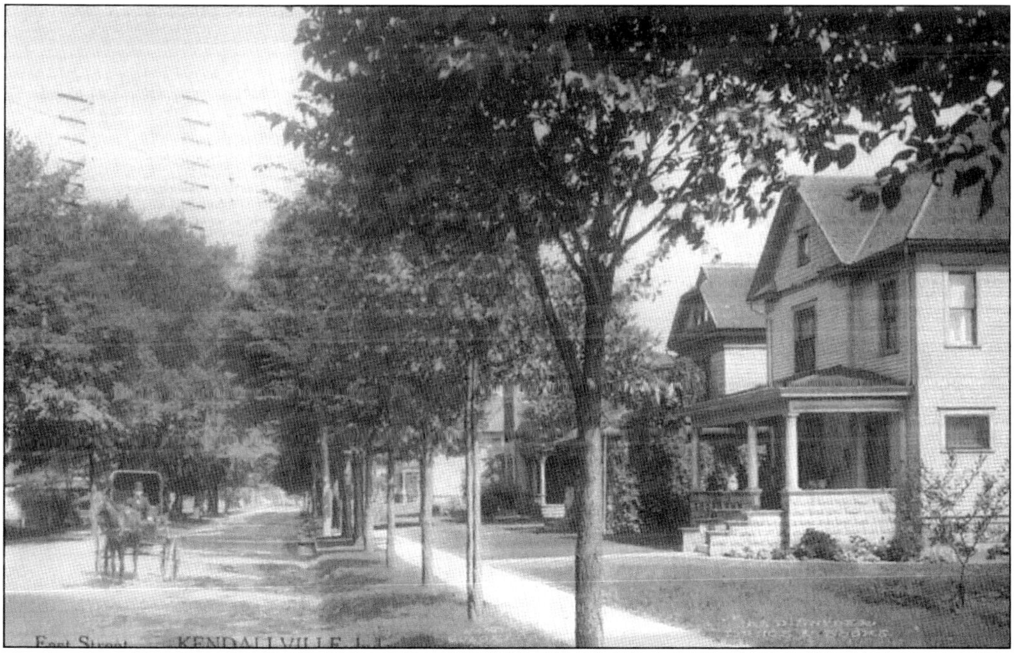

EAST STREET, KENDALLVILLE, INDIANA, *C.* 1913. A horse and buggy are on the left.

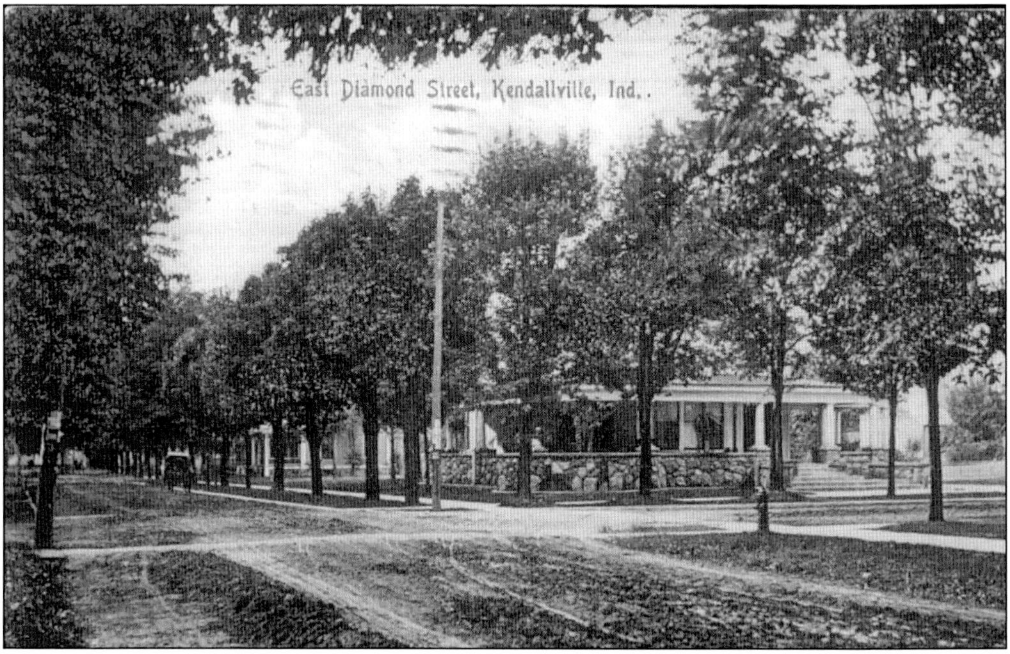

EAST DIAMOND STREET, KENDALLVILLE, INDIANA, *c.* 1910. The dirt streets were adequate but muddy and dirty.

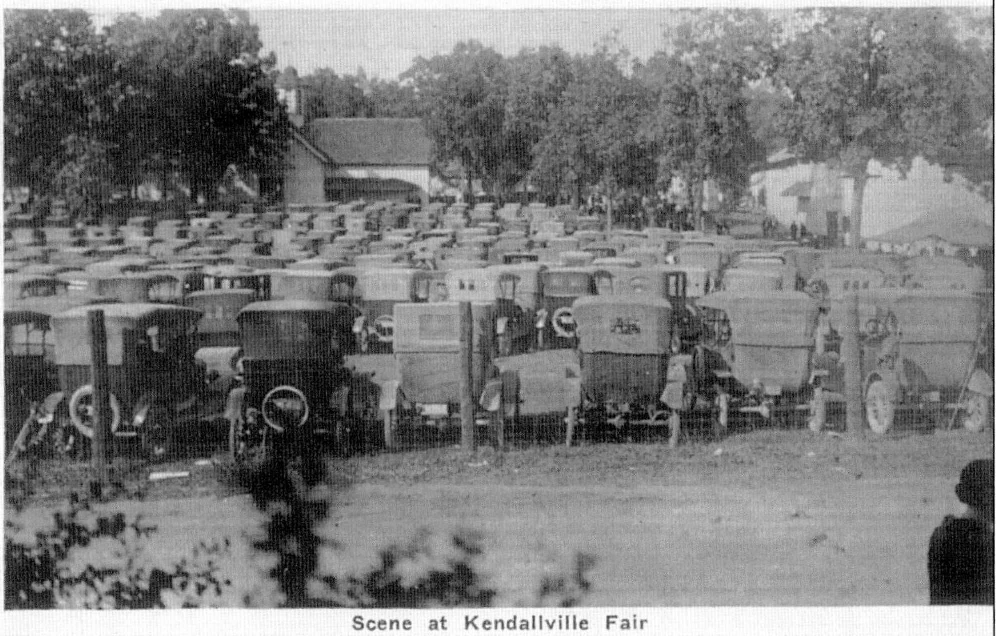

Scene at Kendallville Fair

SCENE AT KENDALLVILLE FAIR. Most of the automobiles are Model T Ford Touring Cars.

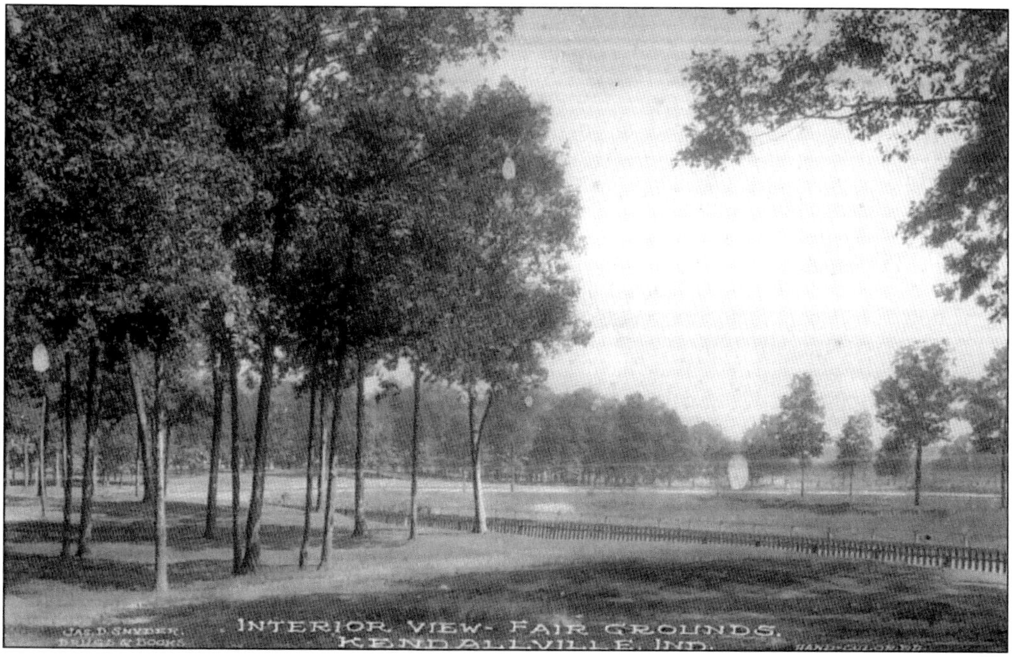

Interior View, Fair Grounds, Kendallville, Indiana. The grounds were maintained like a park.

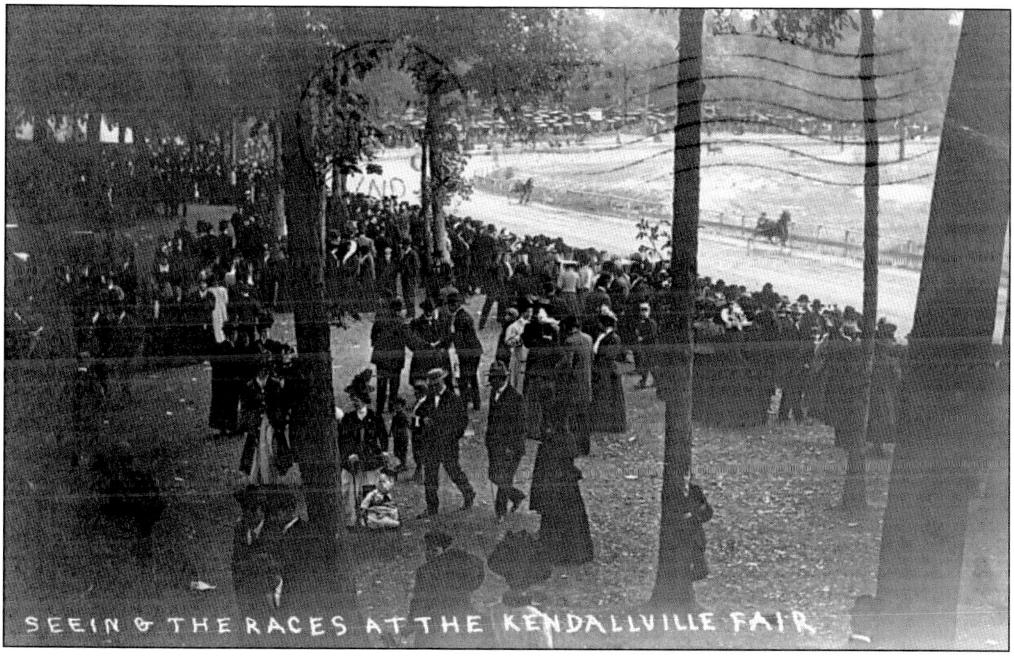

Seeing the Races at the Kendallville Fair, c. 1909. Both ladies and gentlemen are very well dressed. Many buggies are parked just beyond the track. Horse racing was very popular.

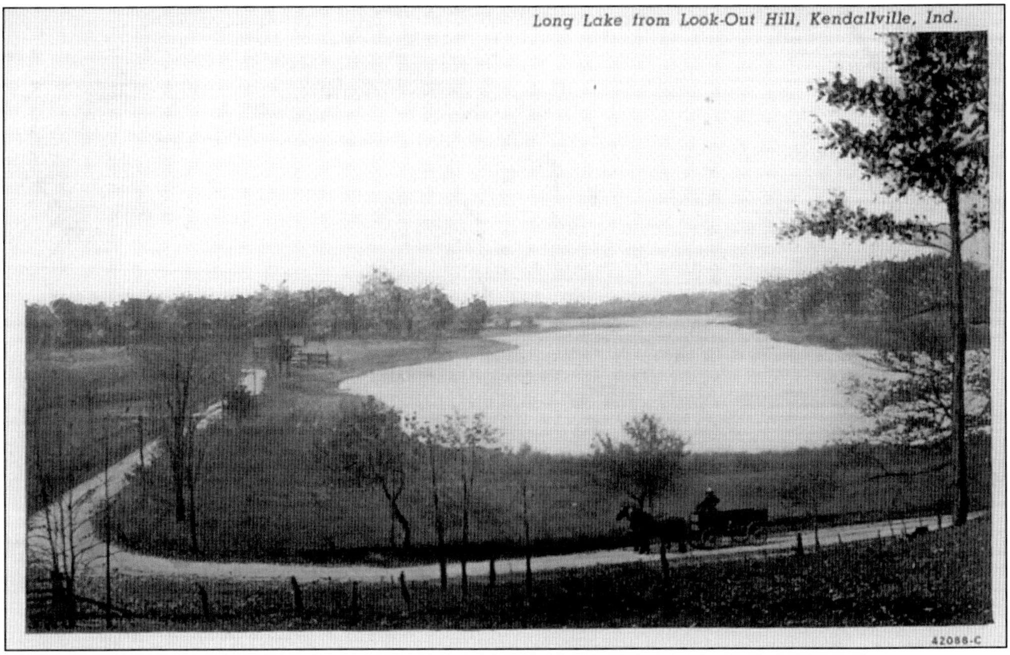

LONG LAKE FROM LOOK-OUT HILL, KENDALLVILLE, INDIANA. A horse and wagon are in the foreground.

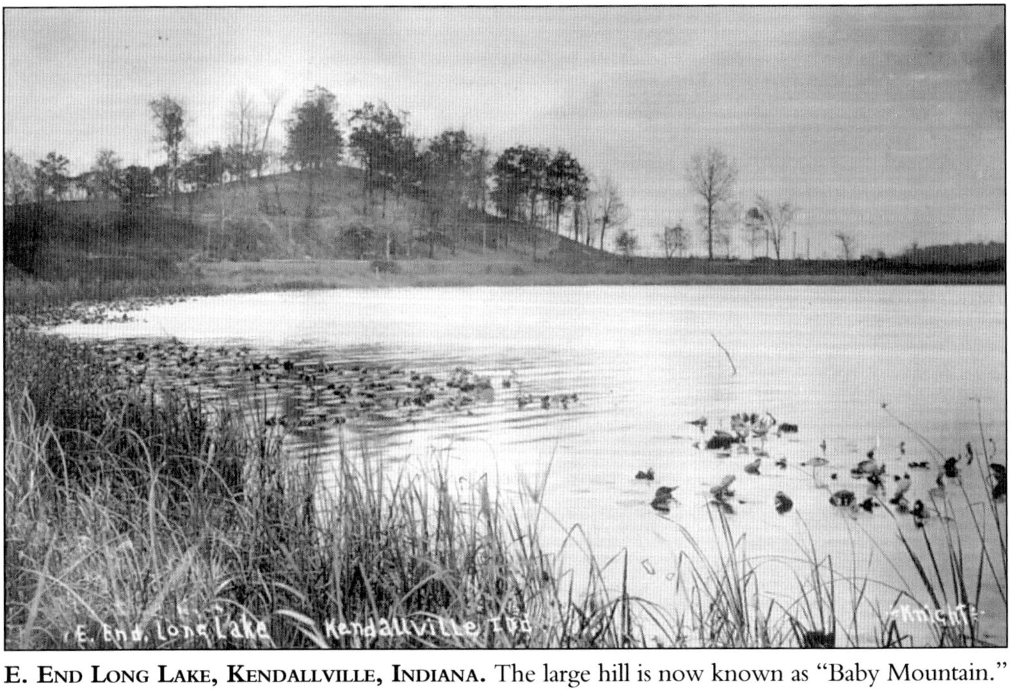

E. END LONG LAKE, KENDALLVILLE, INDIANA. The large hill is now known as "Baby Mountain."

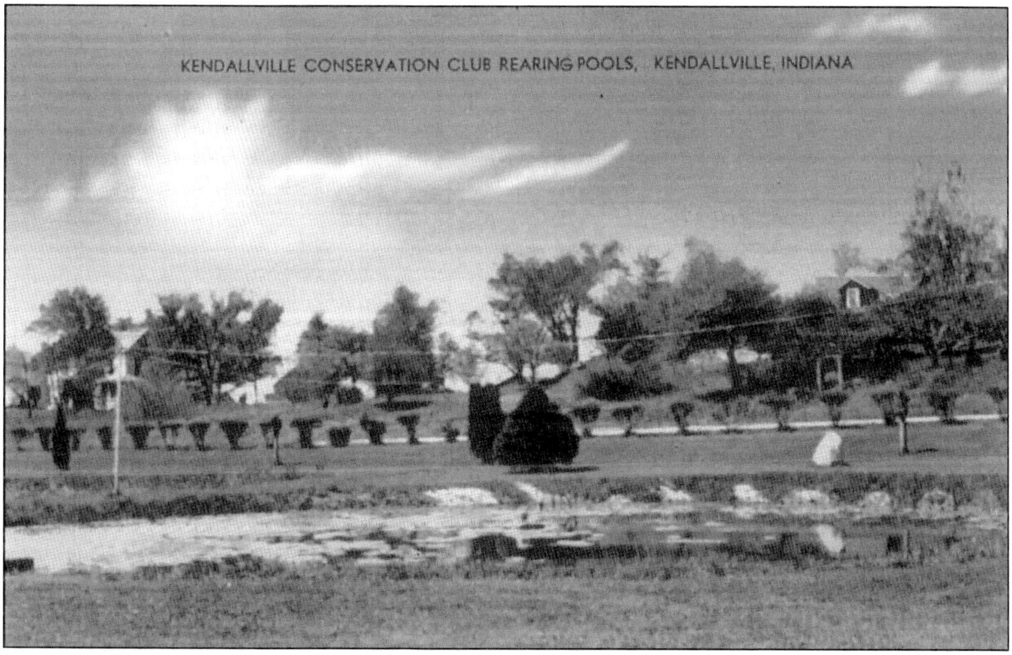

KENDALLVILLE CONSERVATION CLUB REARING POOLS, KENDALLVILLE, INDIANA. Fish were raised to be released in the nearby lakes.

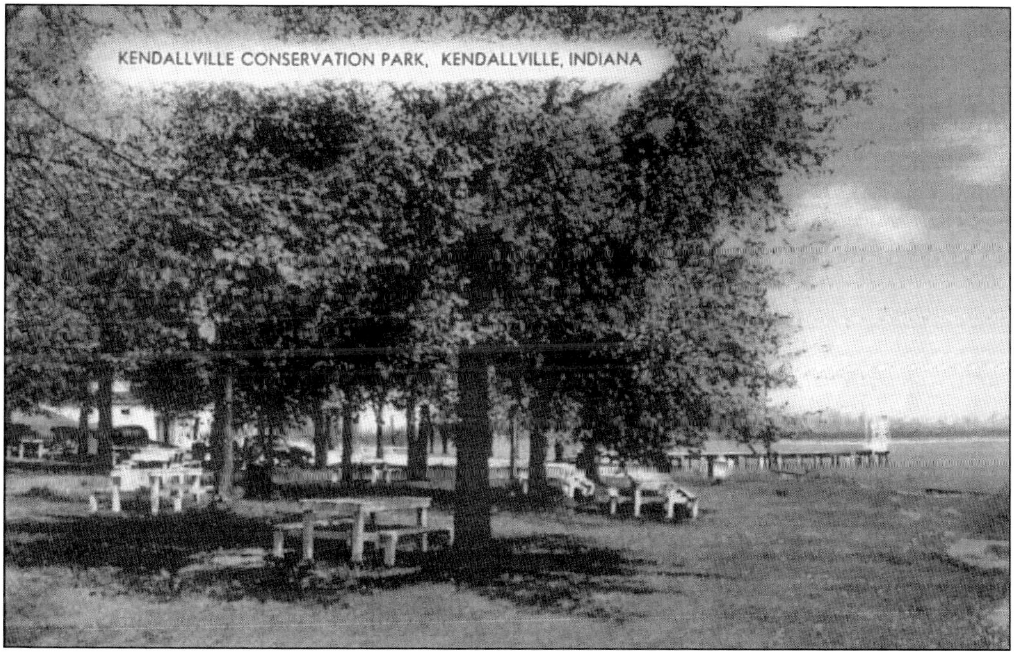

KENDALLVILLE CONSERVATION PARK, KENDALLVILLE, INDIANA. The park was a popular place for picnics.

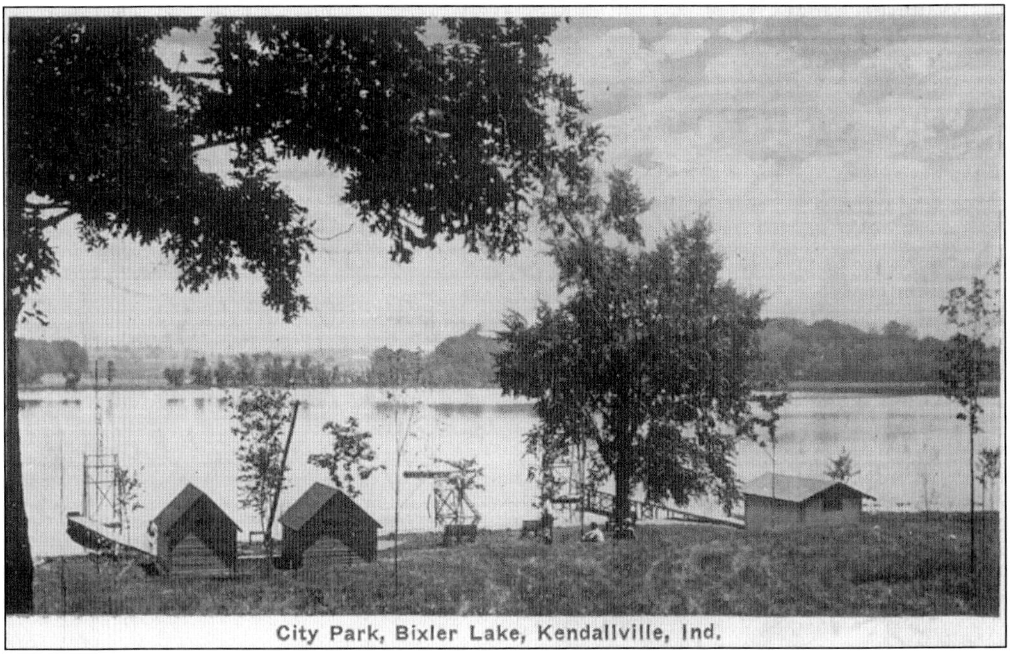

City Park, Bixler Lake, Kendallville, Indiana. The lake, located on the east side of Kendallville, was used by citizens for swimming, fishing, and boating.

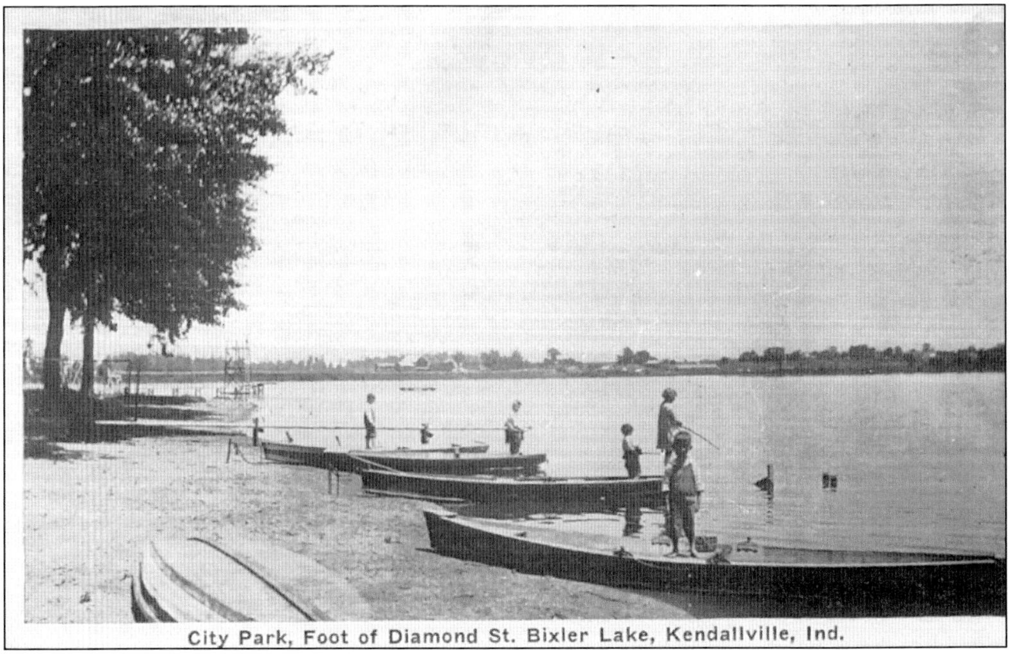

City Park, Foot of Diamond Street, Bixler Lake, Kendallville, Indiana, *c.* 1910. Long, slim boats were easy to row by hand.

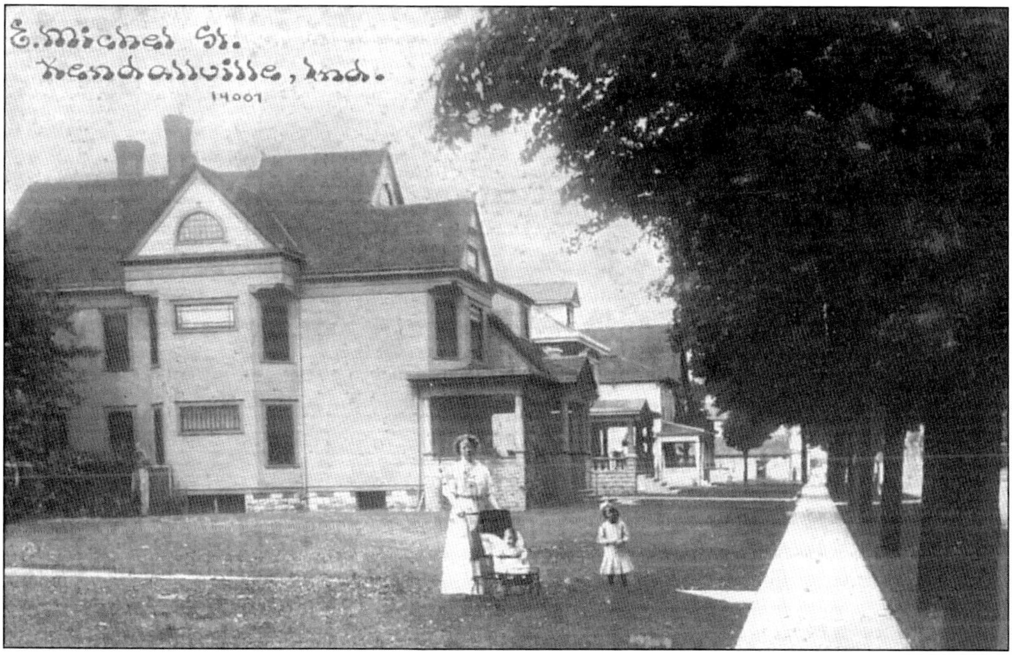

East Michel Street, Kendallville, Indiana. The mother and two children in this picture are not identified.

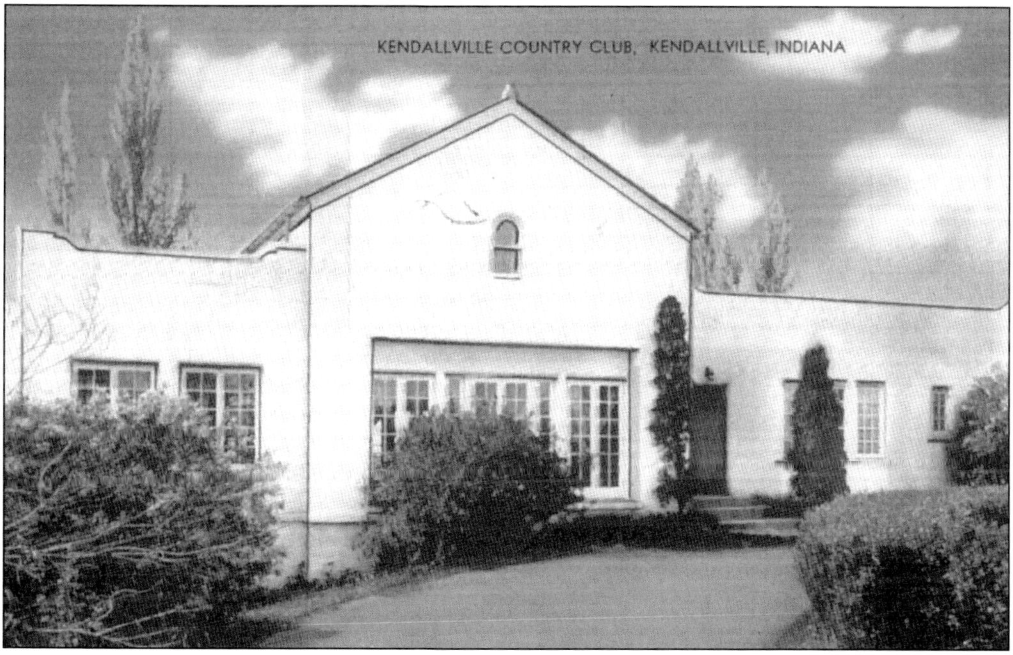

Kendallville Country Club, Kendallville, Indiana. Kendallville Country Club was a popular place.

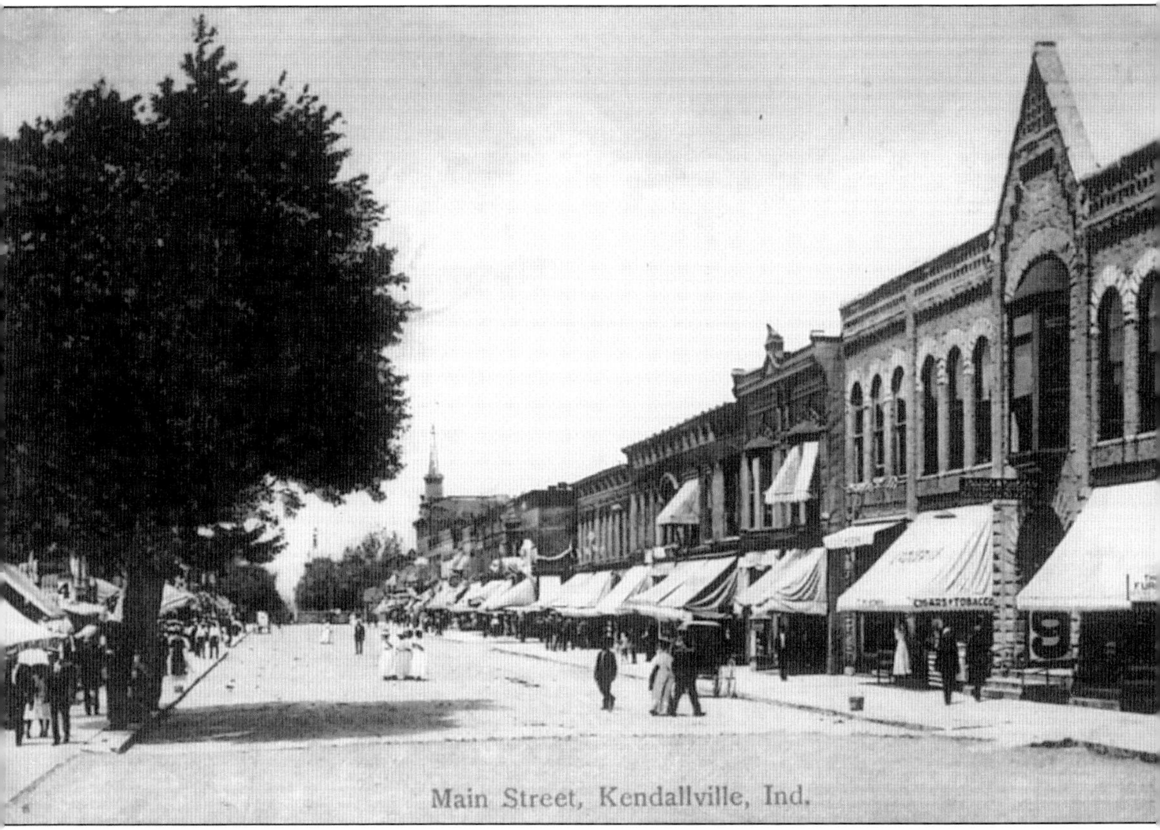

Main Street, Kendallville, Indiana, c. 1909. Mailed from Kendallville to James in Garrett, the message states, "My dear friend—Wasn't that a glorious time we had last night? You're a dandy. I never thought it of you ...Eula."

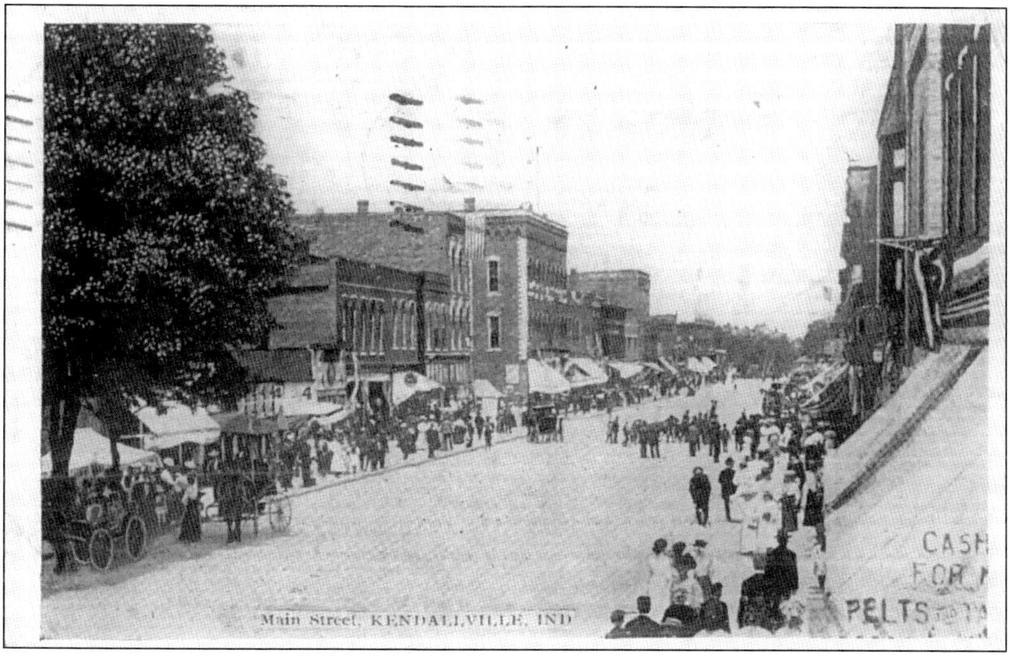

Main Street, Kendallville, Indiana. The sign at lower right reads, "Cash for Pelts." Many farmers trapped fur bearing animals during the winter months. The pelts were sold to local buyers who then sold them to brokers in large cities, usually New York.

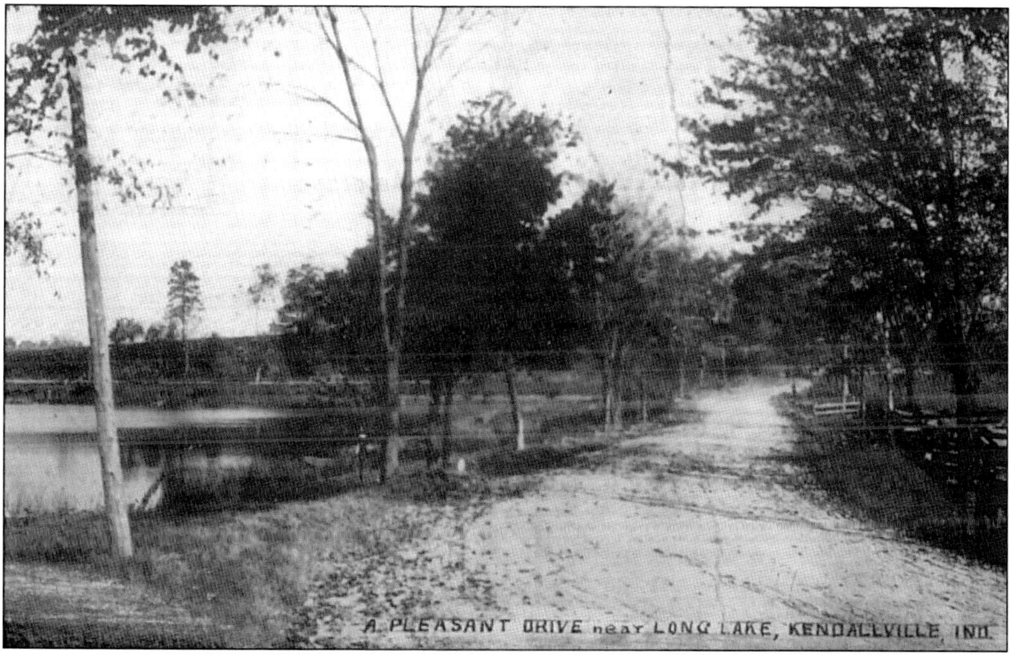

A Pleasant Drive Near Long Lake, Kendallville, Indiana. The message states, "Am in Kendallville seeing the sights, Ha Ha. Going to work Monday night?… I will explain about the party. If you don't come on. Meet us out the Transfer Cor. At 7:30 that is going out there at 7:45. Now you be sure. Don't forget. B.W."

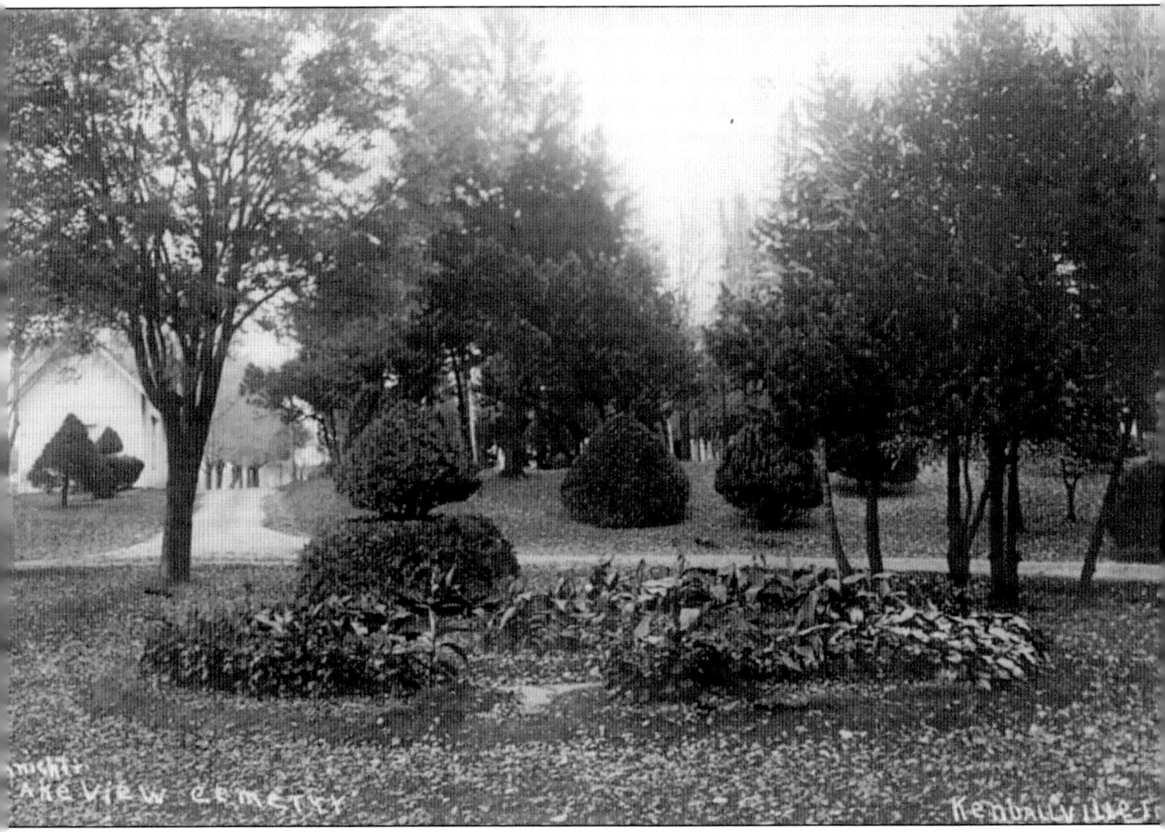

Lakeview Cemetery, Kendallville, Indiana. A tranquil place to spend eternity!

Two

Albion

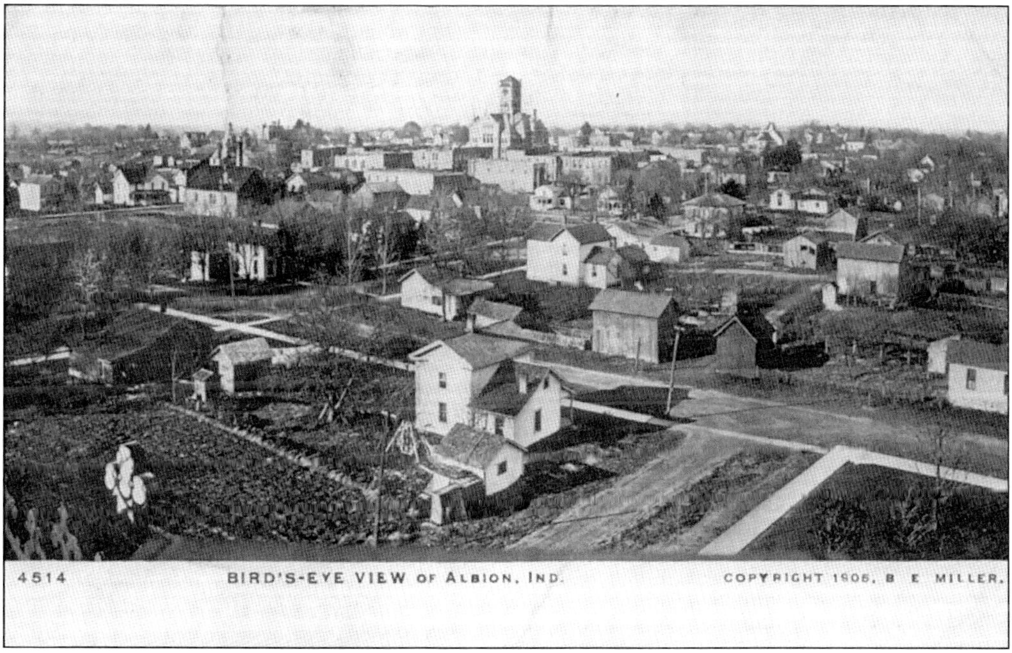

Bird's-Eye View of Albion, Indiana, *c.* 1905. The sidewalks appear to be concrete, but the white streets are still dirt. Part of the cornice of the schoolhouse from which roof the photograph was taken can be seen in the lower left.

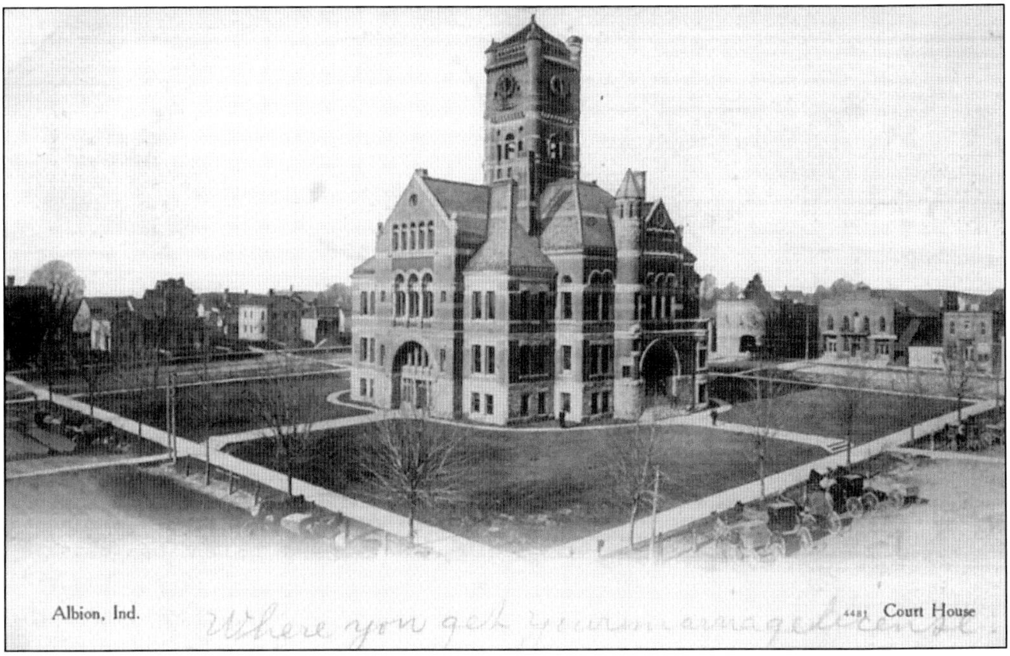

ALBION, INDIANA, *C.* 1907. This card is interesting for its message. Addressed to Miss Rosa Schlotterer, it hints "where you get your marriage license."

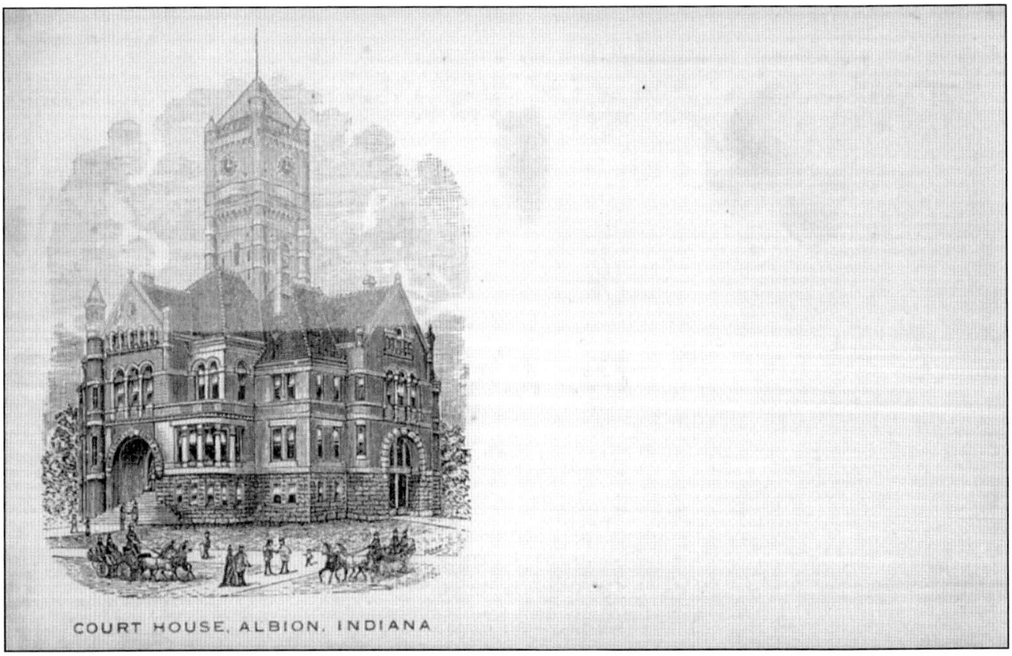

COURTHOUSE, ALBION, INDIANA. This is a "Private Mailing Card" authorized by Act of Congress—May 19, 1899. The printed addressee is Dr. R.S. Malong, Albion, Indiana. The etching of the courthouse was a stock image. Space was left for a message on the front of the card.

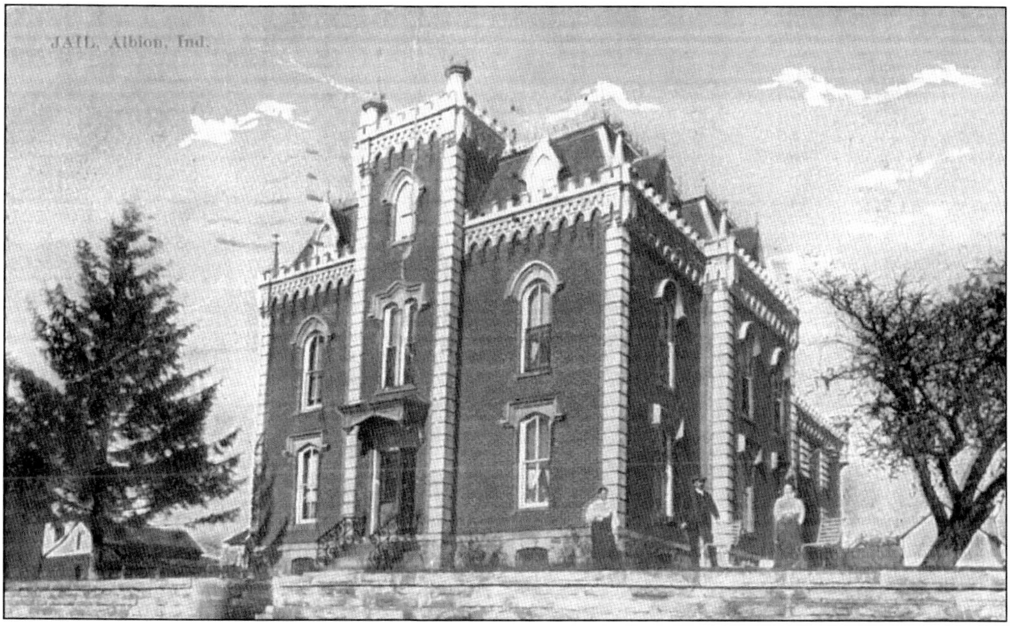

JAIL, ALBION, INDIANA. This handsome Italianate structure provided a residence for the sheriff and his family in the front and jail cells in the rear. The sheriff's wife was usually the jail matron and provided meals for the prisoners.

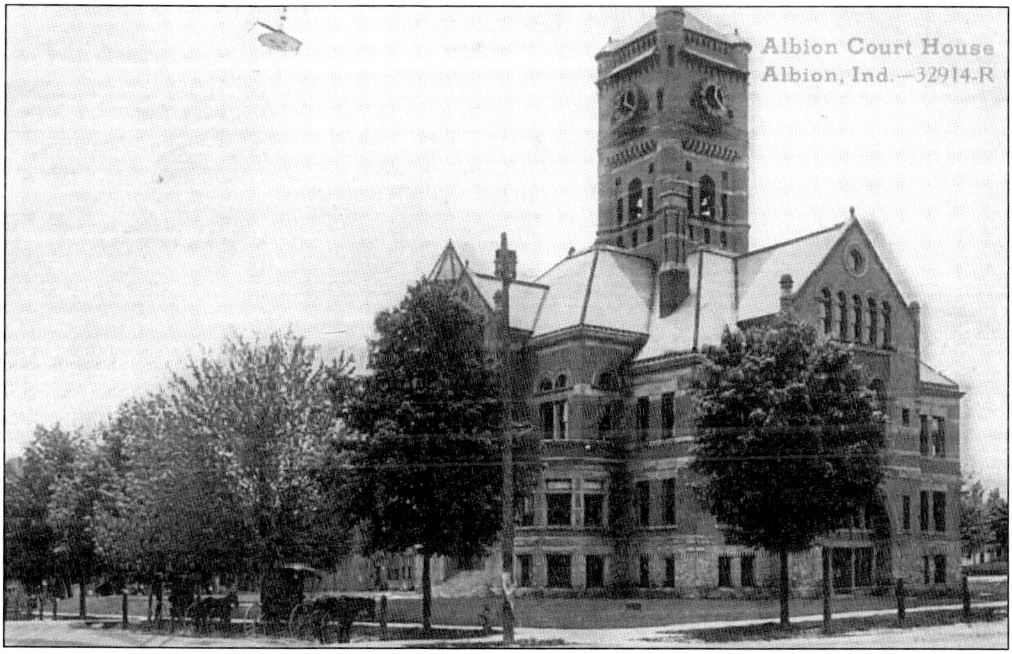

ALBION COURT HOUSE, ALBION, INDIANA, *c.* 1914. Note the streetlight in upper left and buggies tied to hitching post. The message states, "Yesterday I was to Albion. Papa went to pay his taxes. We went up with Uncle John's in the Auto. We went by Ligonier and came back by Ligonier. You no that the best way. Ha. Ha. … I have not got any girl now. I cut that one out but she does not no it I guess."

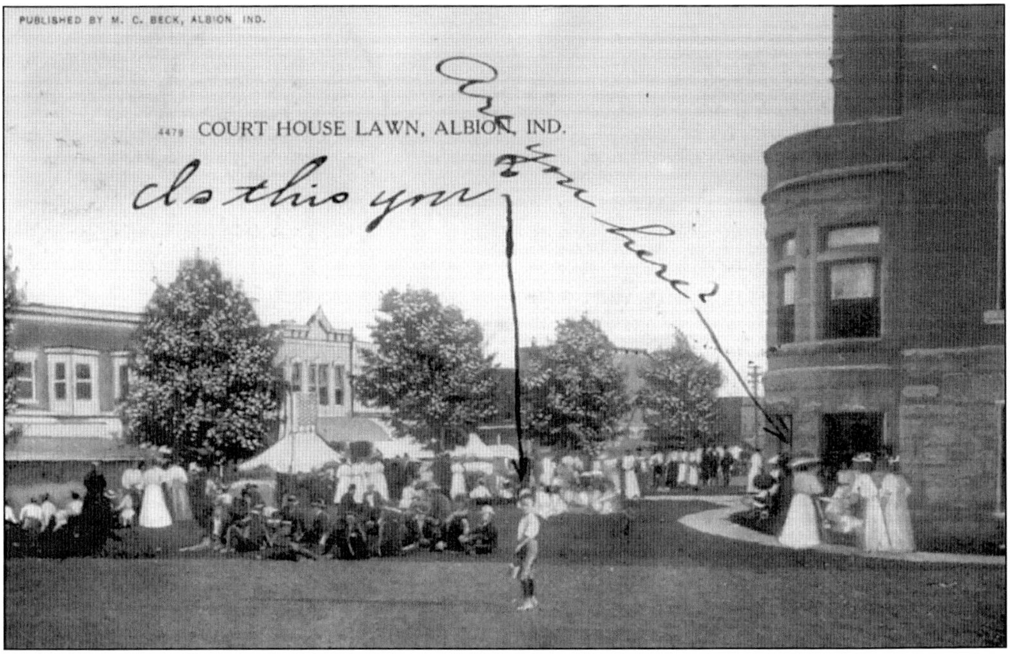

COURT HOUSE LAWN, ALBION, INDIANA, *c.* 1908. This picture was probably taken during the street fair.

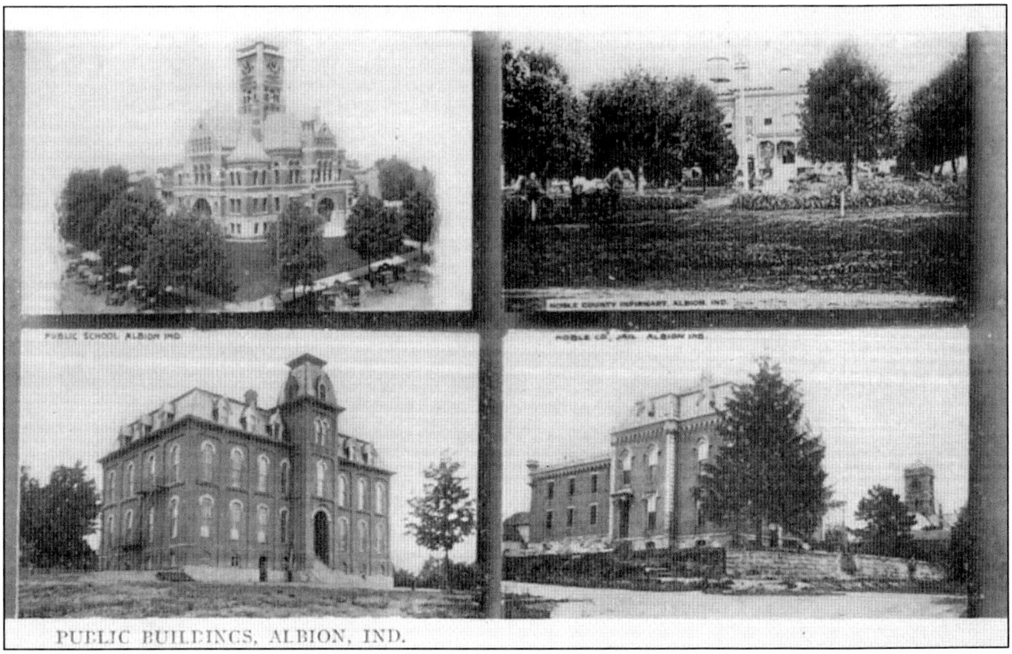

PUBLIC BUILDINGS, ALBION, INDIANA. Seen here are the Noble County Infirmary, Public School, and Noble County Jail.

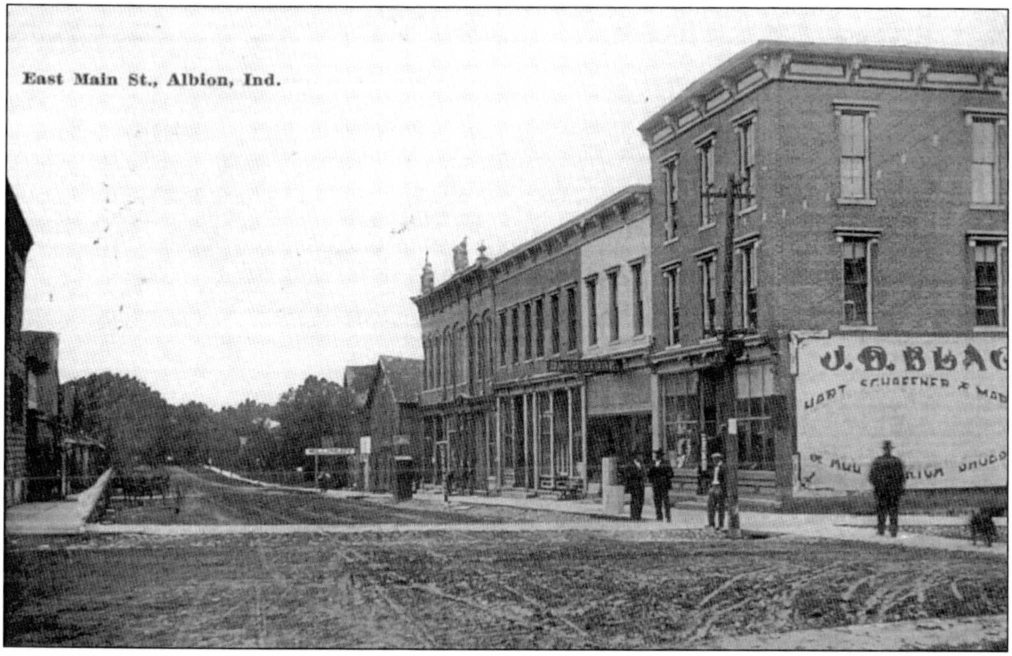

EAST MAIN STREET, ALBION, INDIANA. The sign on the building on the right states, "J.D. Black—Hart Schaeffner & Marx." The sign at the end of the street states, "Millinery."

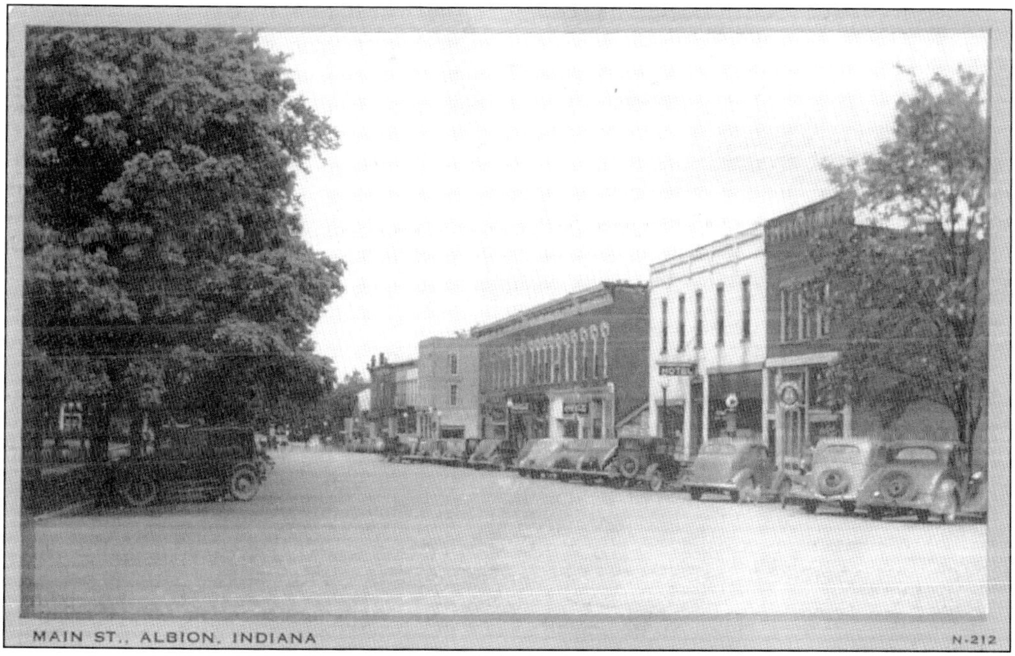

MAIN STREET, ALBION, INDIANA, C. 1940. This is the south side of the public square.

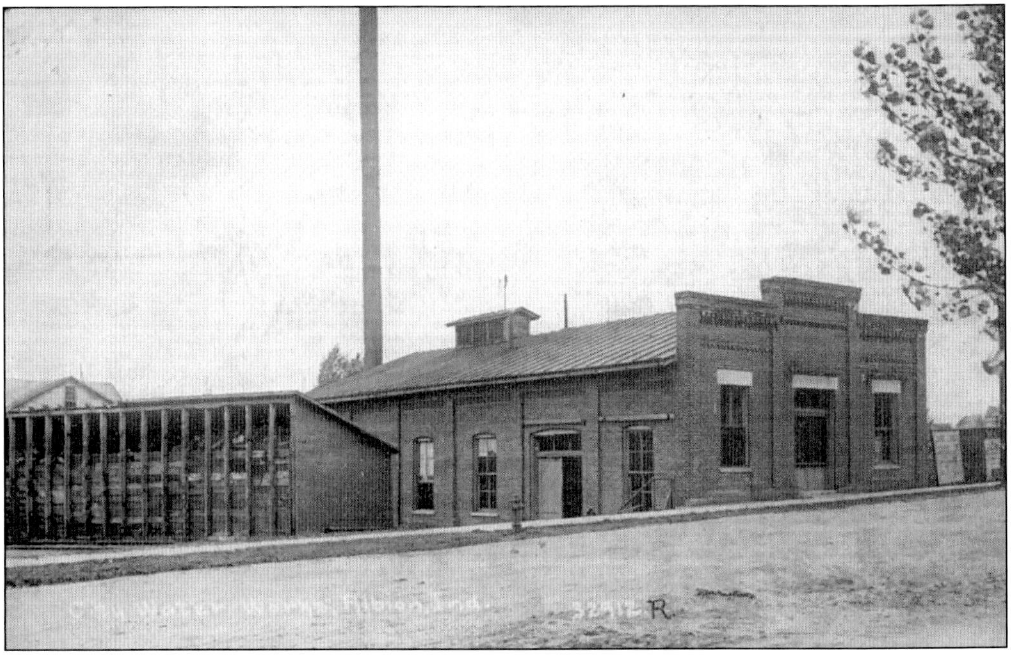

CITY WATER WORKS, ALBION, INDIANA. Citizens were proud that their town had a public water system.

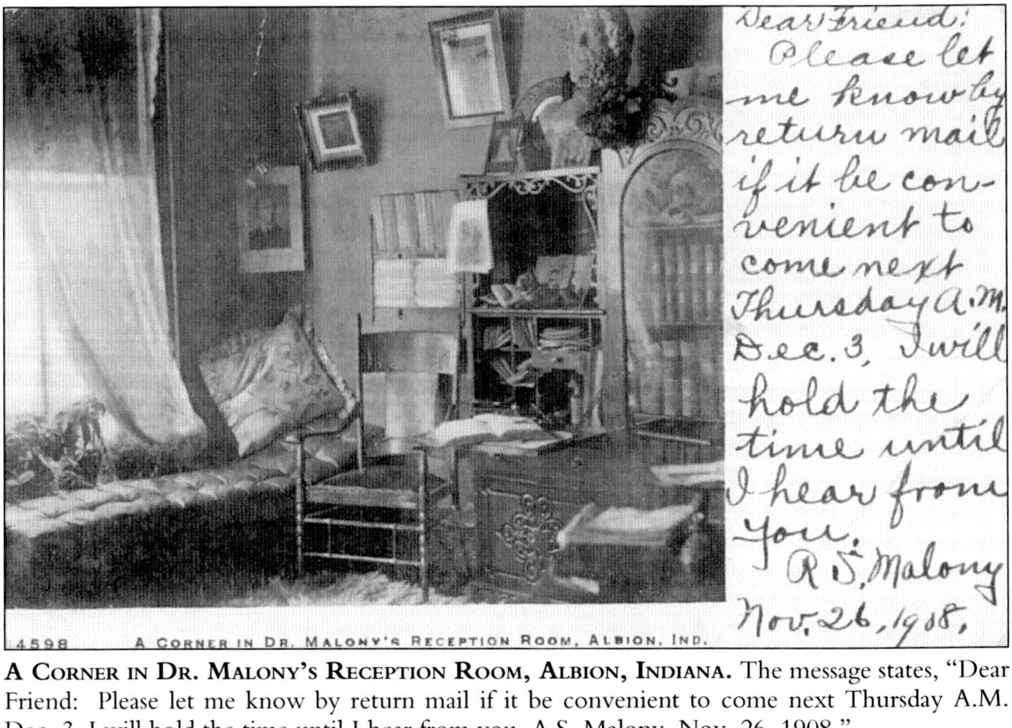

A CORNER IN DR. MALONY'S RECEPTION ROOM, ALBION, INDIANA. The message states, "Dear Friend: Please let me know by return mail if it be convenient to come next Thursday A.M. Dec. 3. I will hold the time until I hear from you. A.S. Malony. Nov. 26, 1908."

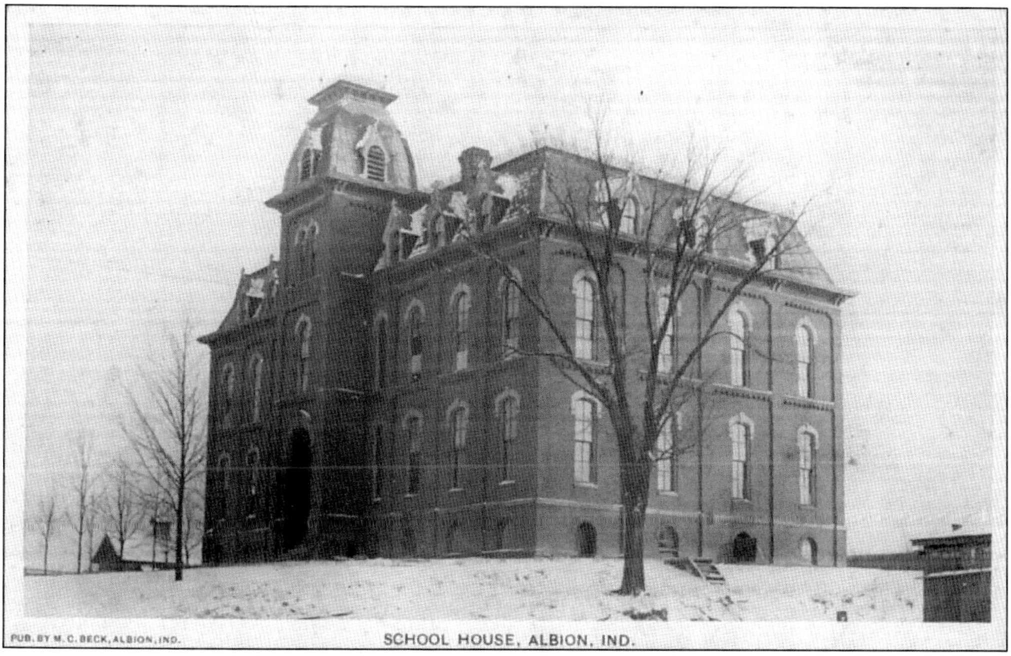

School House, Albion, Indiana. This winter view shows the building in profile.

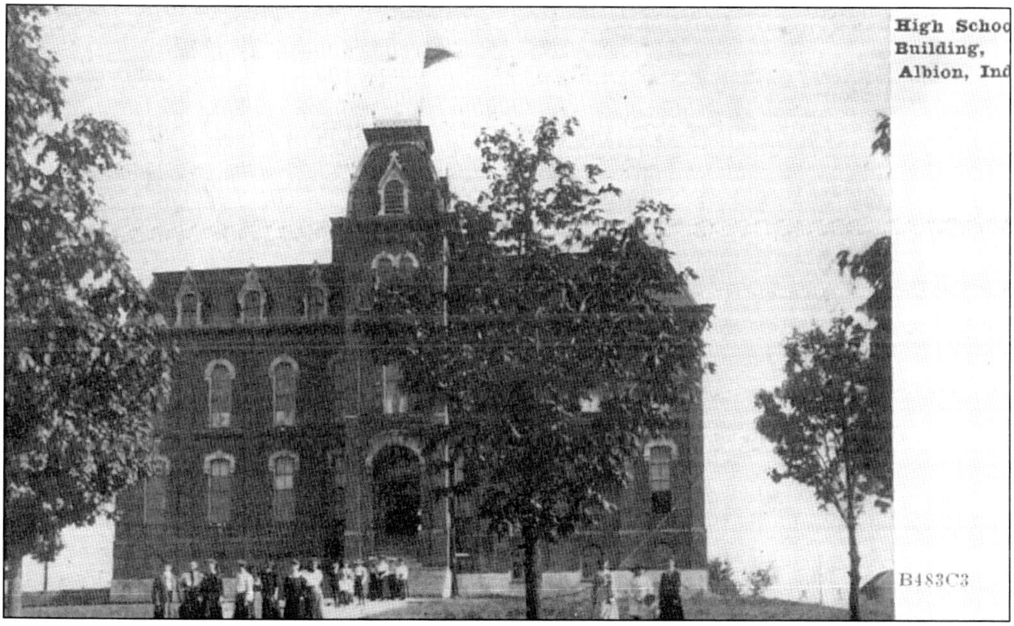

High School Building, Albion, Indiana. The students are on the front walk. Note the long skirts.

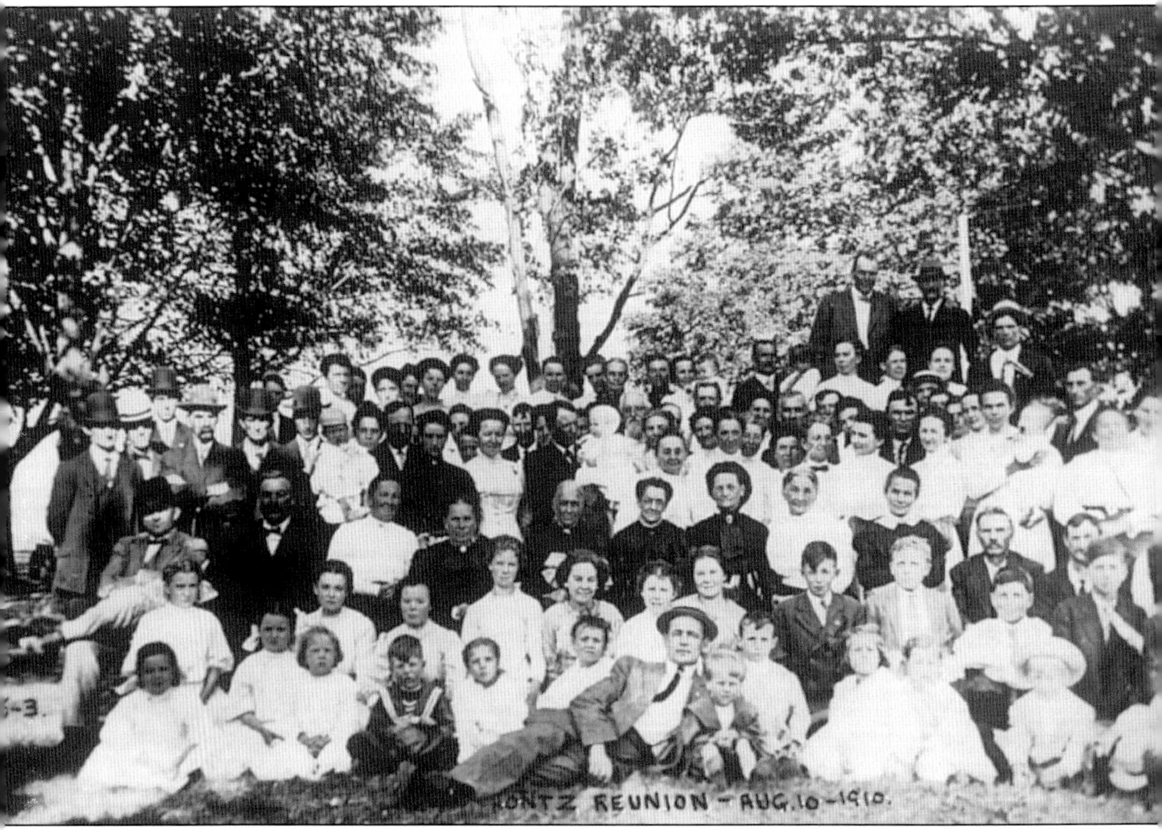

HONTZ REUNION, AUGUST 10, 1910. This Noble County Reunion Scene is typical of group photographs taken at reunions. The Hontz Family seems overdressed for a hot August day!

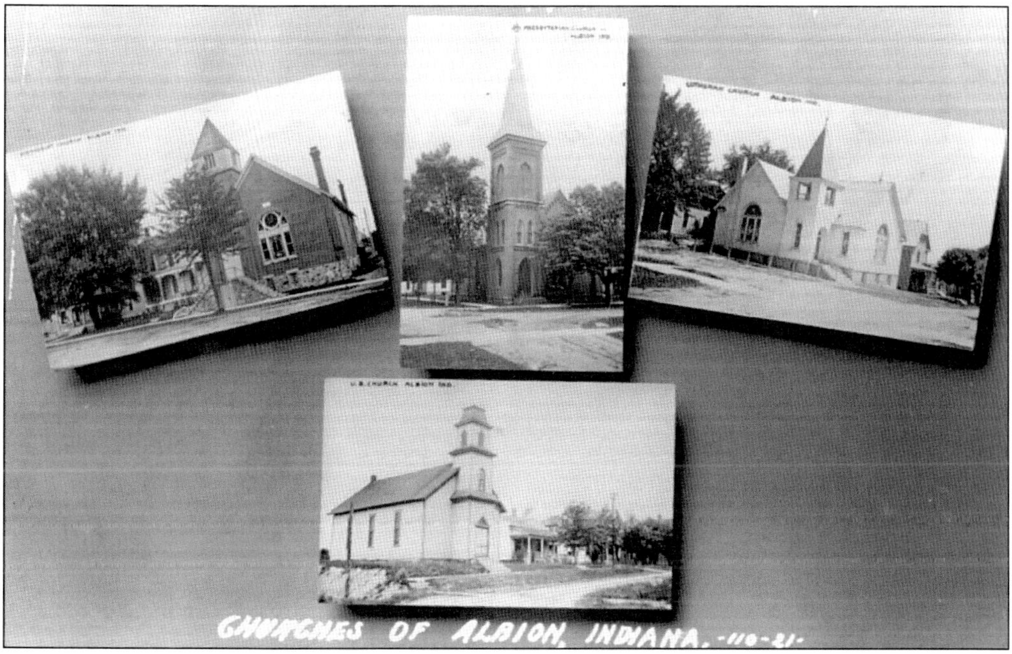

CHURCHES OF ALBION, INDIANA. Pictured here, from left to right, are as follows: Methodist Church, Presbyterian Church, and Lutheran Church; (lower) U.B. Church.

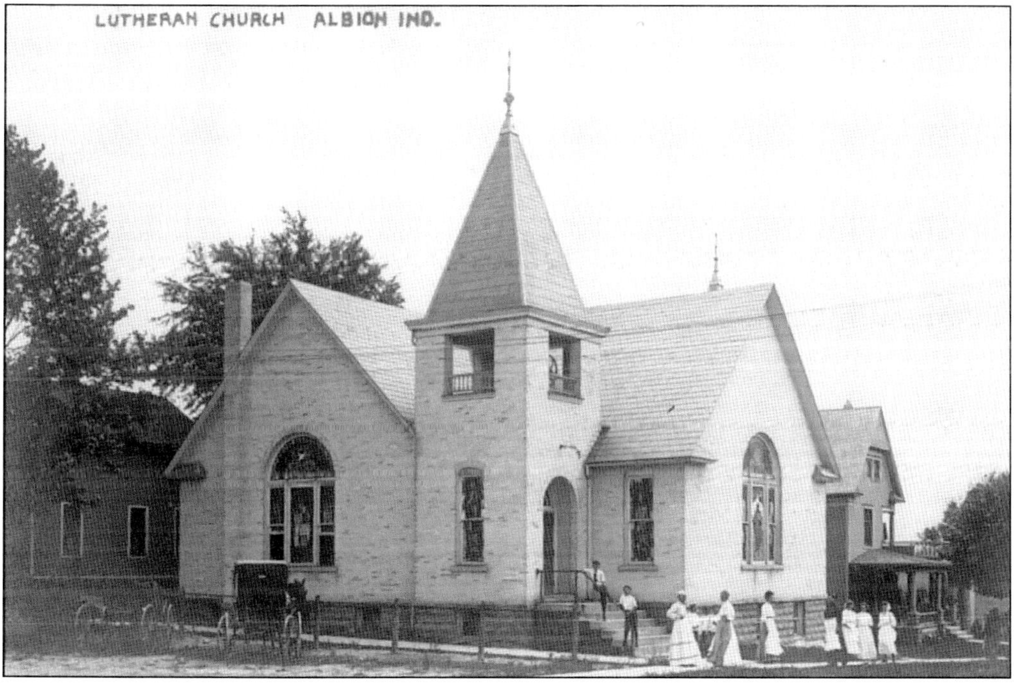

LUTHERAN CHURCH, ALBION, INDIANA. Note hitching rack and buggies at left.

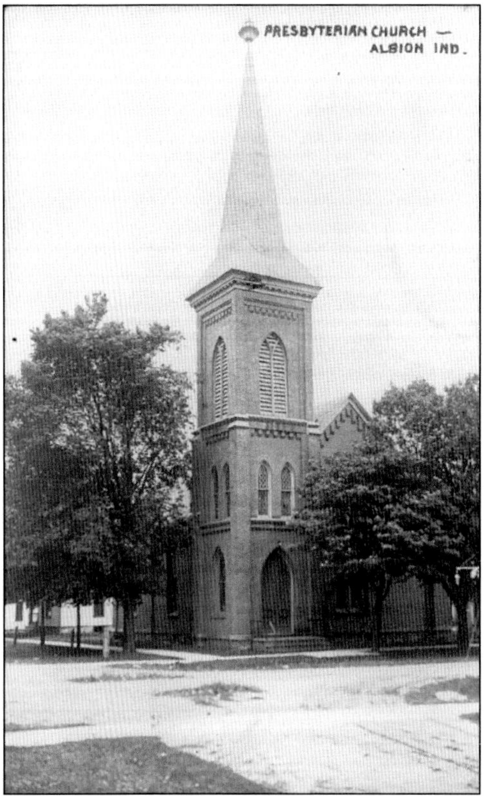

PRESBYTERIAN CHURCH, ALBION, INDIANA. The tower contained the bell which rang to call worshipers to services.

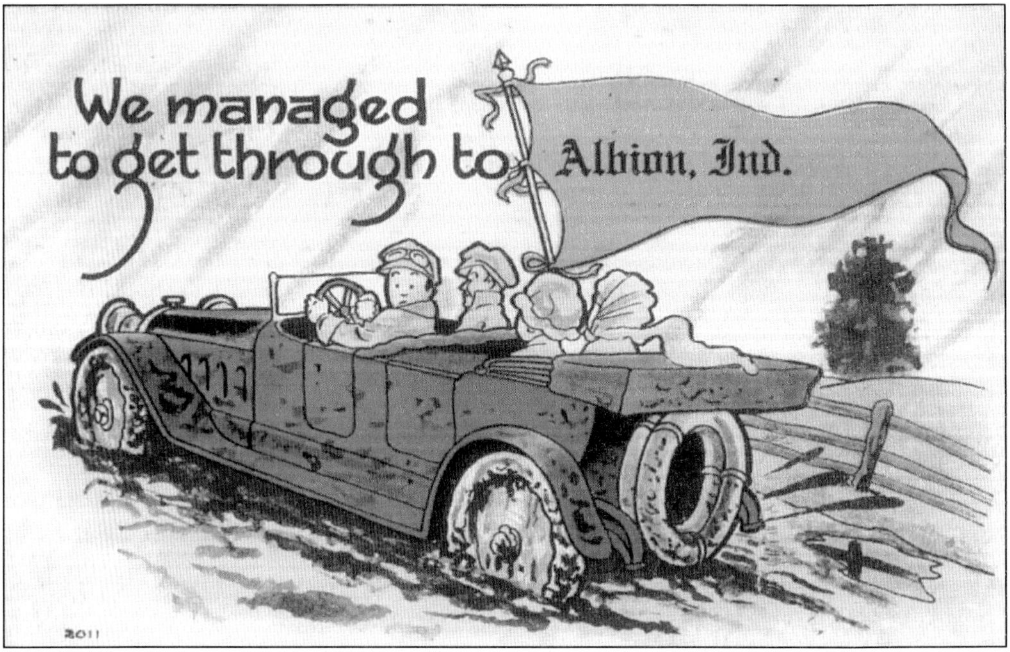

WE MANAGED TO GET THROUGH TO ALBION, INDIANA, *c.* 1916. This stock novelty card has an Albion imprint.

Three

Avilla

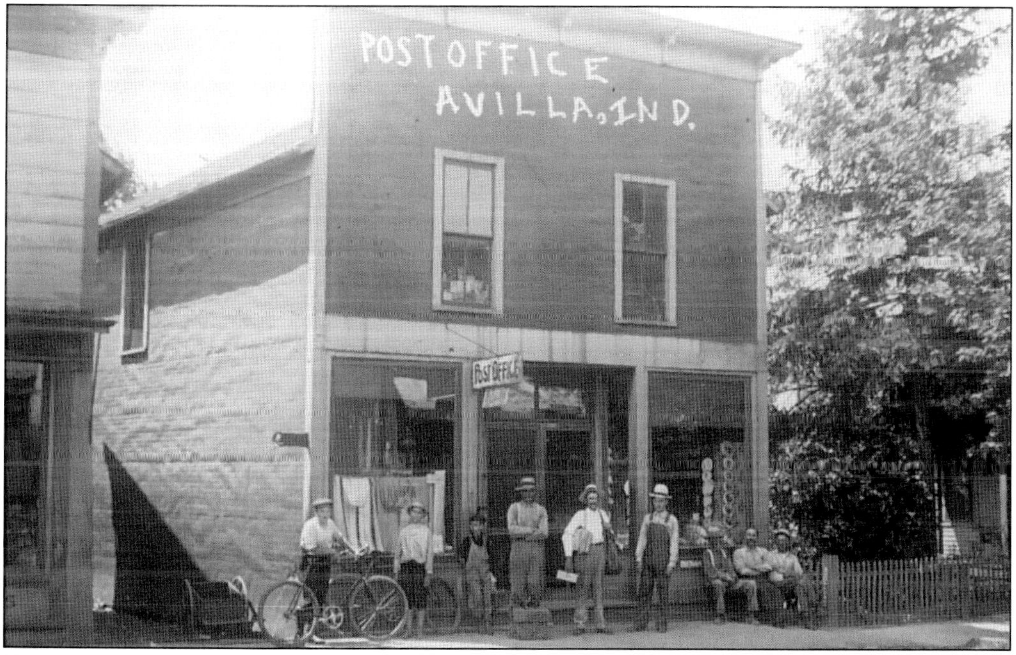

Post Office, Avilla, Indiana, c. 1911. This post office was also a general store. The two men in front of the doors have pouches and appear to be mail carriers.

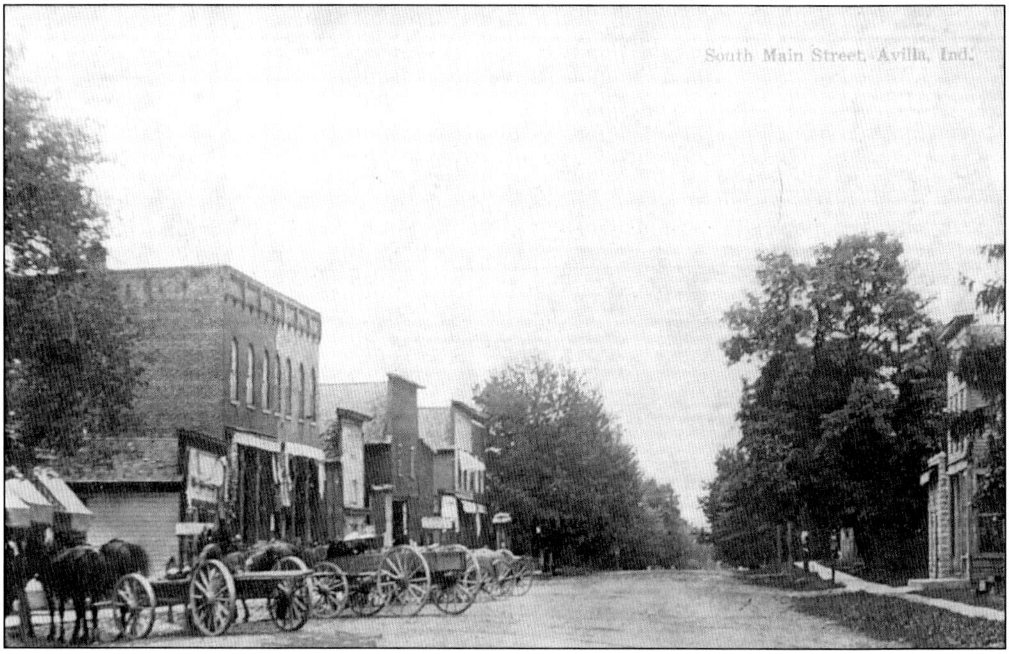

South Main Street, Avilla, Indiana. Horses and wagons are lined up at the hitching rack.

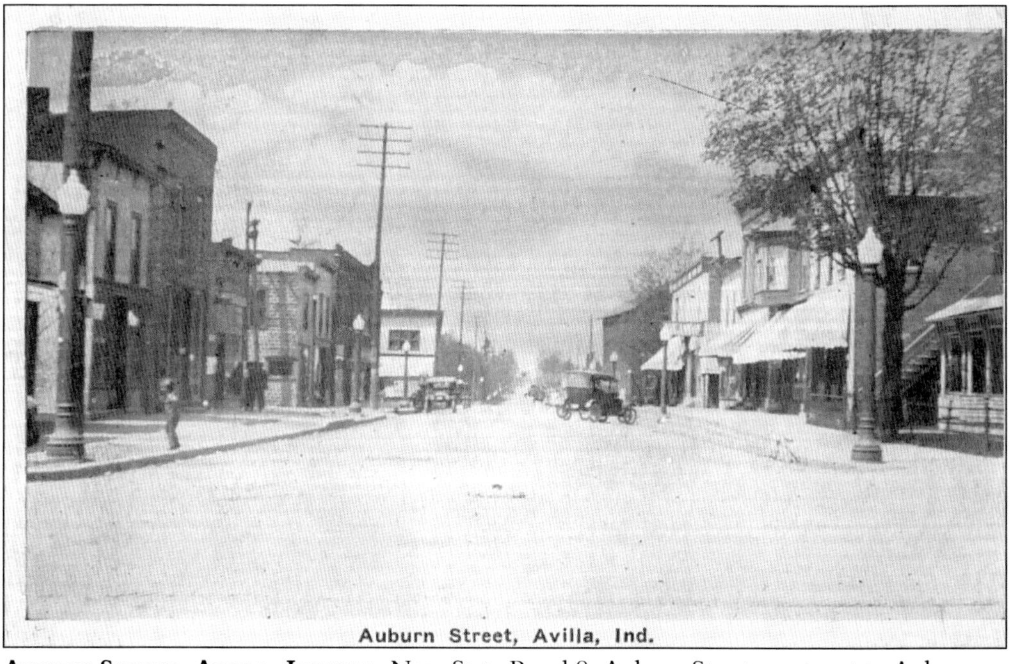

Auburn Street, Avilla, Indiana. Now State Road 8, Auburn Street went east to Auburn.

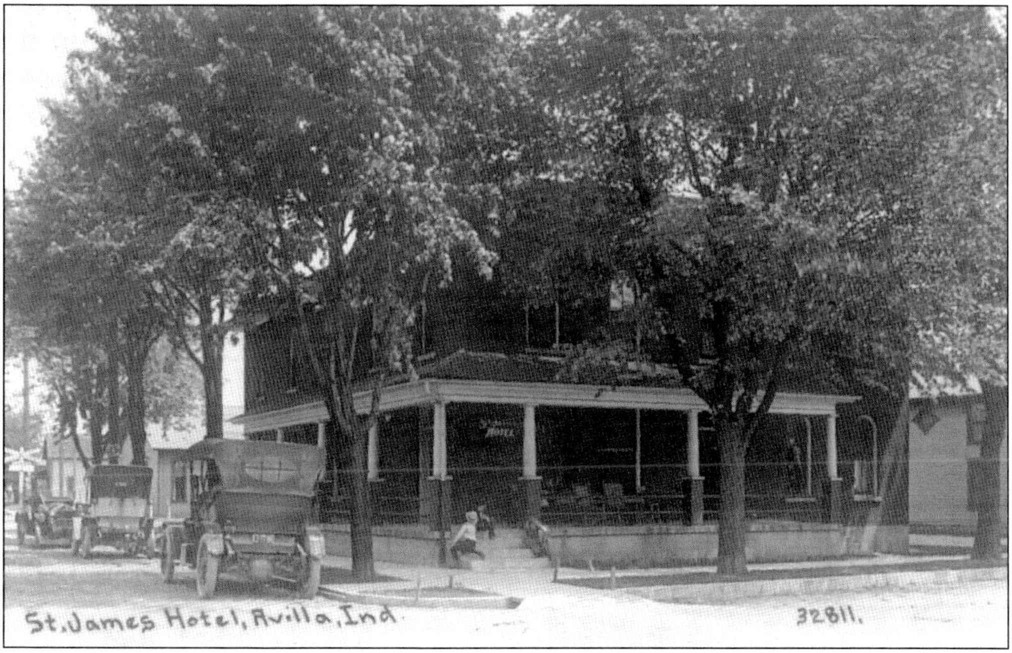

St. James Hotel, Avilla, Indiana. Several automobiles are along the street to the left.

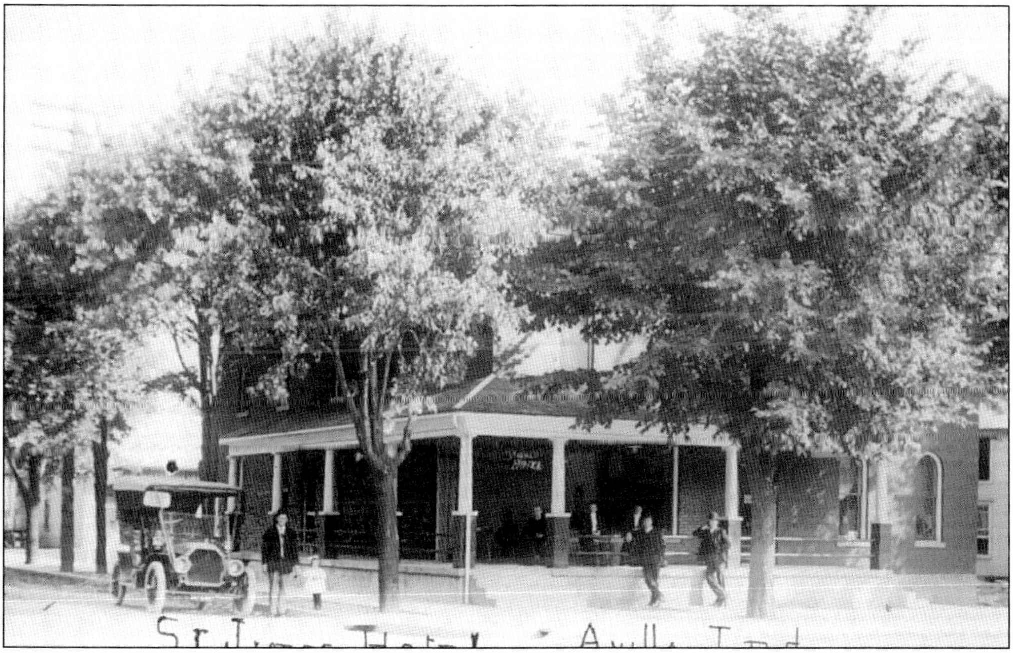

St. James Hotel, Avilla, Indiana. The St. James is now a popular restaurant.

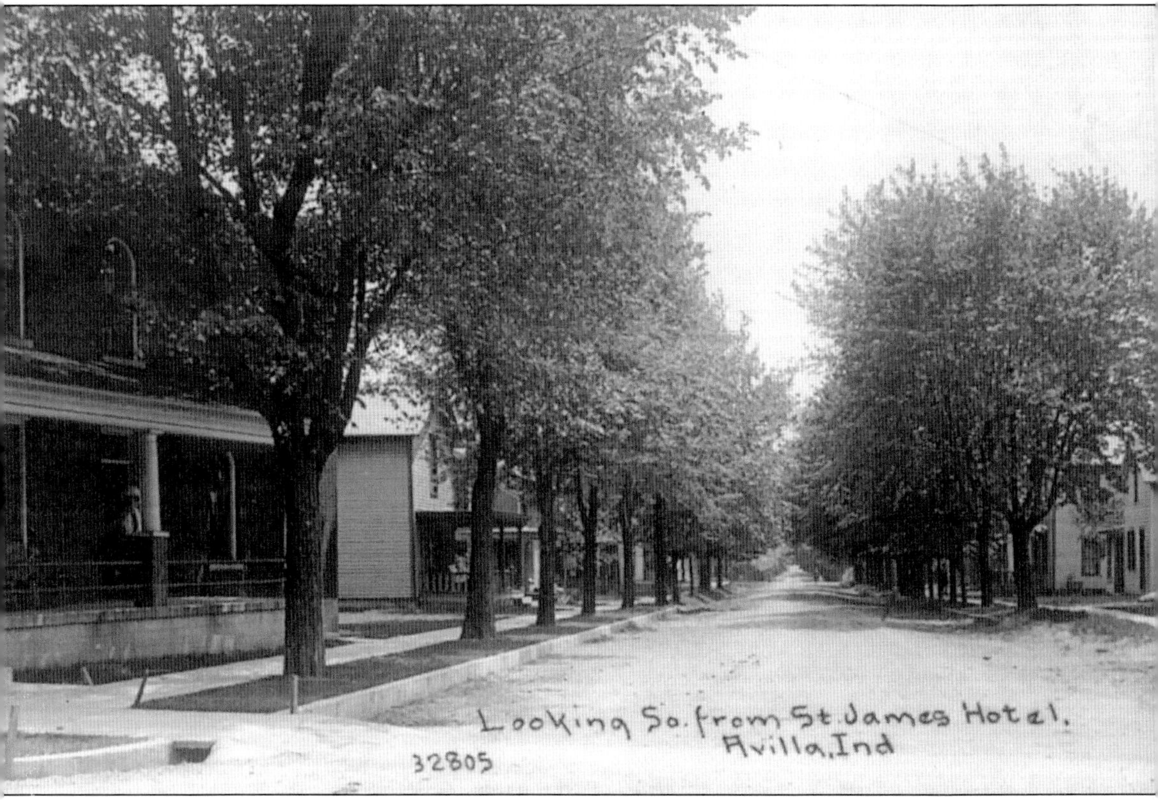

LOOKING SOUTH FROM ST. JAMES HOTEL, AVILLA, INDIANA, *c.* 1911. Mailed from Avilla to Route 5, Columbia City, the message states, "I'm in the big city having a nice time."

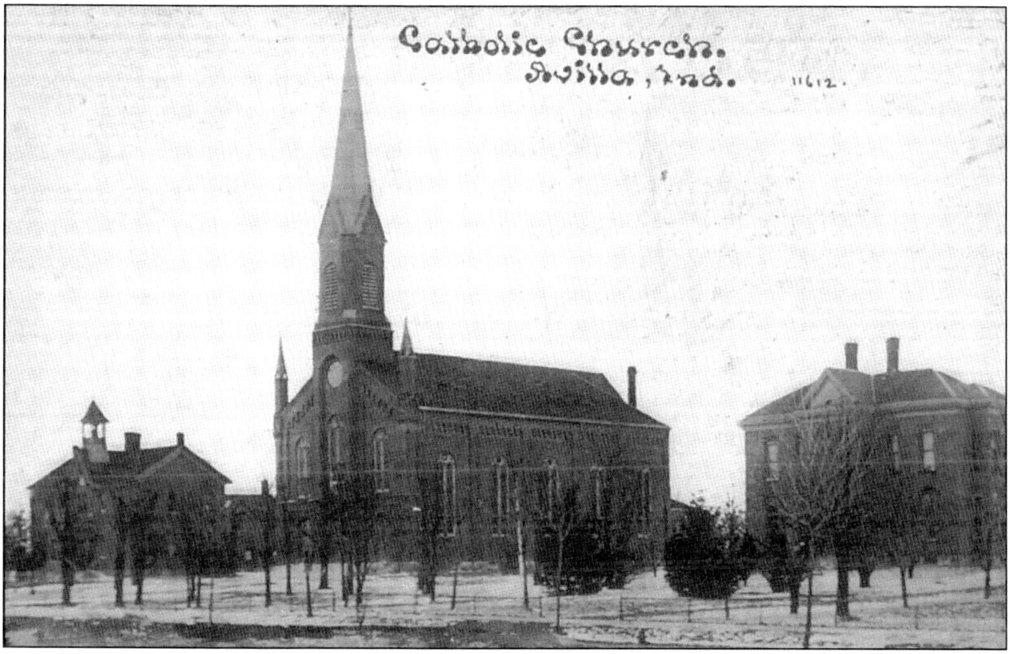

Catholic Church, Avilla, Indiana. Avilla was a Catholic community. The church and other buildings were built much like the European model.

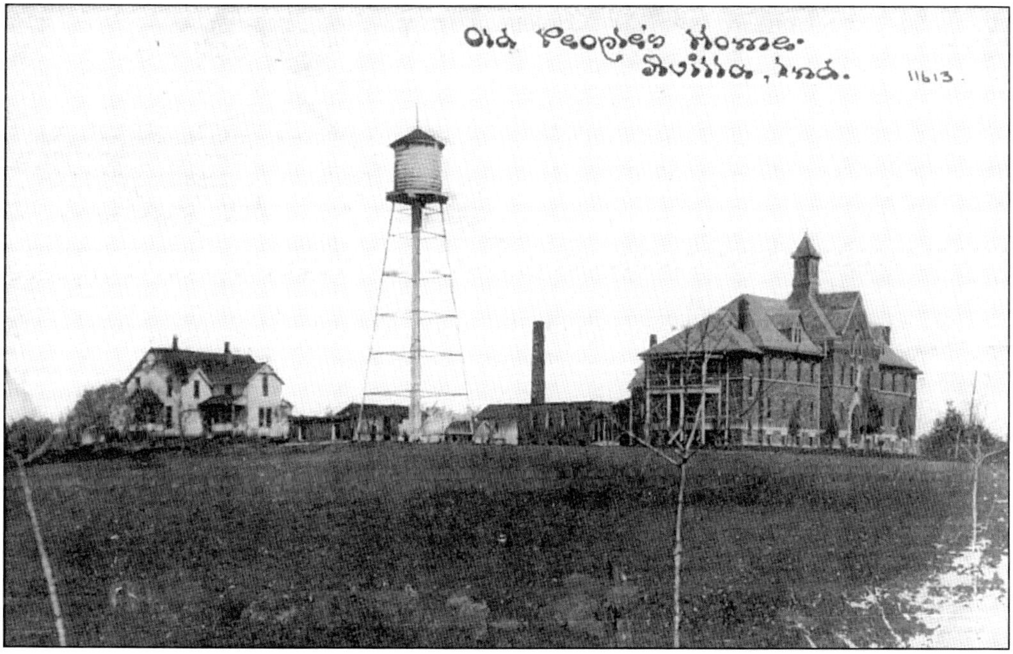

Old People's Home, Avilla, Indiana. Known as the Sacred Heart Home, these buildings were the first "nursing homes" in the area.

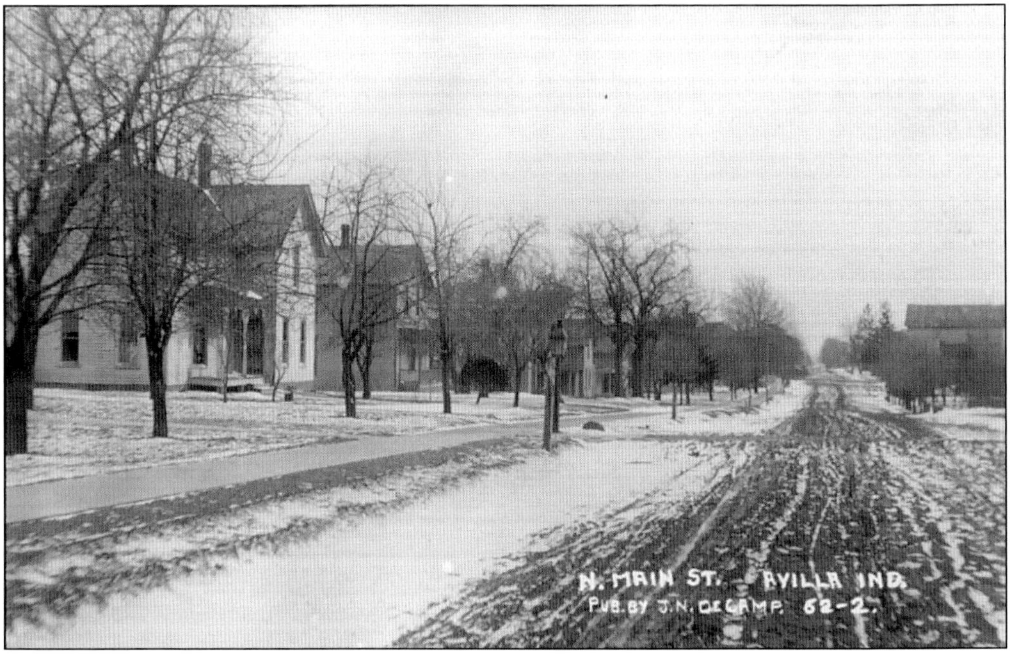

NORTH MAIN STREET, AVILLA, INDIANA. The mud season would have been worse then.

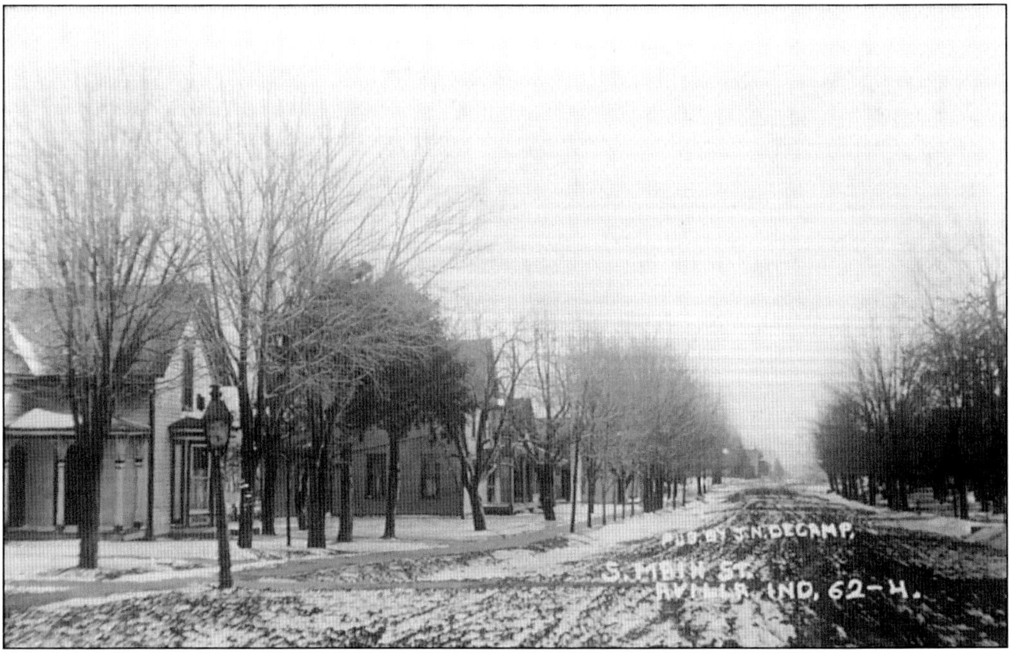

SOUTH MAIN STREET, AVILLA, INDIANA. Wooden, and later concrete, sidewalks crossed the dirt streets.

Four

Brimfield

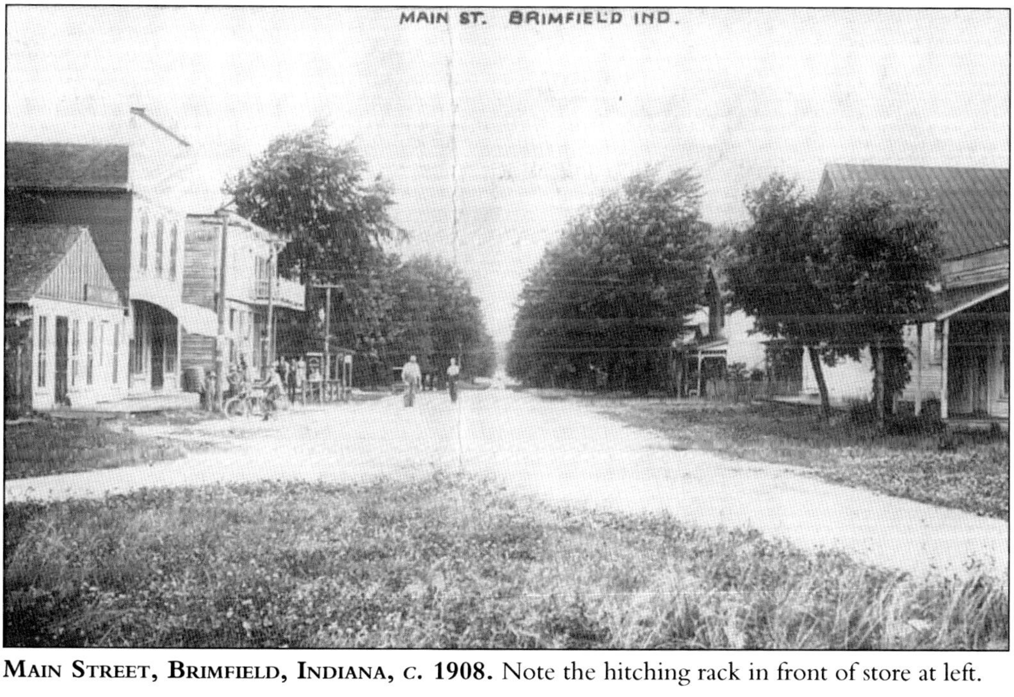

Main Street, Brimfield, Indiana, *c.* 1908. Note the hitching rack in front of store at left.

CROMWELL

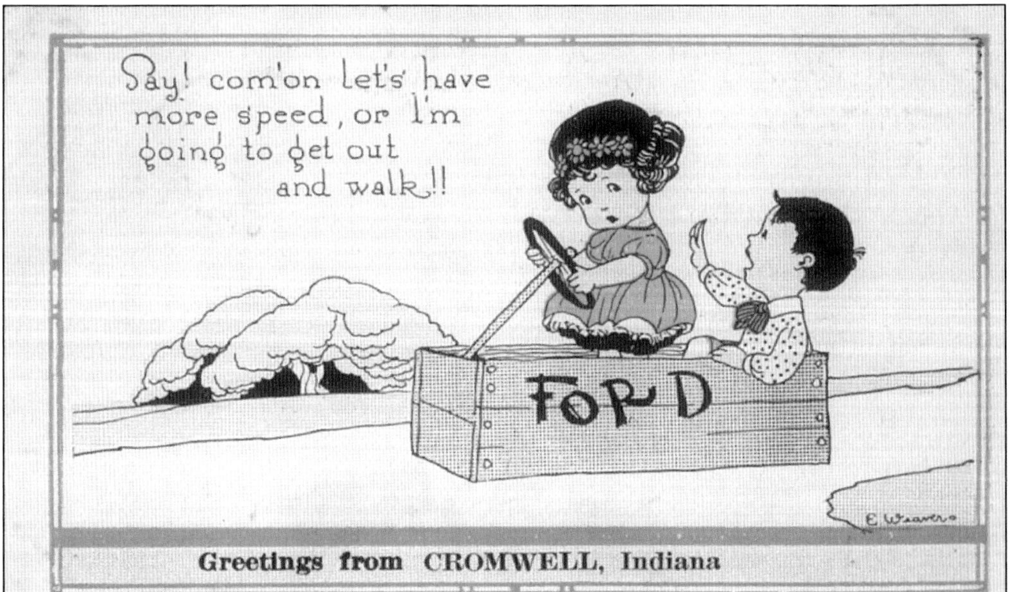

GREETINGS FROM CROMWELL, INDIANA, *c.* 1920. Comic cards were popular from about 1920–1940.

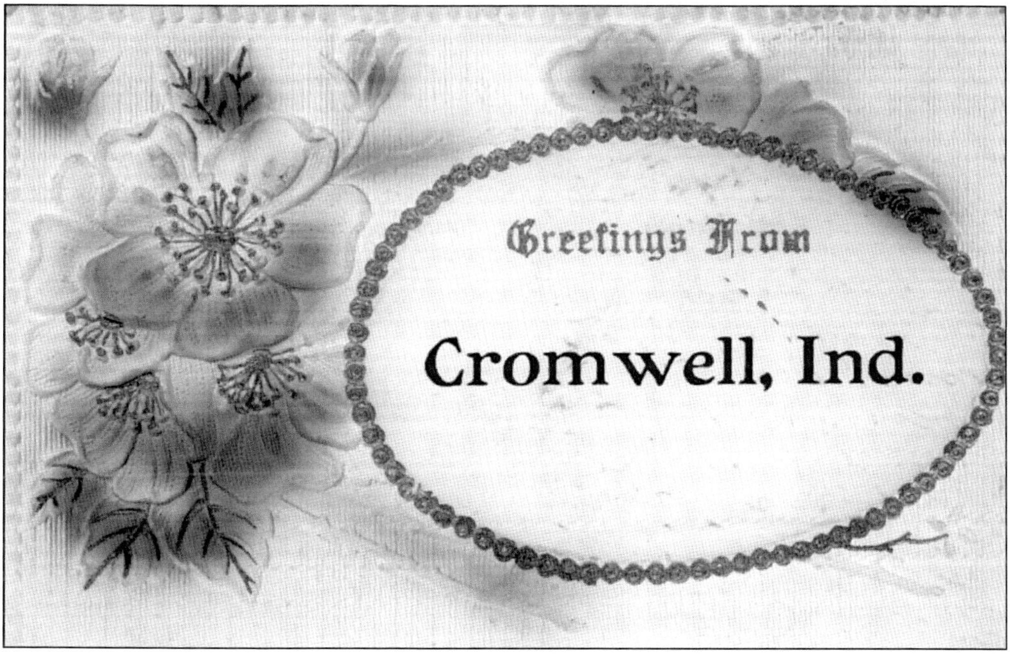

Greetings from Cromwell, Indiana. Stock cards were overprinted with town names.

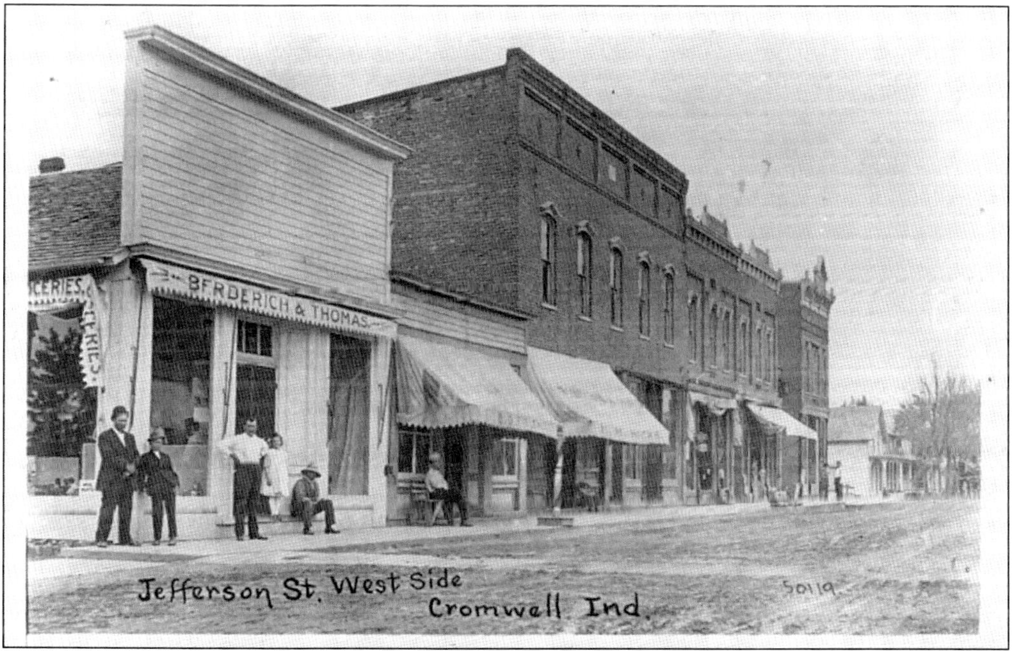

Jefferson Street West Side, Cromwell, Indiana, *c.* 1910. Dirt streets served the light traffic of that era. Note the wooden barber pole in front of second building. The building on the left housed Berberick & Thomas Grocery Store.

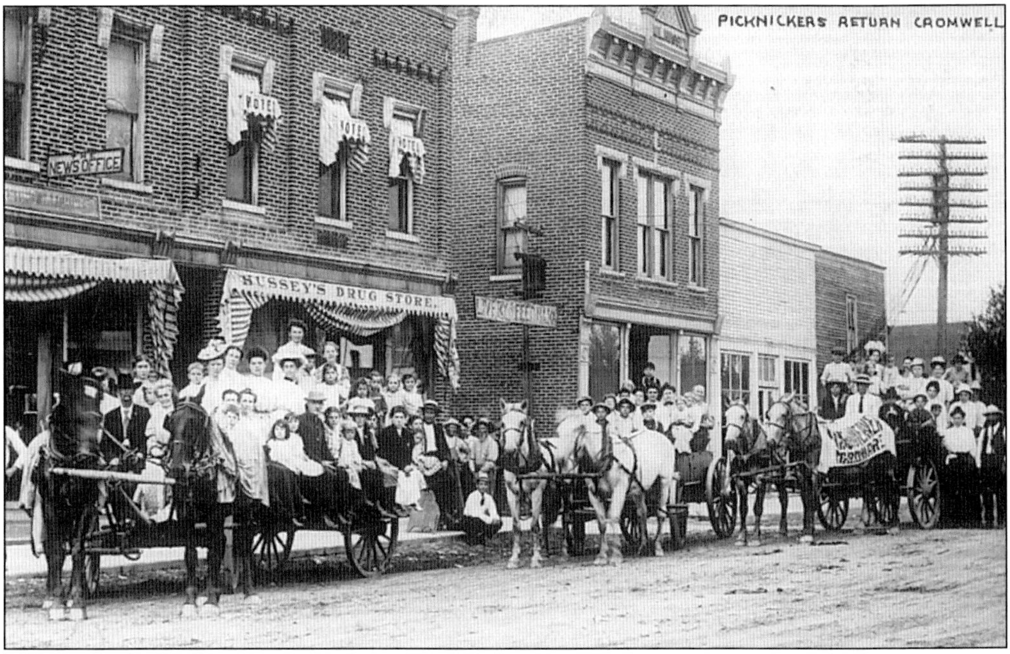

PICKNICKERS RETURN, CROMWELL, *c.* 1908. Pictured here is probably a church group. Note the telephone wires.

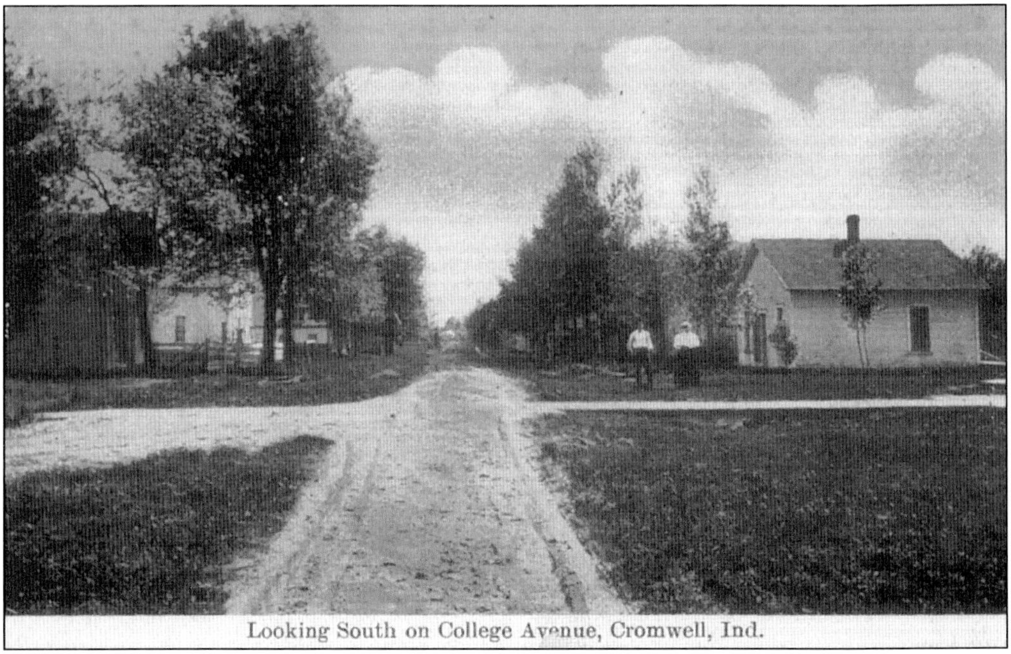

LOOKING SOUTH ON COLLEGE AVENUE, CROMWELL, INDIANA, *c.* 1916. A couple, proud of their modest home, are shown on the right.

KIMMELL

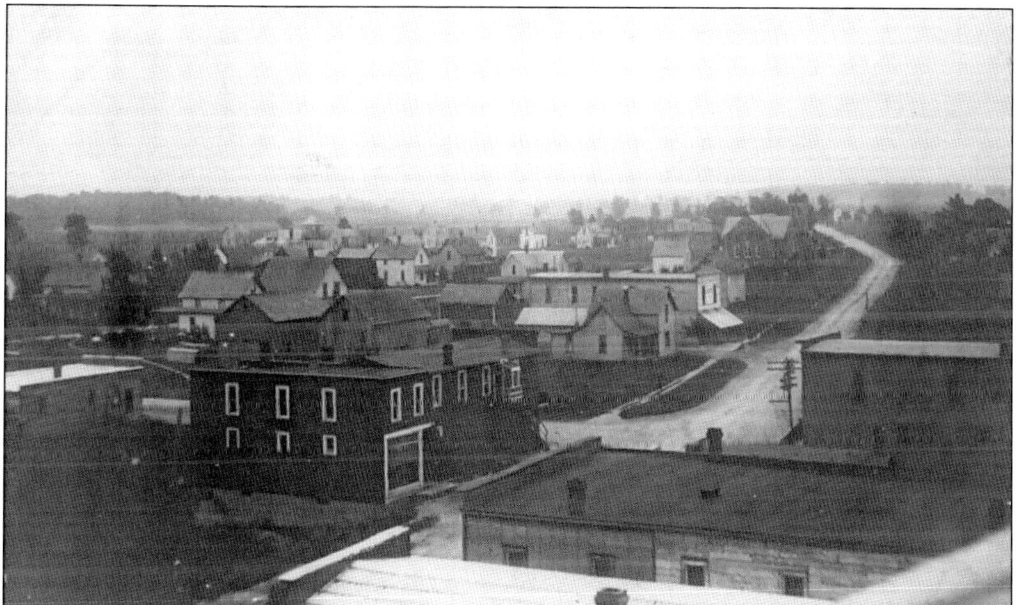

BIRD'S-EYE VIEW OF KIMMELL, INDIANA. This card is dated December 23, 1909.

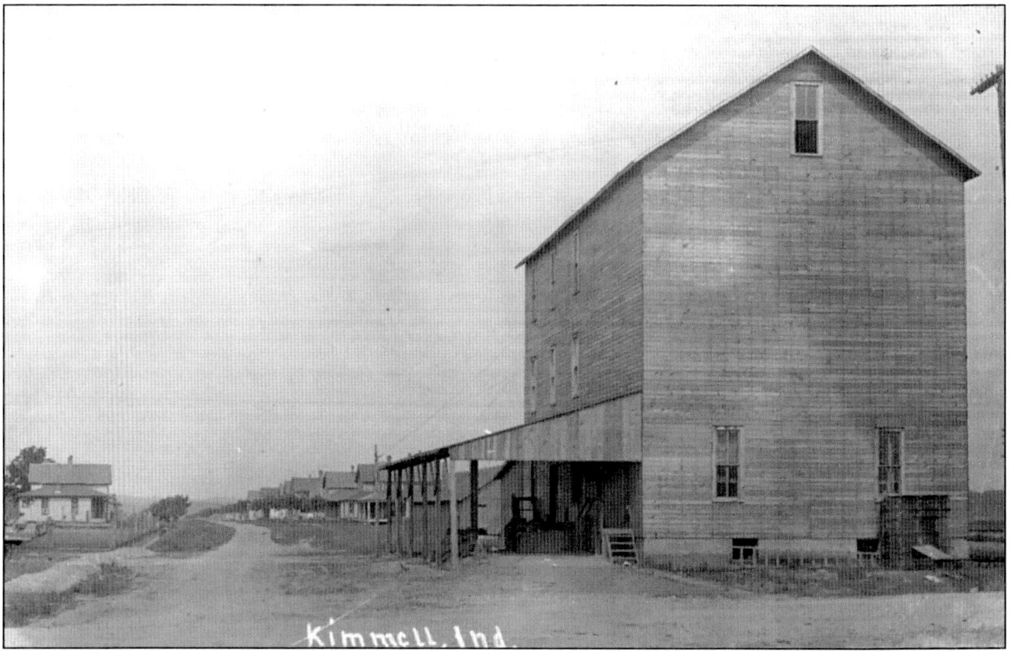

KIMMELL, INDIANA. "This is a picture of the new mill," is the message on the back of the card.

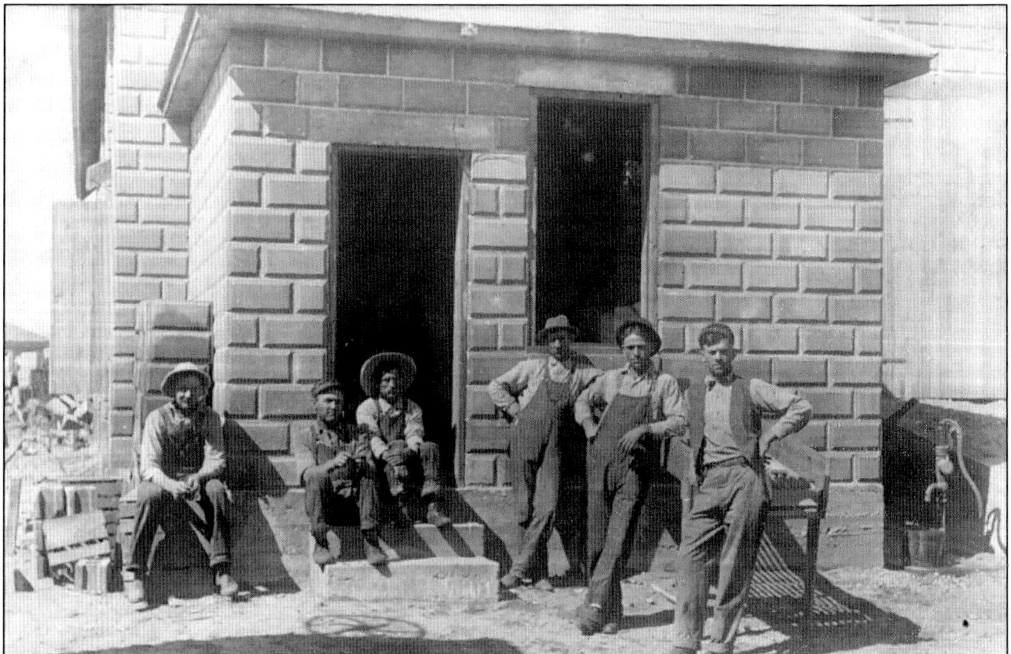

MEN IN KIMMELL, INDIANA. Workers pause for a photograph. Note pump in the lower right.

LaOtto

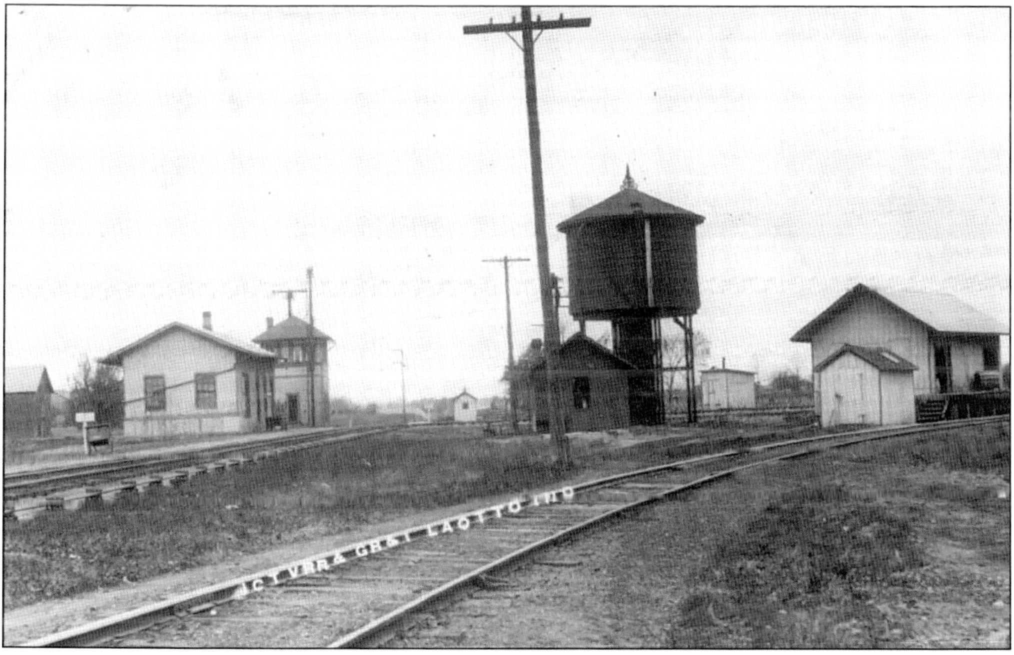

Junction V.R.R. & G.R.&I., LaOtto, Indiana, c. 1910. The initials represent Junction Vandalia Railroad and Grand Rapids & Indiana Railroad. Shown is the "Y" where trains could be turned around.

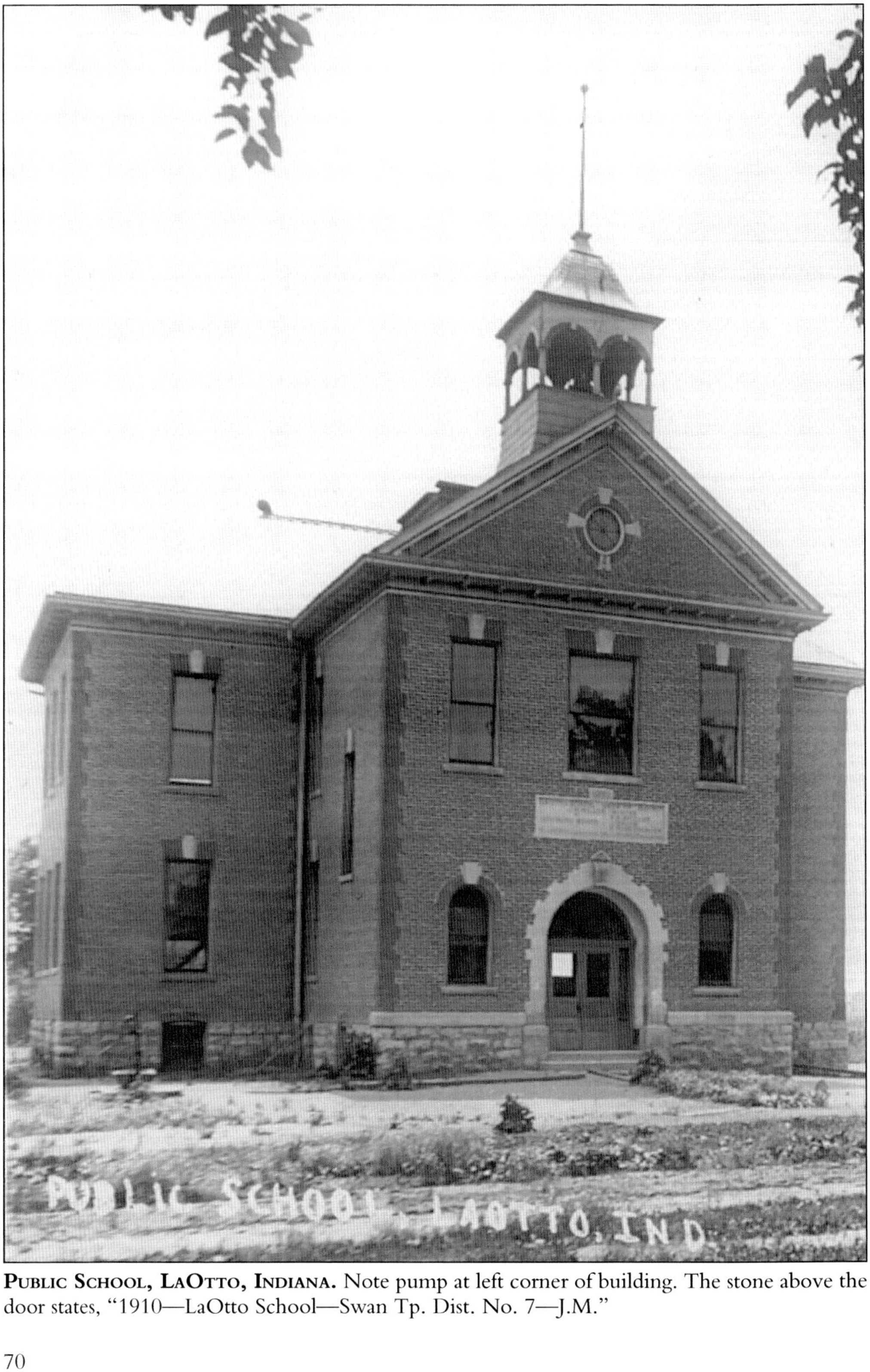

PUBLIC SCHOOL, LAOTTO, INDIANA. Note pump at left corner of building. The stone above the door states, "1910—LaOtto School—Swan Tp. Dist. No. 7—J.M."

Five

Ligonier

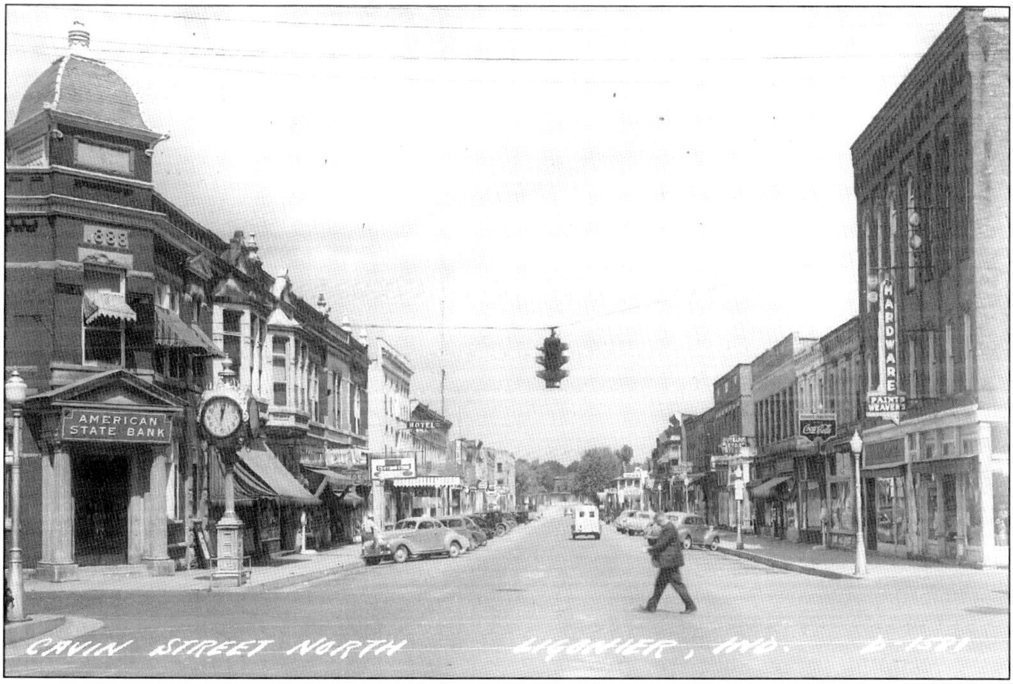

Cavin Street North, Ligonier, Indiana, *c.* 1941. Note the clock in front of American State Bank on the left.

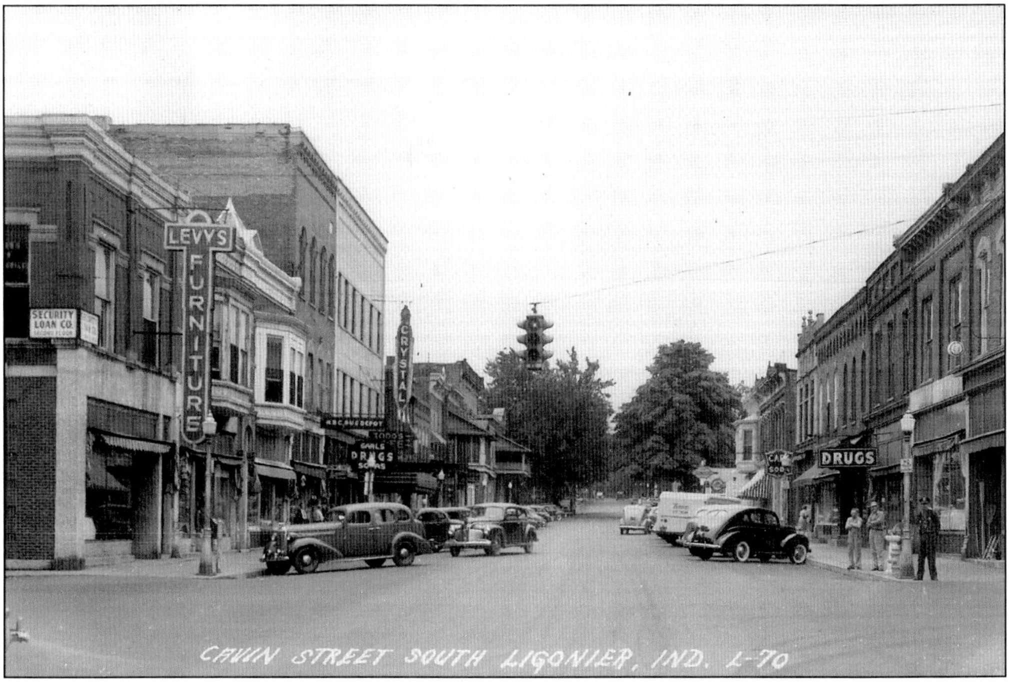

Cavin Street South, Ligonier, Indiana. Levy Furniture and Crystal Theatre are on the left.

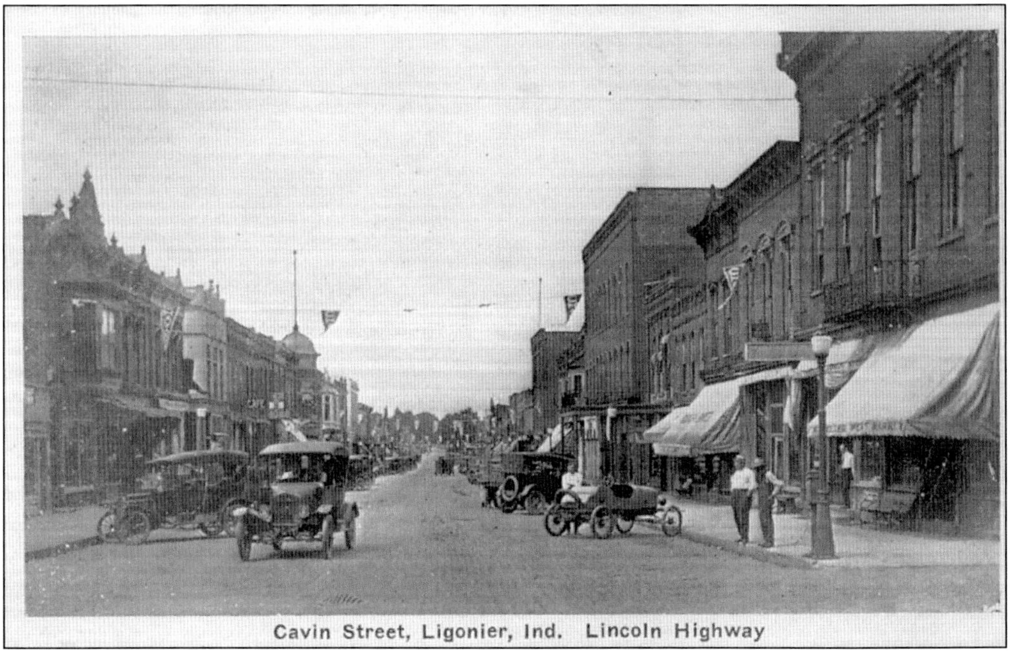

Cavin Street, Ligonier, Indiana Lincoln Highway, c. 1925. Most of the cars are Model T Fords. Note the Model T Speedster in the right foreground.

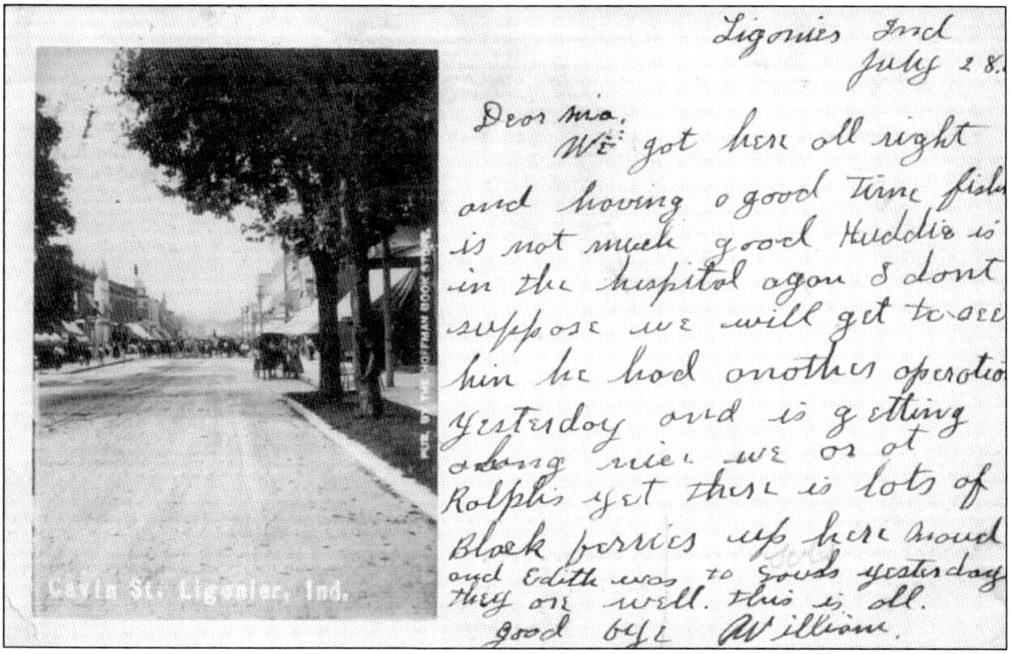

CAVIN ST. LIGONIER, INDIANA, C. 1908. Note the brick street. The message states, "We got here all right and having a good time fishing is not much good. Huddie is in the hospital again I dont suppose we will get to see him he had another operation yesterday and is getting along nice we are at Ralph's yet there is lots of Black berries up here around and Edith was to Souls yesterday they are well this is all. good bye William."

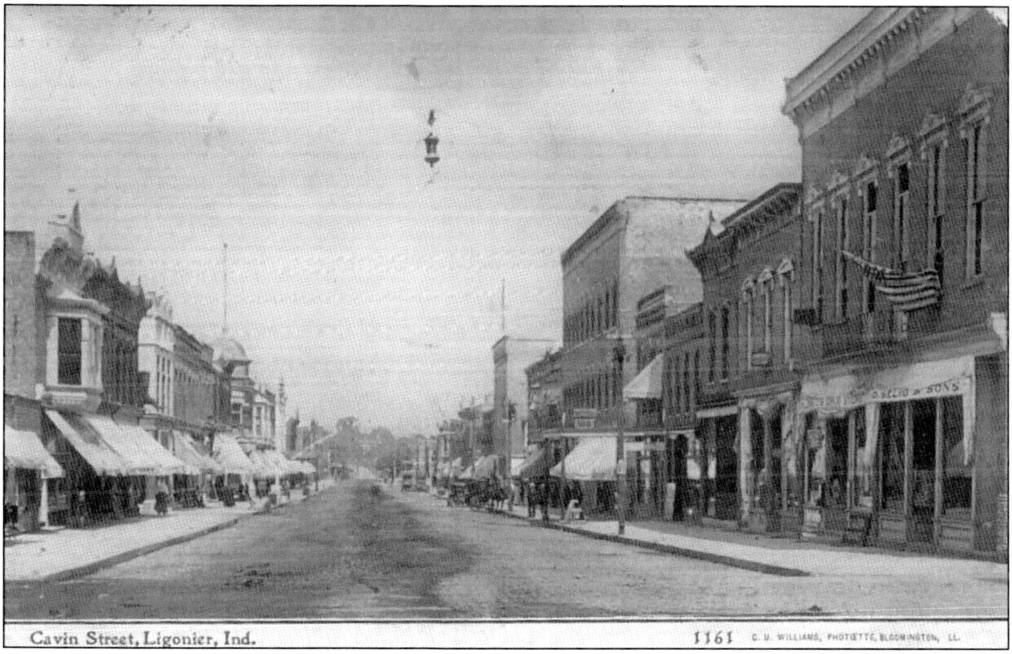

CAVIN STREET, LIGONIER, INDIANA, C. 1909. Several buggies and at least one automobile can be seen. The card was addressed to Shelbyville, Indiana, but mis-sent to Shelbyville, Illinois.

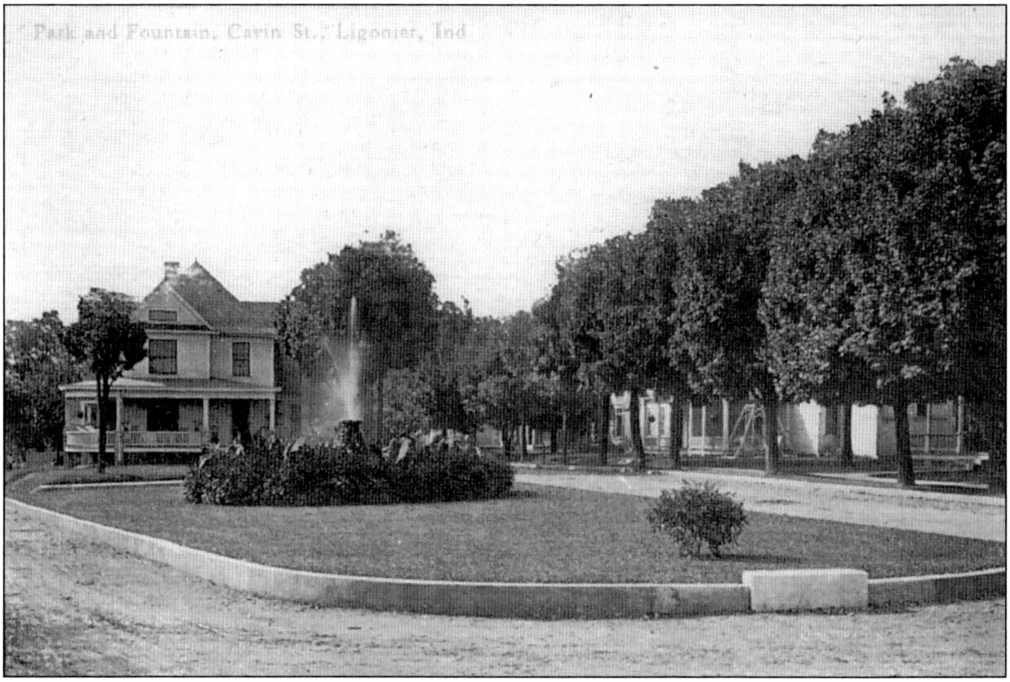

Park and Fountain, Cavin Street, Ligonier, Indiana. The streets here are still dirt.

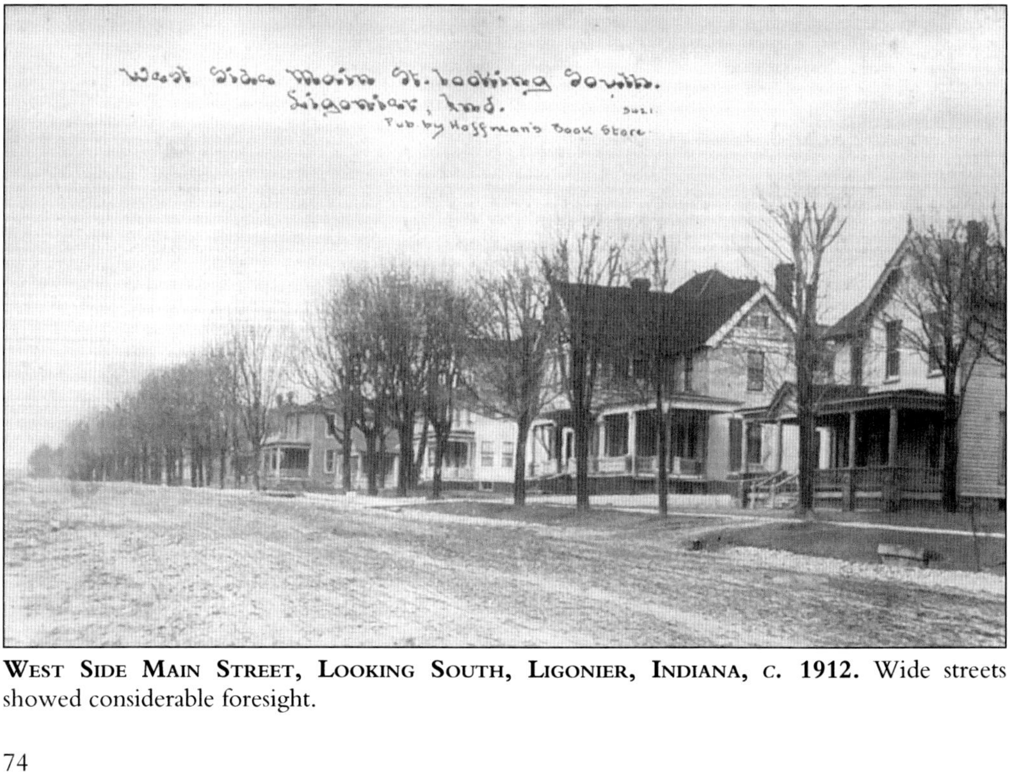

West Side Main Street, Looking South, Ligonier, Indiana, *c.* 1912. Wide streets showed considerable foresight.

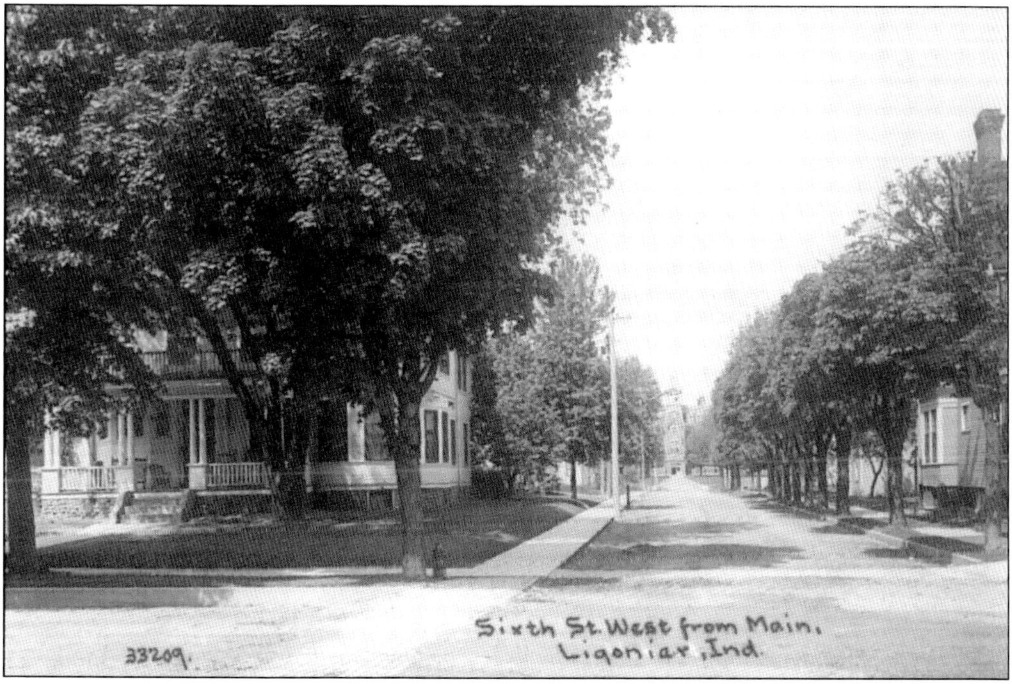

Sixth Street West from Main, Ligonier, Indiana, *c.* 1915. Shade trees and porches provided a pleasant venue.

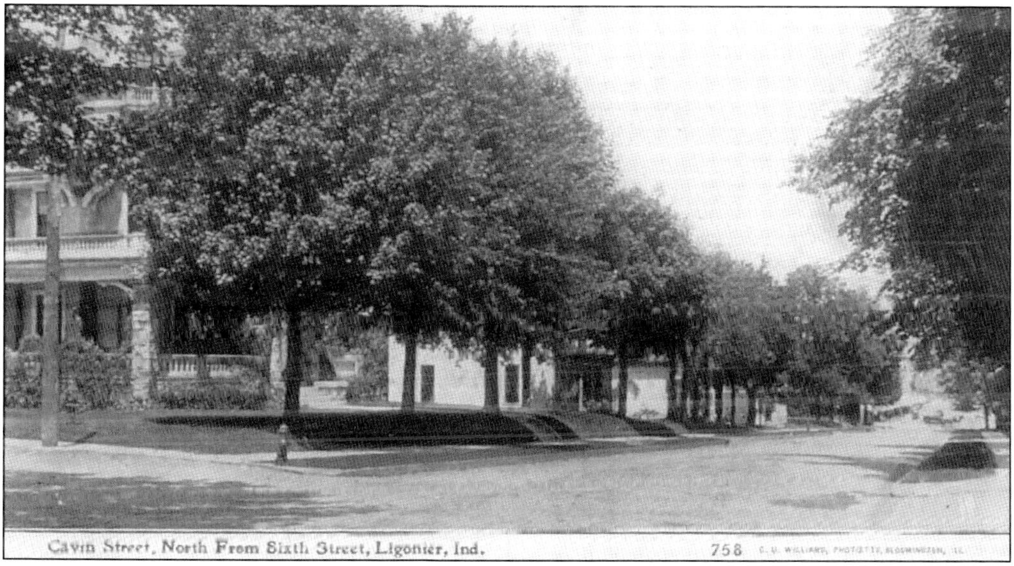

Cavin Street, North from Sixth Street, Ligonier, Indiana. Dated September 6, 1908, from Ligonier. The message is interesting. "Well Justus: Suppose you wonder what I think of the Jews. Have thought till my head is dizzy and dont no. But do no that the first week I was about home sick girl you ever saw. Dident no anybody, knew about half that they said to me, when they spoke their best English. And when dear Dutch friends came in and all got to talking, O heavens. And their goose grease is old enough to vote. I have canned 69 qt. Fruit in the week today since we came."

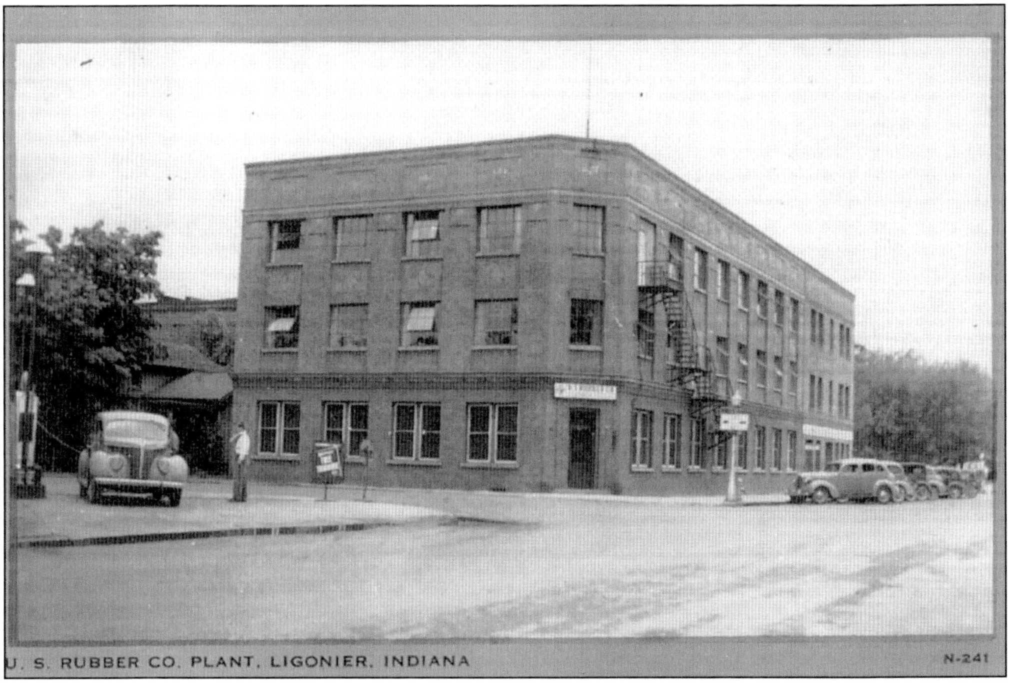

UNITED STATES RUBBER CO. PLANT, LIGONIER, INDIANA, *c.* 1941. The United States Rubber Company was a major industry.

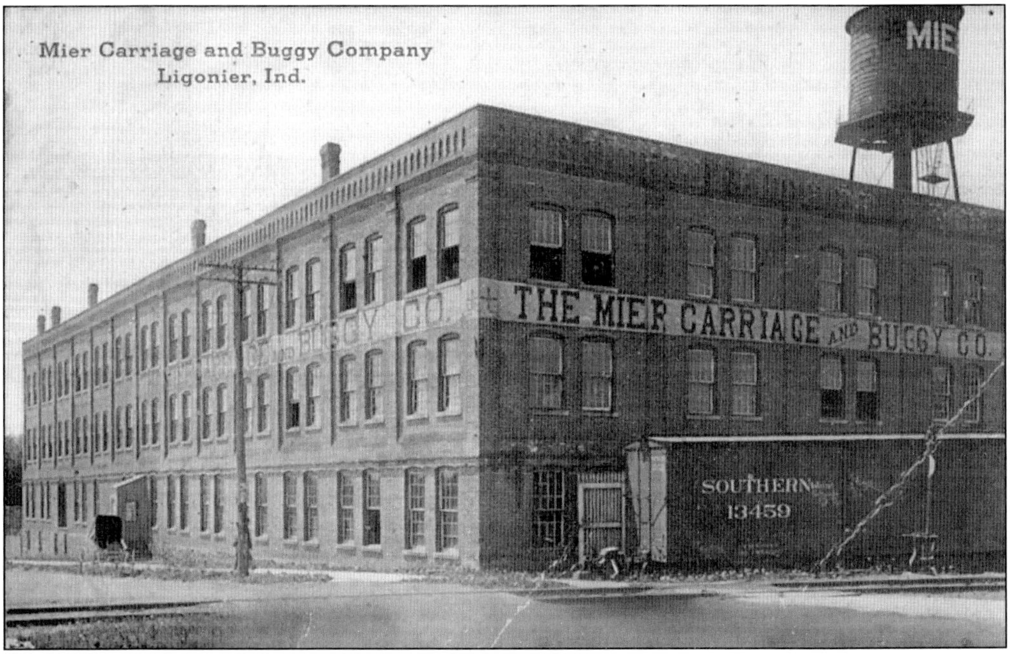

MIER CARRIAGE AND BUGGY COMPANY, LIGONIER, INDIANA. The company also built a high wheel automobile.

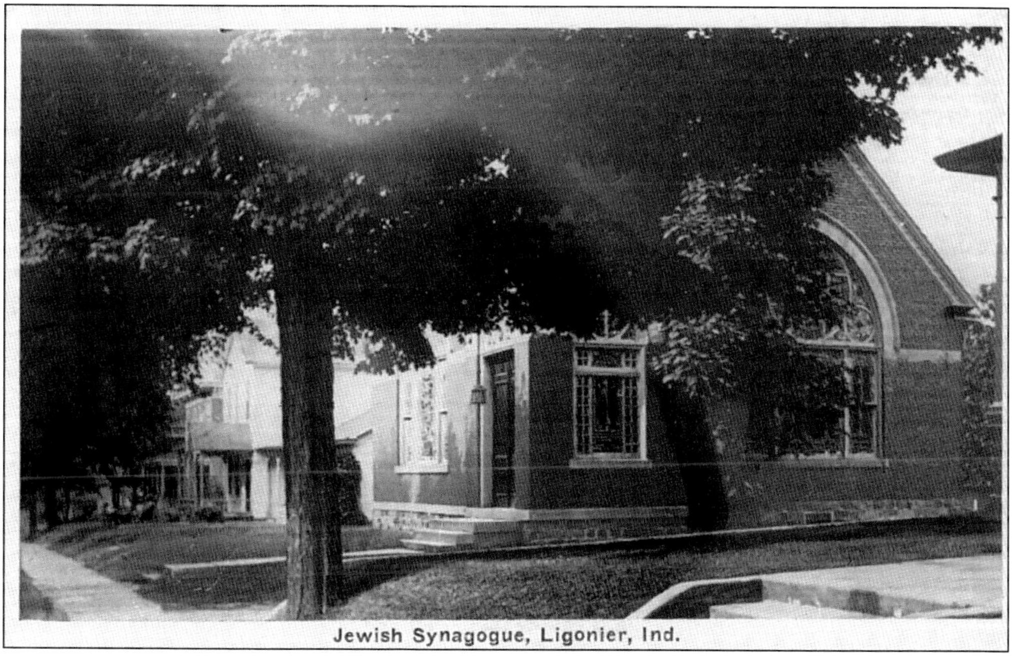

Jewish Synagogue, Ligonier, Indiana. Many Jewish people lived in Ligonier.

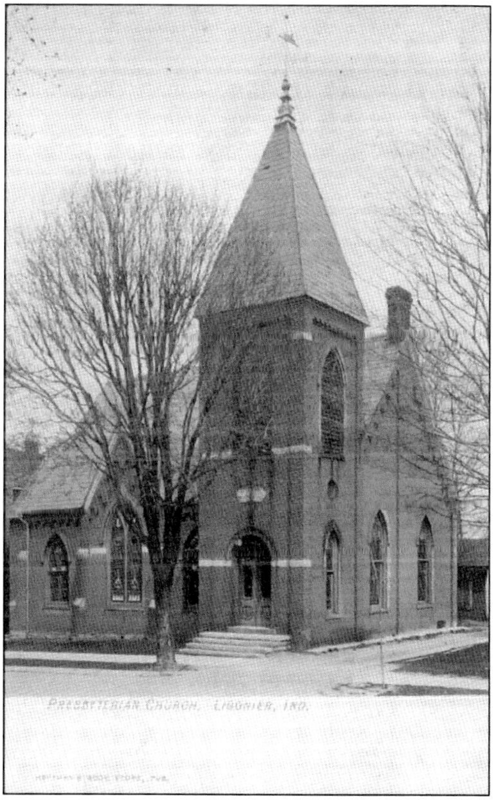

Presbyterian Church, Ligonier, Indiana, c. 1910. The card was mailed but there is no message. Apparently a gentle reminder from the church to a wayward member.

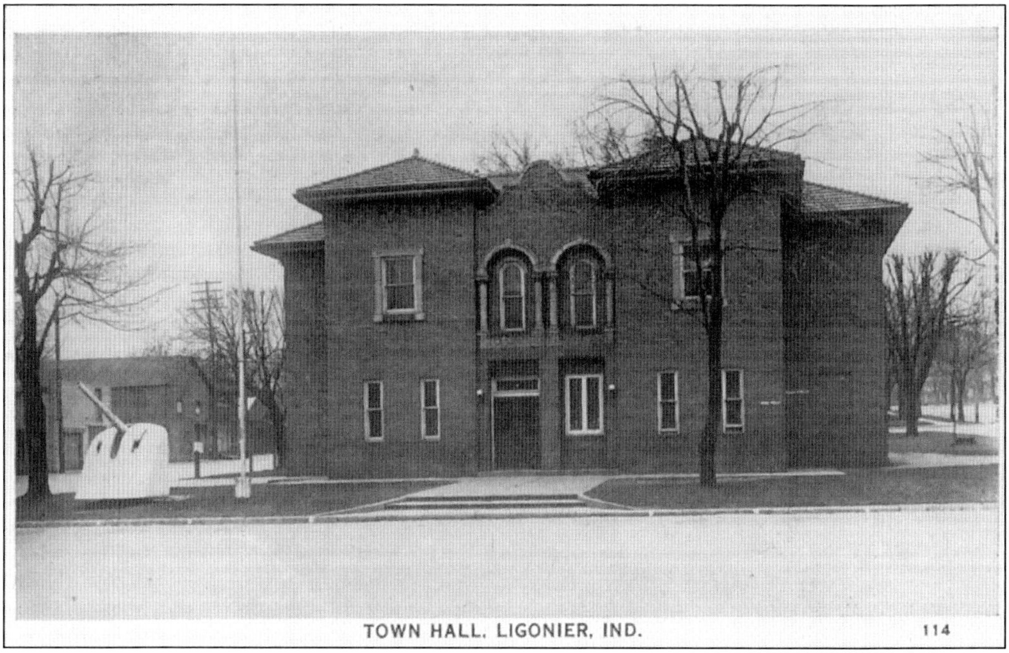

TOWN HALL, LIGONIER, INDIANA. The canon on the left commemorated World War I.

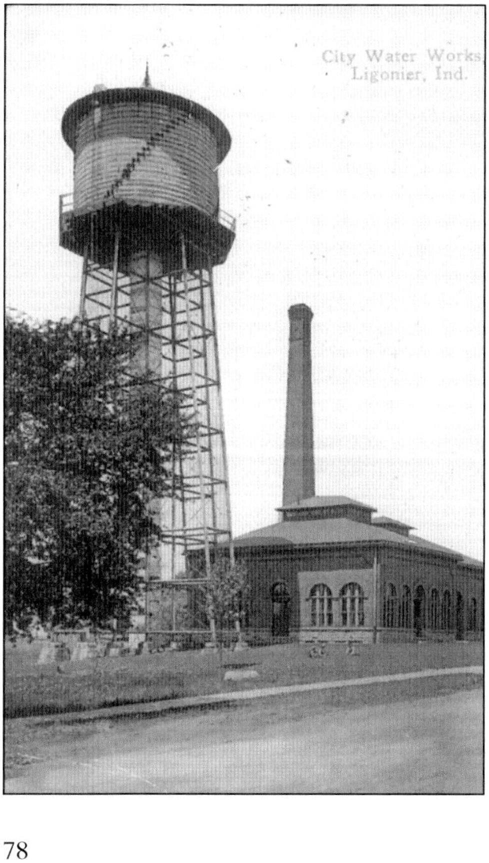

CITY WATER WORKS, LIGONIER, INDIANA, *c.* 1916. The water tank is made of wood stoves held together by iron rings.

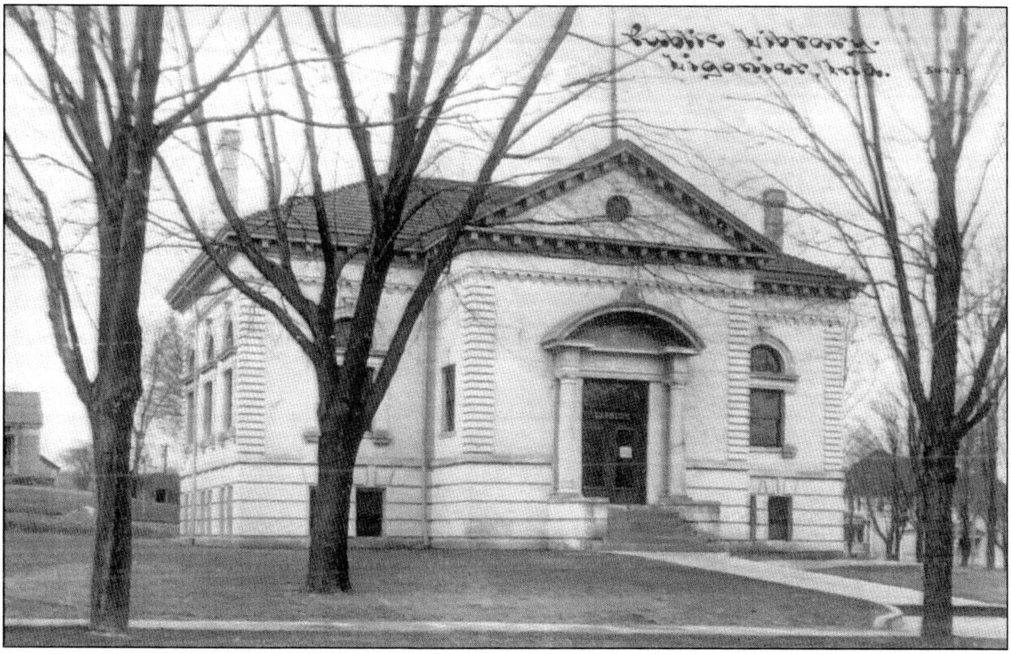

Public Library, Ligonier, Indiana, *c.* 1920. The public library is a classic structure which has served the town well.

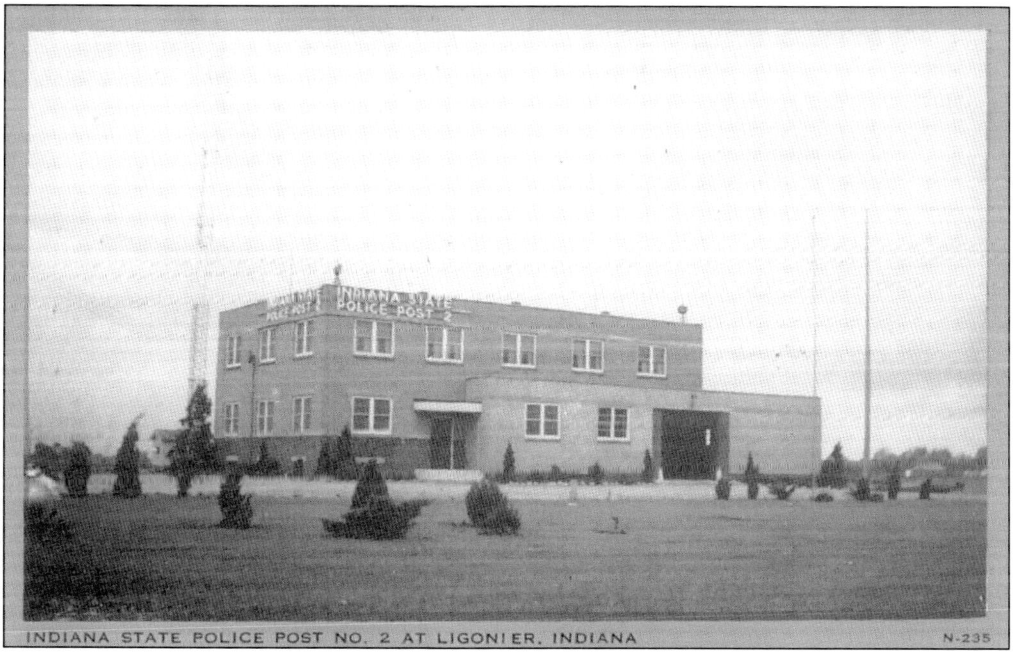

Indiana State Police Post No. 2 at Ligonier, Indiana. The Indiana State Police Post serves Northeastern Indiana.

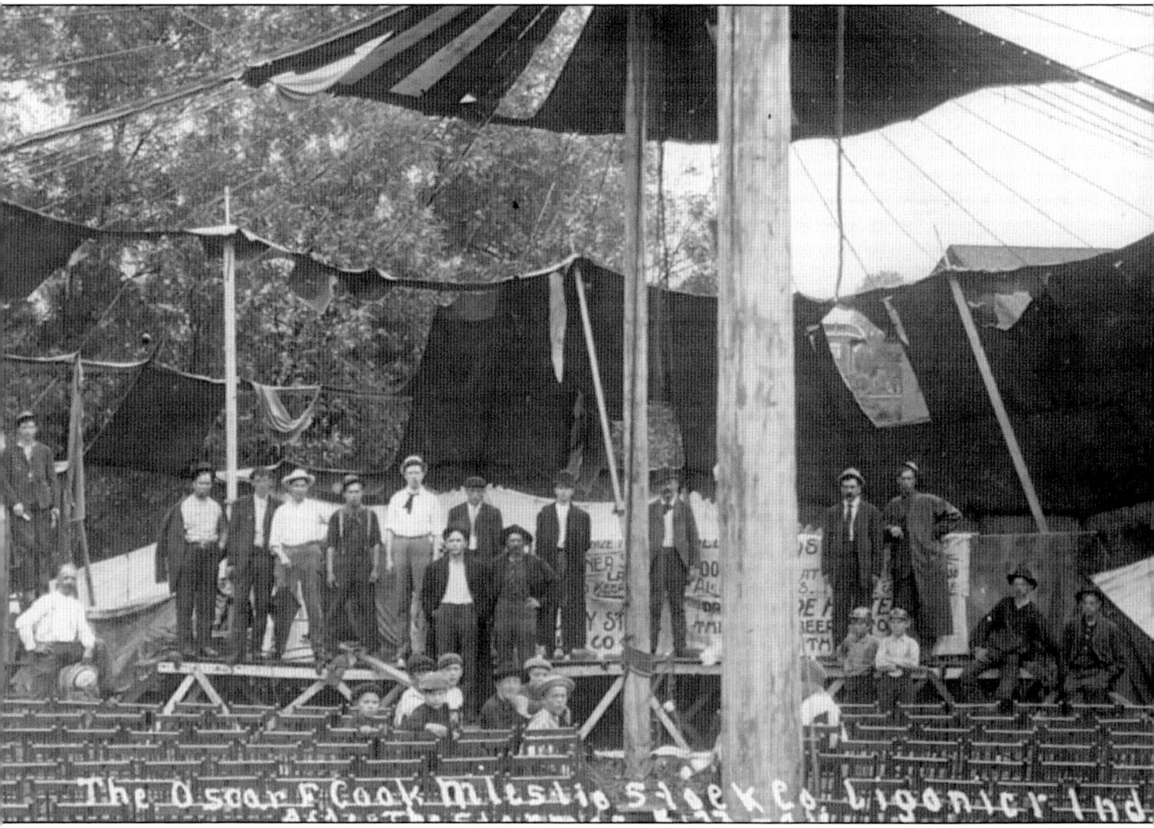

The Oscar F. Cook Miesteo Stock Co. Ligonier, Indiana, After The Storm of May 23, 1908. A railroad car can be seen in the background through a hole in the tent.

Six

Lisbon

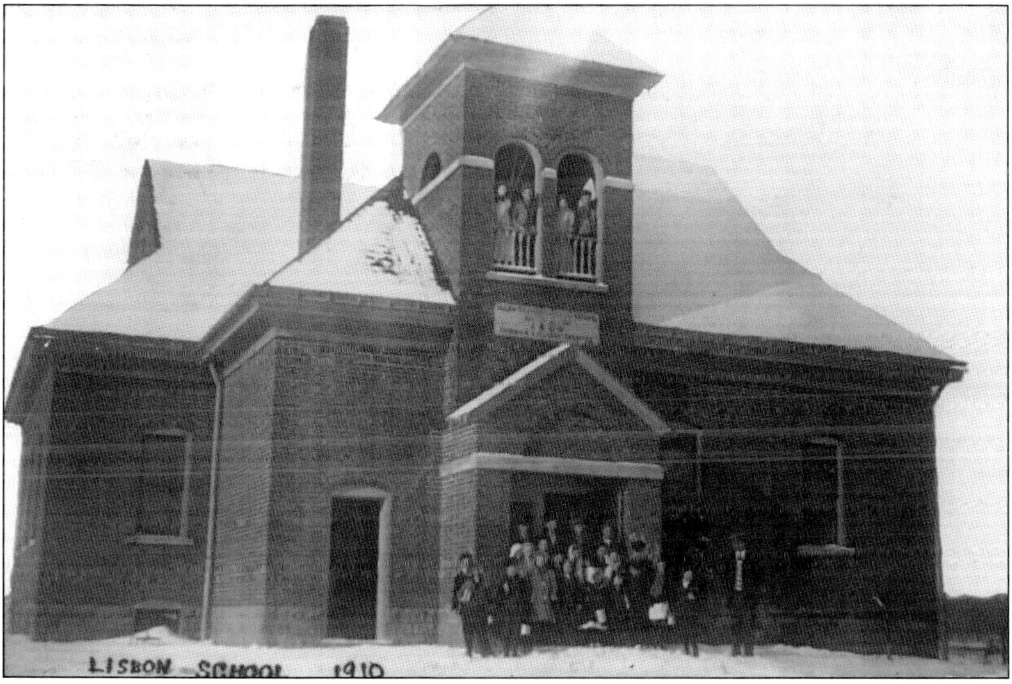

Lisbon School, 1910. Carved stone above door appears to read, "Allen Township High School—District No. 24—1906—Thomas Kelham, Trustee." Mailed from Lisbon to Fort Wayne, the message states, "Dear Pappa—Don't think I have forgotten you. I am having such a good time that I don't get much time to write—Love to all—Clara."

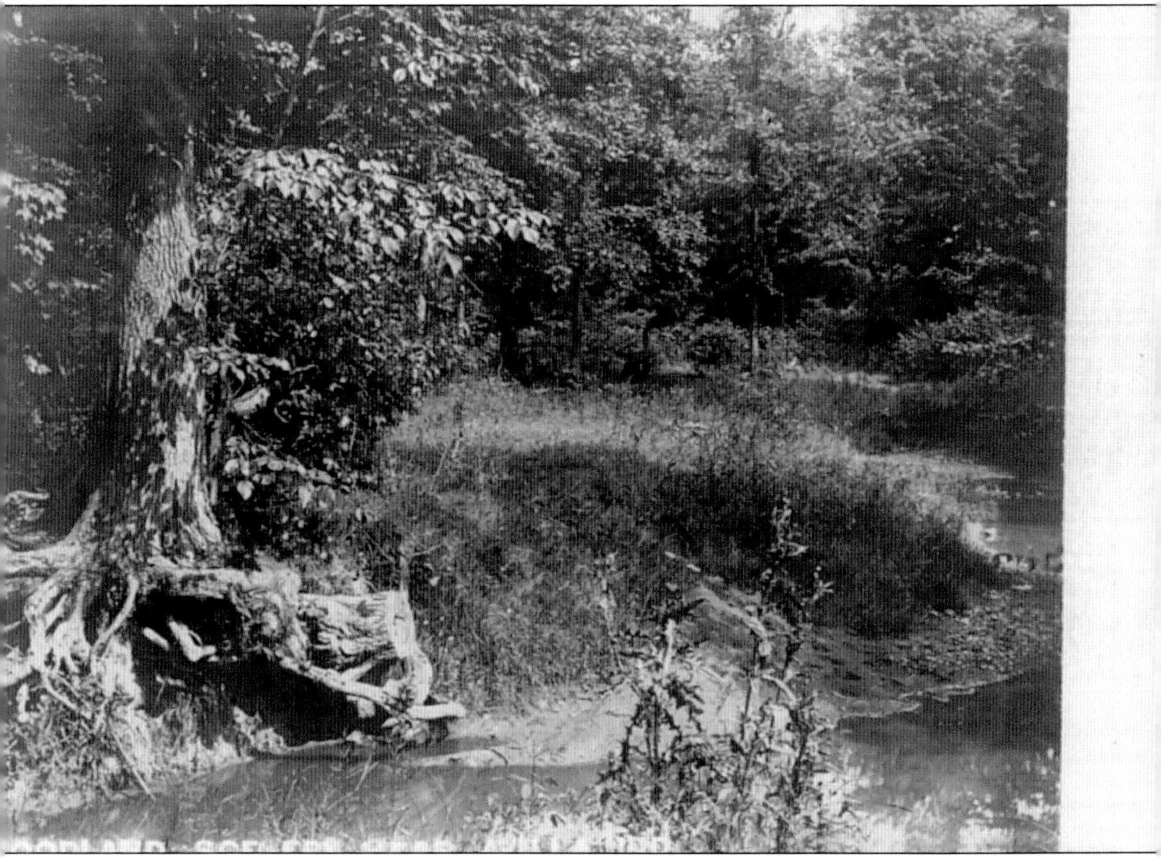

WOODLAND SCENERY NEAR AVILLA, INDIANA. Pictured here is an old tree with exposed roots.

Seven

Rome City

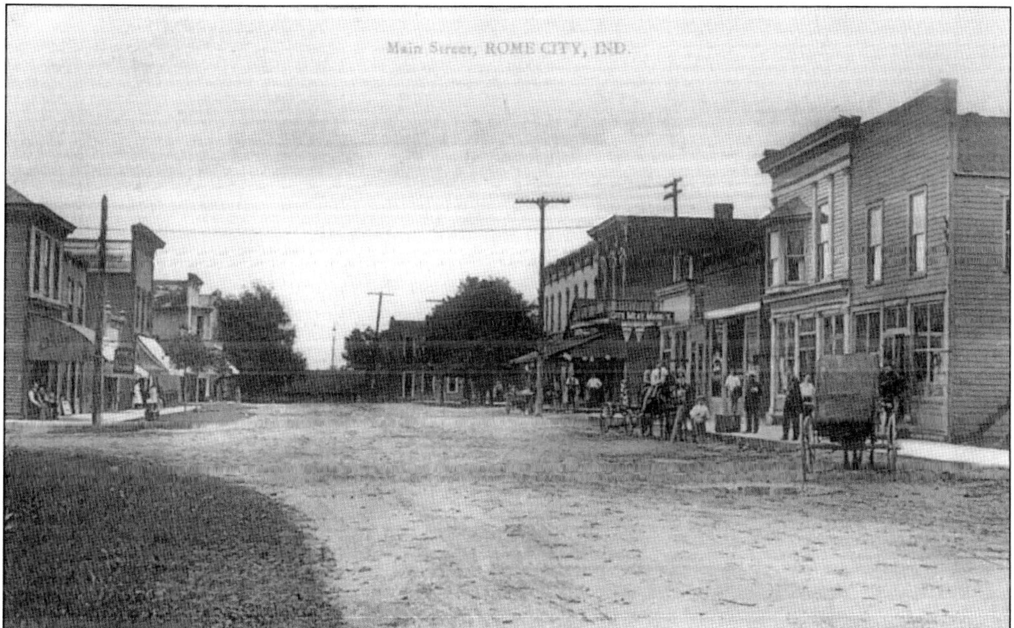

Main Street, Rome City, Indiana, *c.* 1911. The only sign visible is "City Meat Market" on the right.

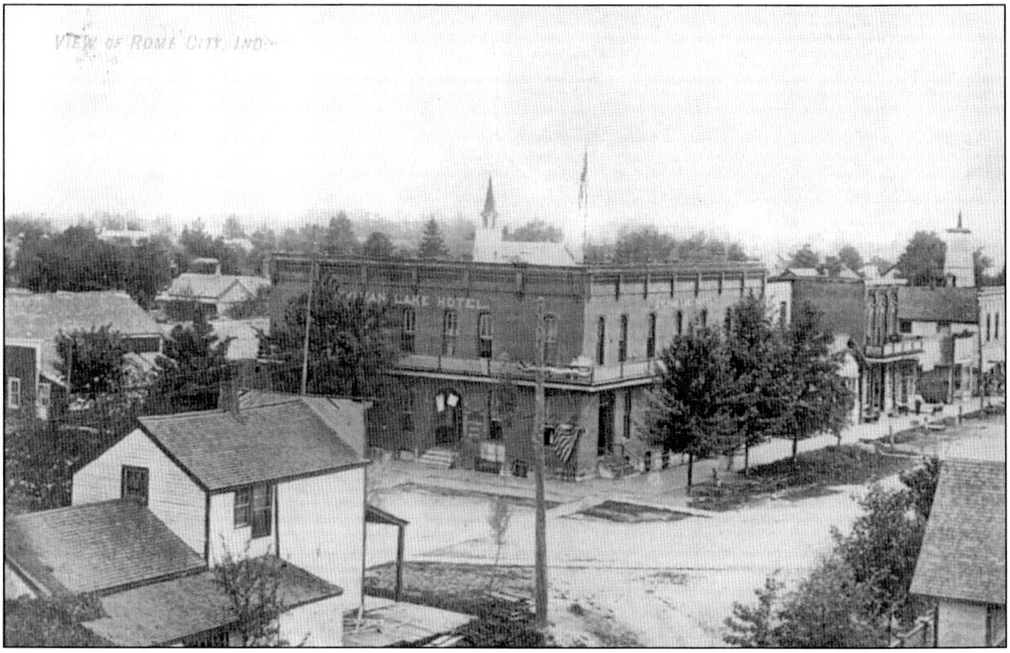

View of Rome City, Inc., c. 1907. The message states, "Add this to your collection." Many persons collected postcards.

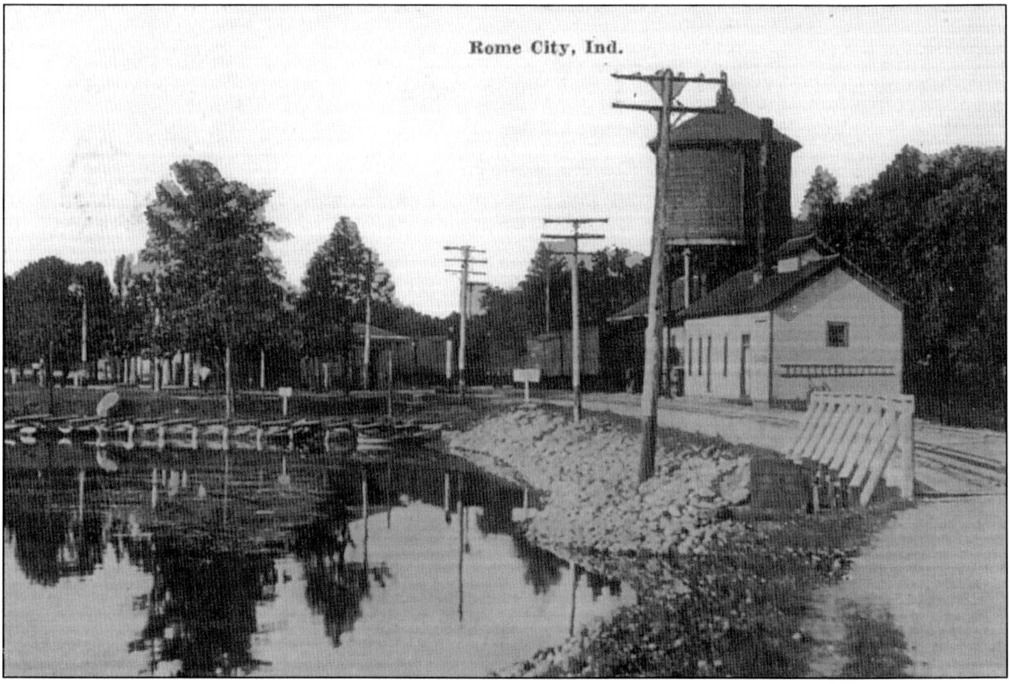

Rome City, Indiana. Sylvan Lake is on the left. The railroad dam is on the right.

Kneipp Sanitarium

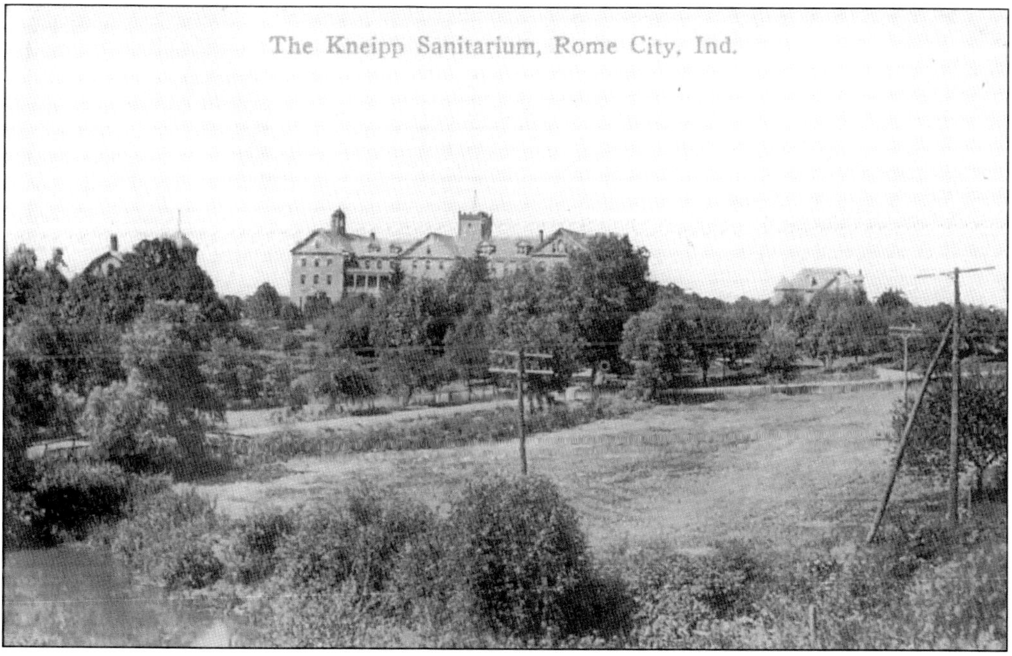

The Kneipp Sanitarium, Rome City, Indiana. This view is taken from a distance.

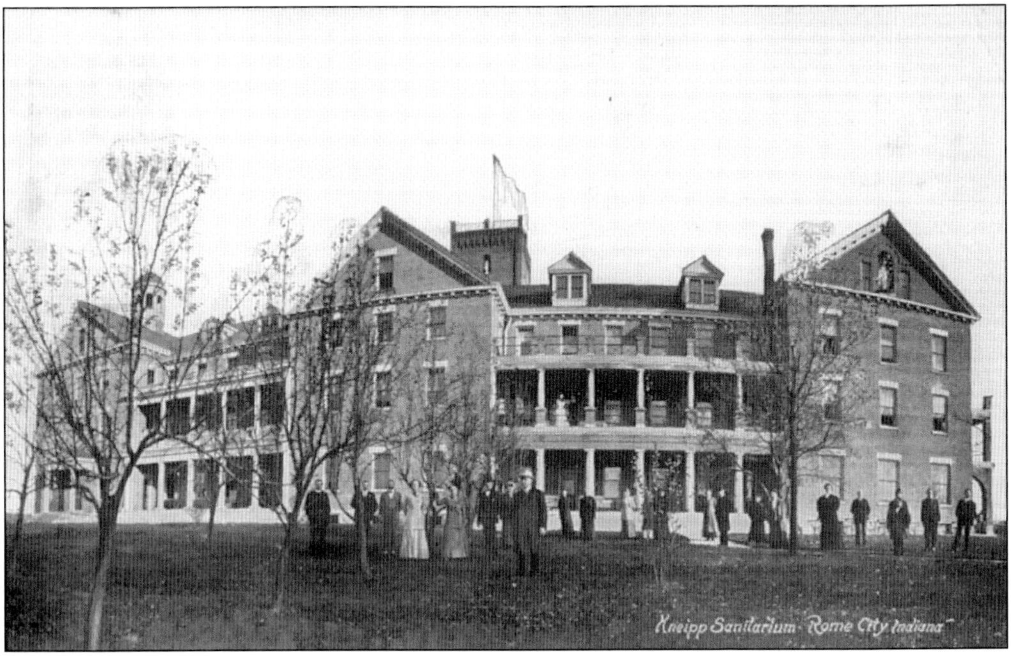

Kneipp Sanitarium, Rome City, Indiana. This was a popular spa.

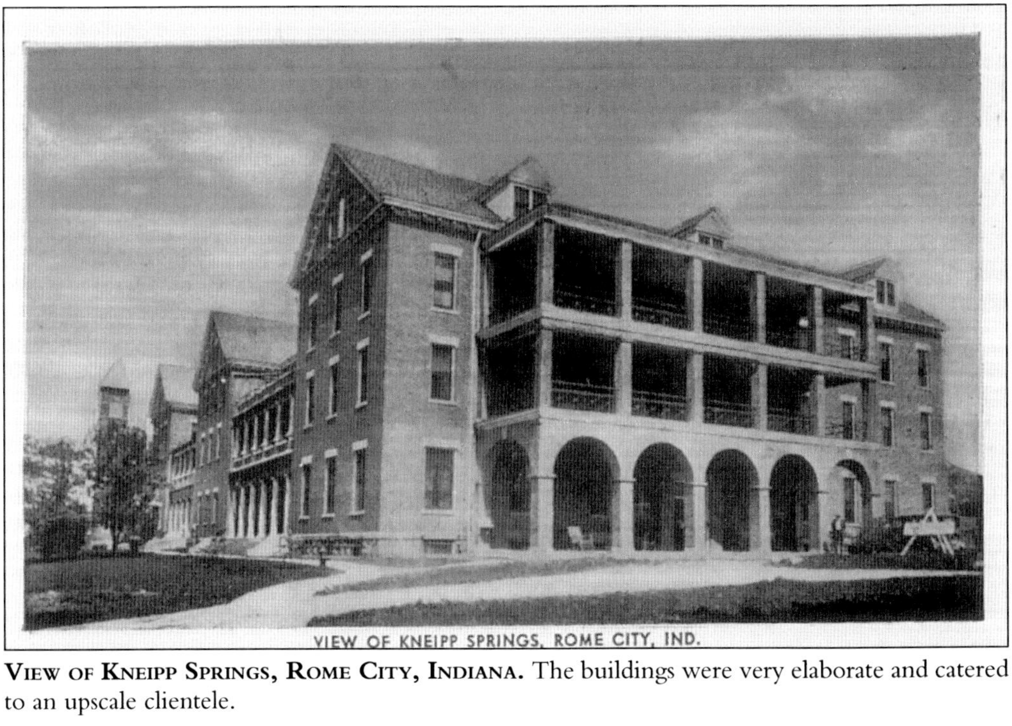

View of Kneipp Springs, Rome City, Indiana. The buildings were very elaborate and catered to an upscale clientele.

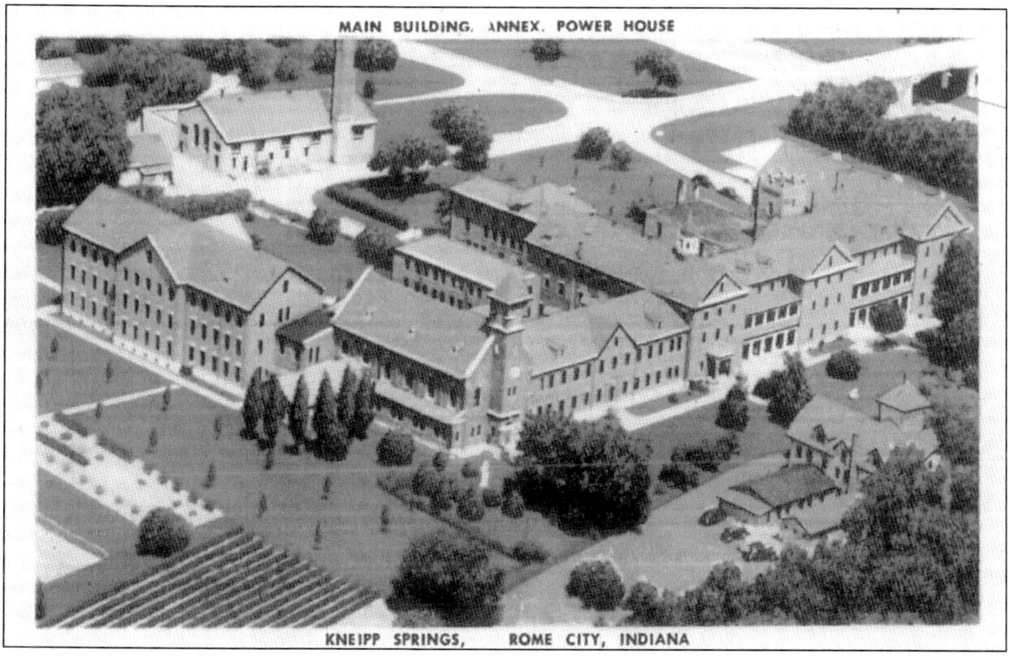

KNEIPP SPRINGS, ROME CITY, INDIANA. This aerial view shows the extent of the complex. The description on the back of the card states, "Kneipp Springs, Rome City, Indiana. For health and recreation. 175 rooms. 950 feet above sea level. On Sylvan Lake, 35 miles northwest of Fort Wayne, 135 miles east of Chicago."

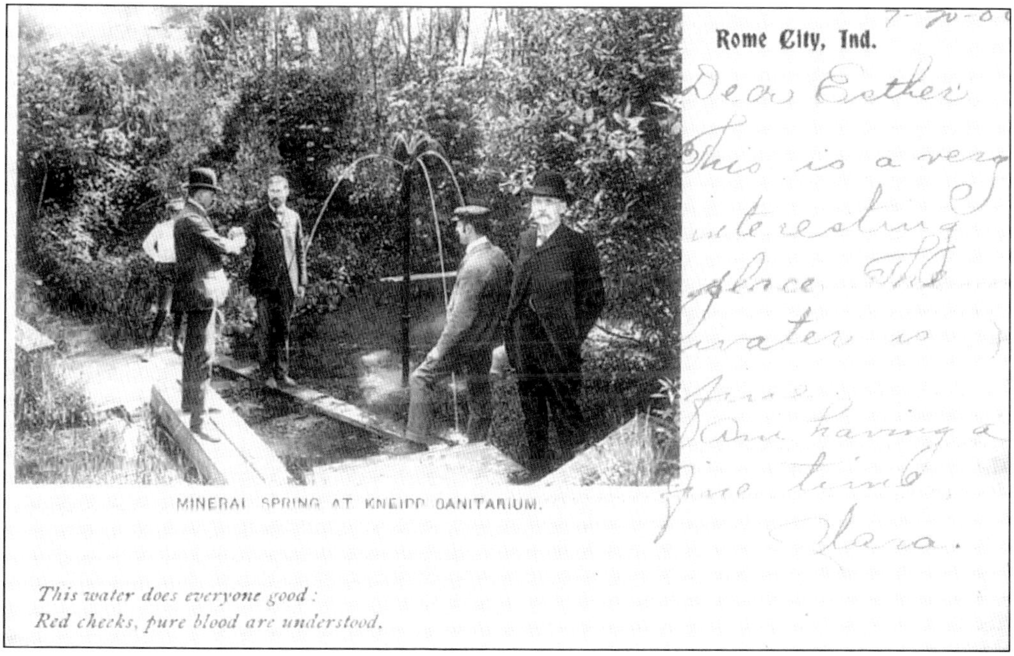

MINERAL SPRING AT KNEIPP SANITARIUM, ROME SPRINGS, INDIANA. This water does everyone good. The message states, "Dear Esther This is a very interesting place. The water is fine. Am having a fine time. Clara." Guests drank and bathed in the natural spring water.

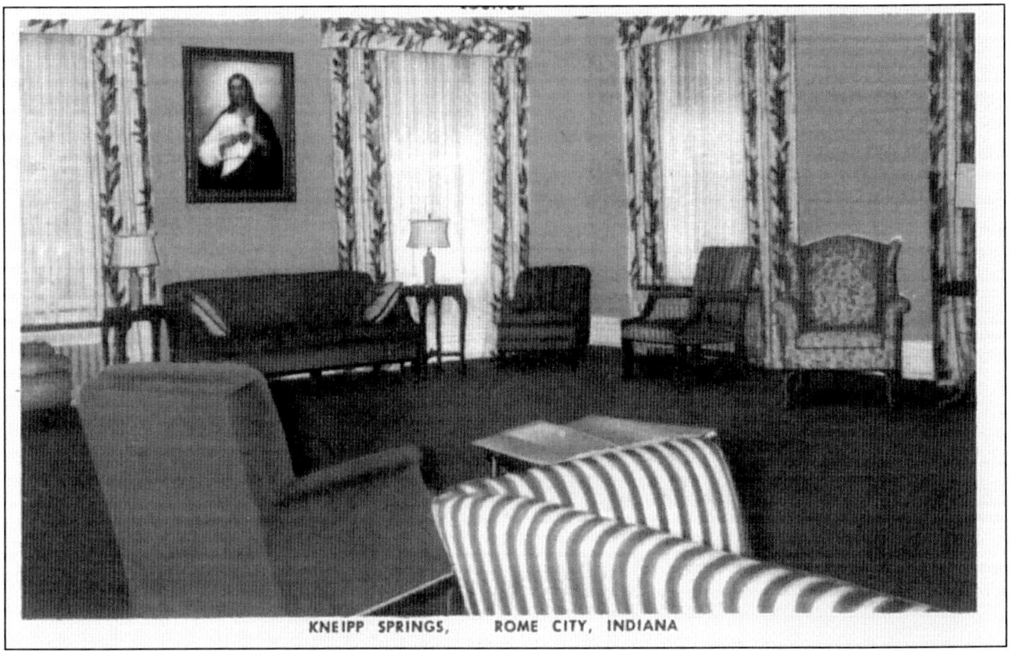

KNEIPP SANITARIUM, ROME CITY, INDIANA. The interior lobby area is shown. The card is postmarked October 3, 1955. The message states, "We did not get here until the twenty seventh. I am taking treatments. I have two kinds of pills and two kinds of treatments to take. The food is fair. Agnes."

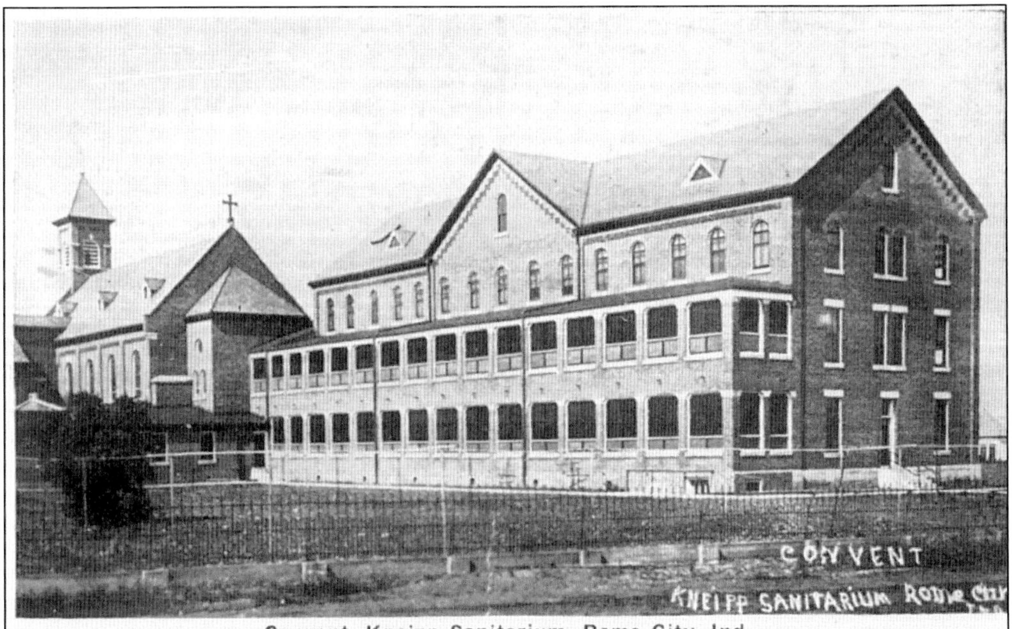

CONVENT KNEIPP SANITARIUM, ROME CITY, INDIANA. The horse and buggy are partially hidden by trees. The staff was primarily nuns who lived in the convent.

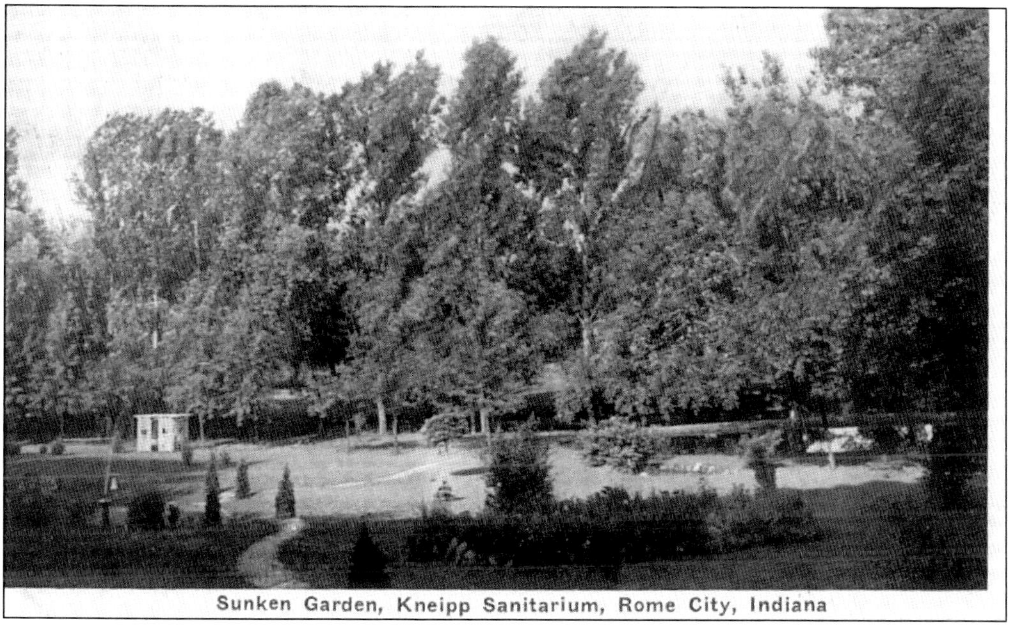

SUNKEN GARDEN, KNEIPP SANITARIUM, ROME CITY, INDIANA, *c.* 1909. The grounds were beautiful and very well maintained. The card is postmarked July 27, 1935. The message states, "We are spending our vacation at Rome City. It sure is a beautiful place to rest. Hope you are both well...."

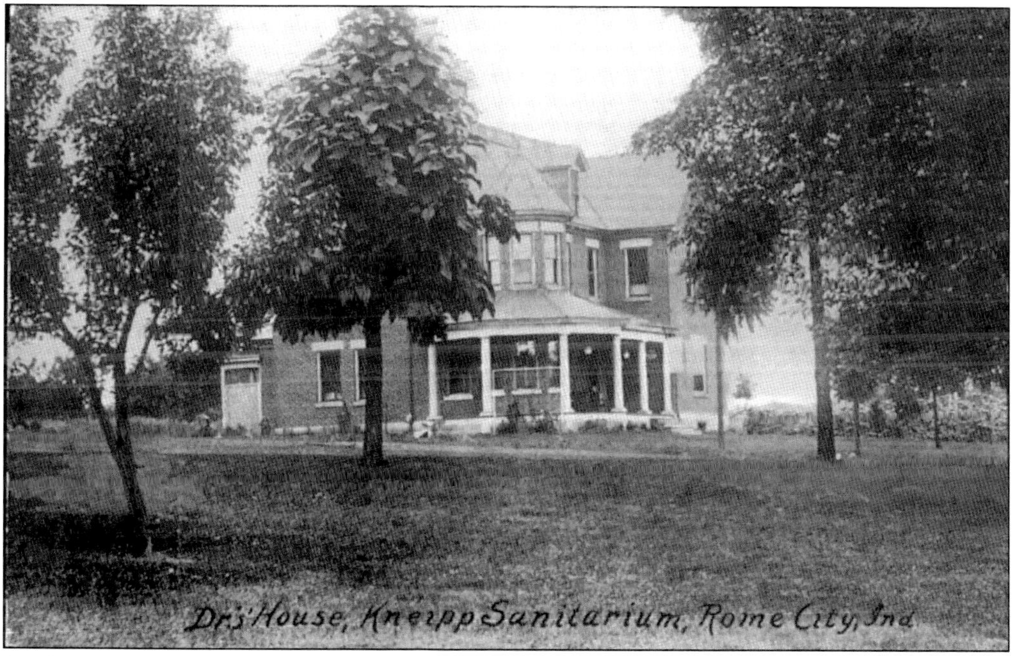

DR.'S HOUSE, KNEIPP SANITARIUM, ROME CITY, INDIANA, *c.* 1913. All treatments were under the supervision of the physician who lived in this house on the grounds.

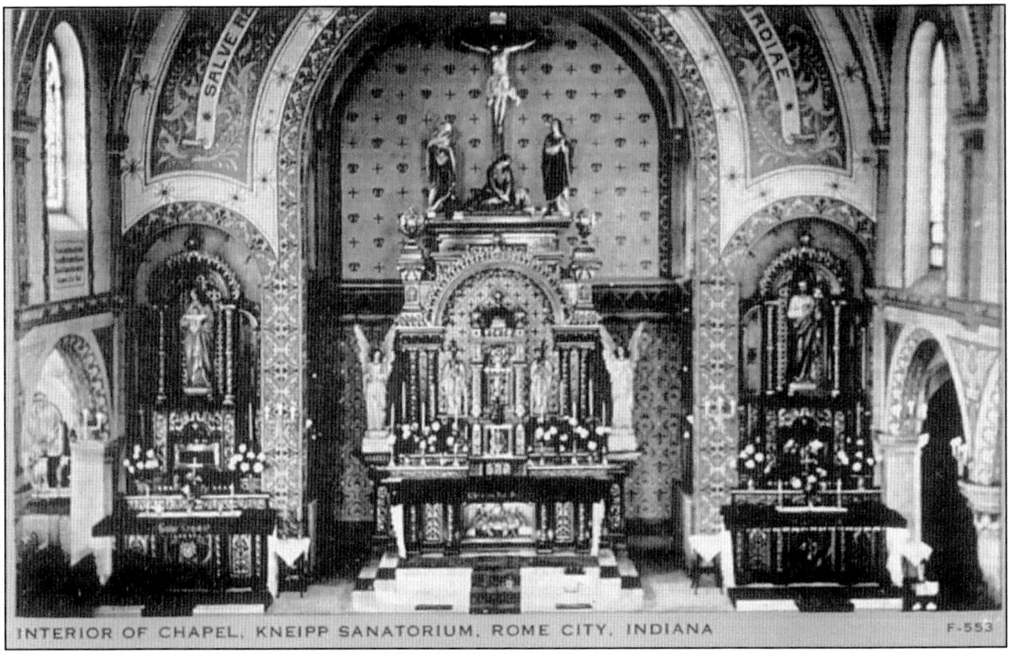

INTERIOR OF CHAPEL, KNEIPP SANATARIUM, ROME CITY, INDIANA. The church was a part of the building complex and was used by the nuns and those patients who were Catholic.

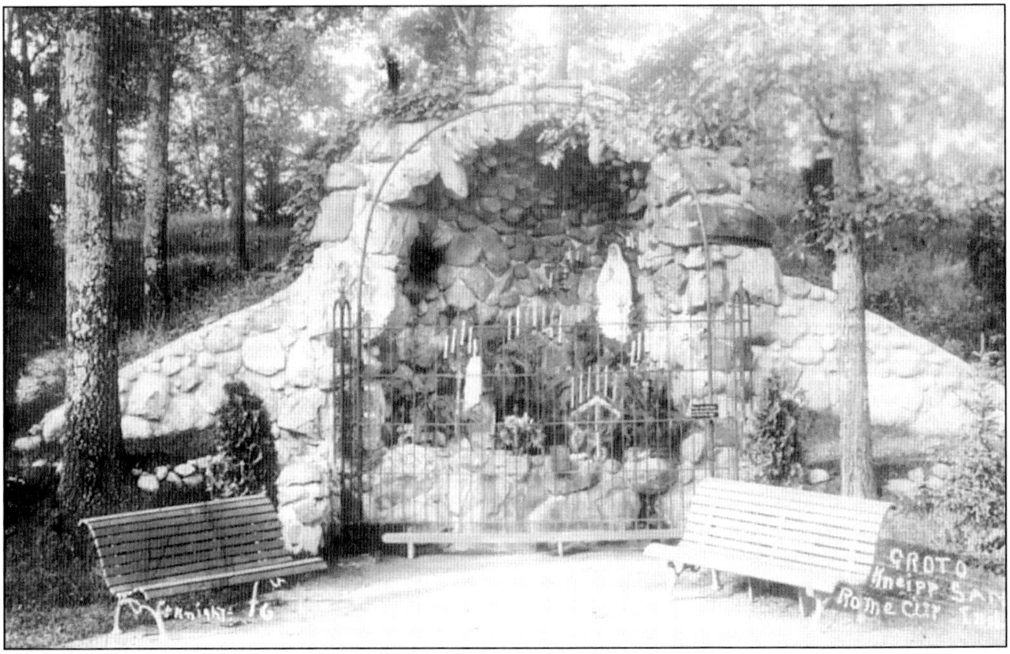

GROTTO, KNEIPP SANITARIUM, ROME CITY, INDIANA, *c.* 1908. The outdoor grotto was a popular destination for a stroll on the grounds.

SYLVAN LAKE

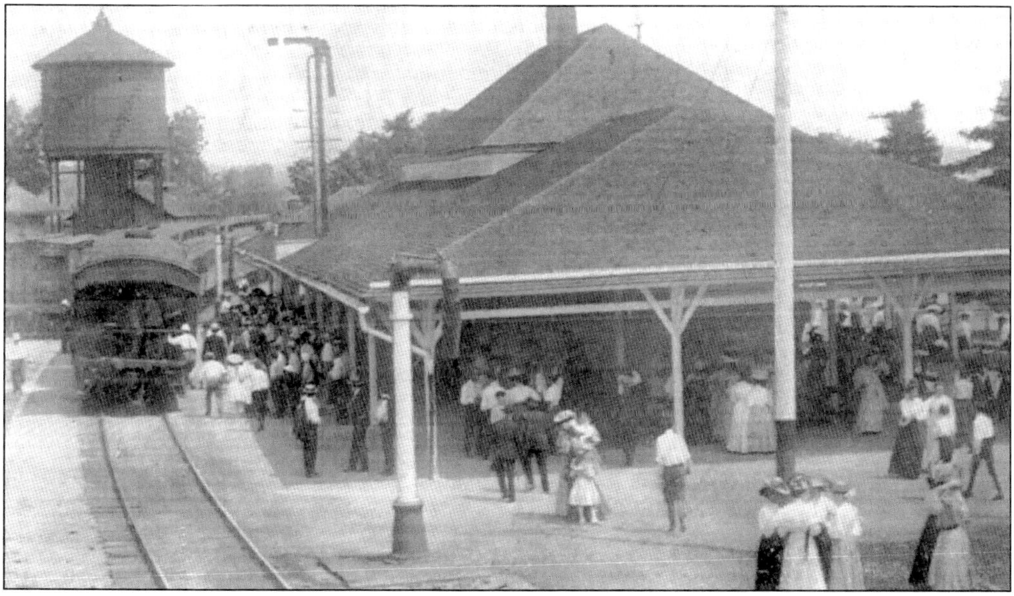

ROME CITY, INDIANA DEPOT, *c.* 1908. The Indiana Depot was a busy place. The good railroad connections were the primary reason for the popularity of Kneipp Sanitarium and Sylvan Lake.

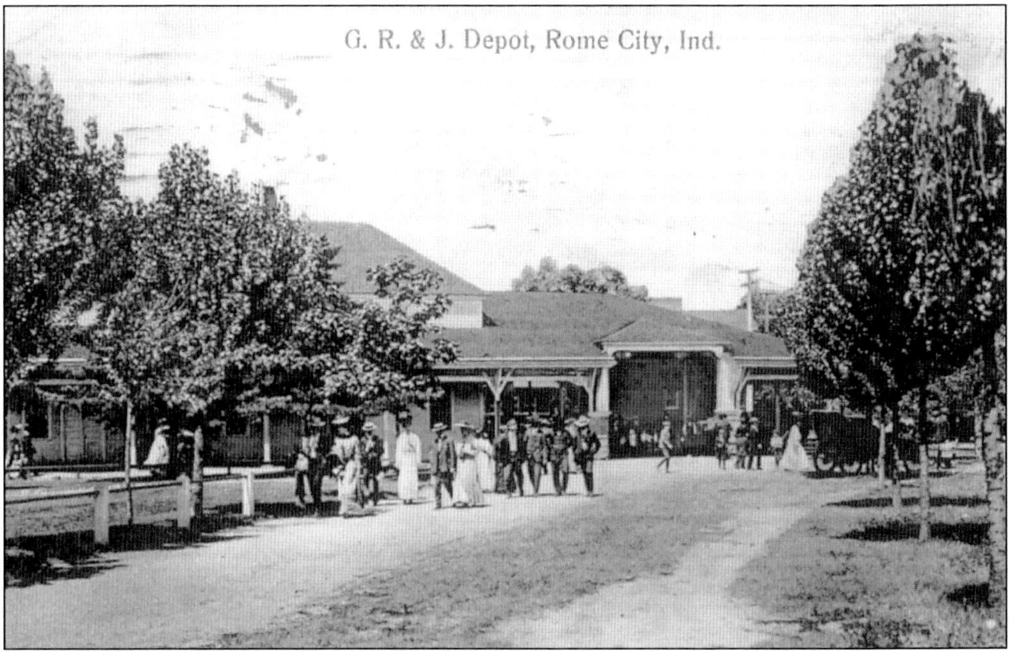

G.R.&I. Depot, Rome City, Indiana, c. 1911. Rome City was a busy place as a resort and health spa. Railroad initials stand for "Grand Rapids & Indiana."

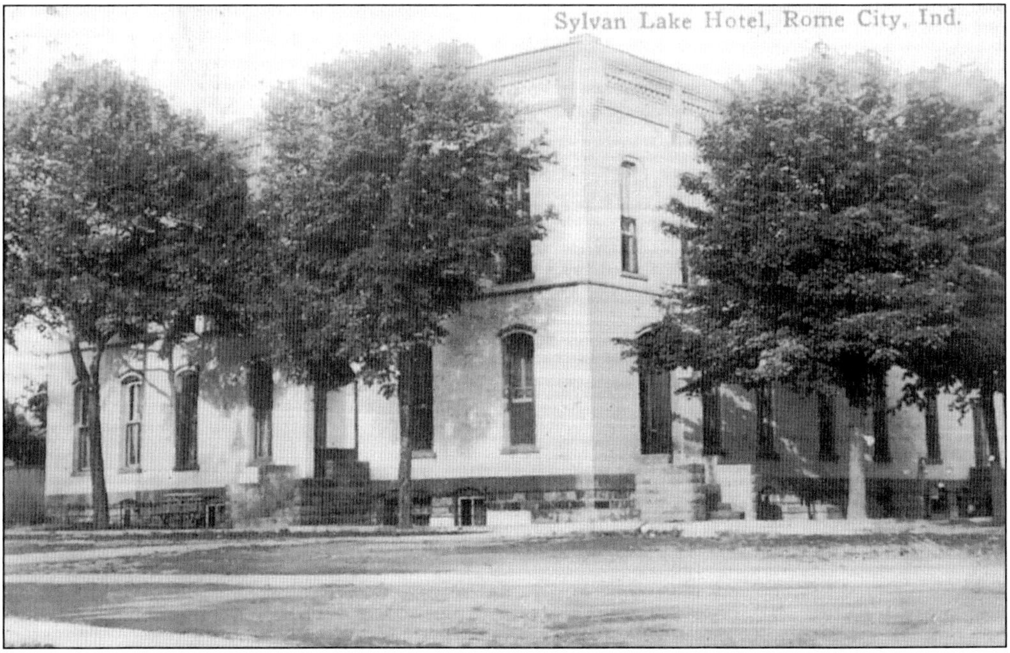

Sylvan Lake Hotel, Rome City, Indiana, c. 1913. The message states, "Went berry hunting about 4:30 this A.M. Got quite a few...some of them were almost as large as my thumb."

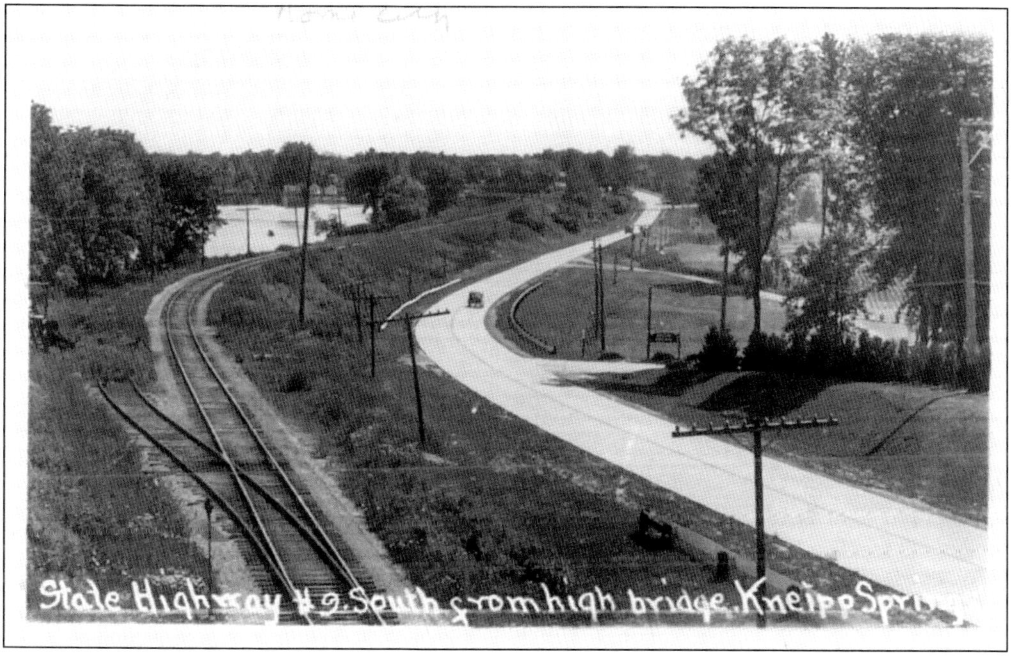

STATE HIGHWAY 9. SOUTH FROM HIGH BRIDGE KNEIPP SPRINGS. The main entrance to Kneipp Springs is on the right. The G.R.&I. Railroad runs along the top of the dam which created Sylvan Lake.

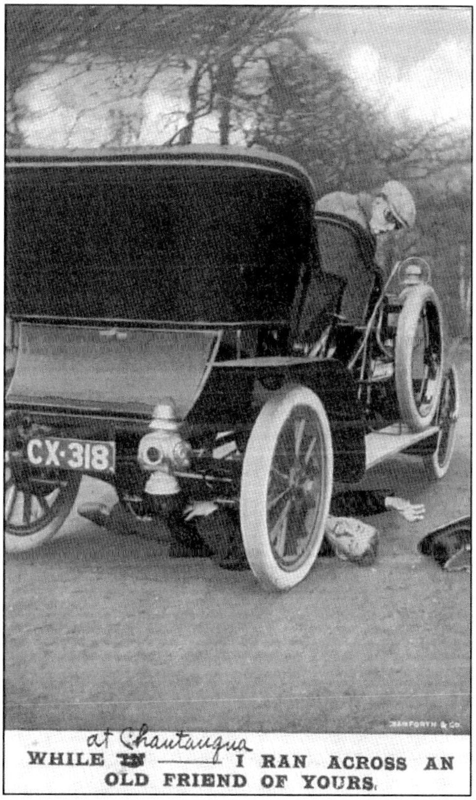

WHILE AT CHAUTAUQUA I RAN ACROSS AND OLD FRIEND OF YOURS. This was a stock card. The Chautauqua was a popular event at Sylvan Lake. The message states, "Yes I ran across an <u>old</u> friend of yours all right, who was a pretty good opinion of you too. How did you get home? You left rather suddenly didn't you? Write to me. Ruby."

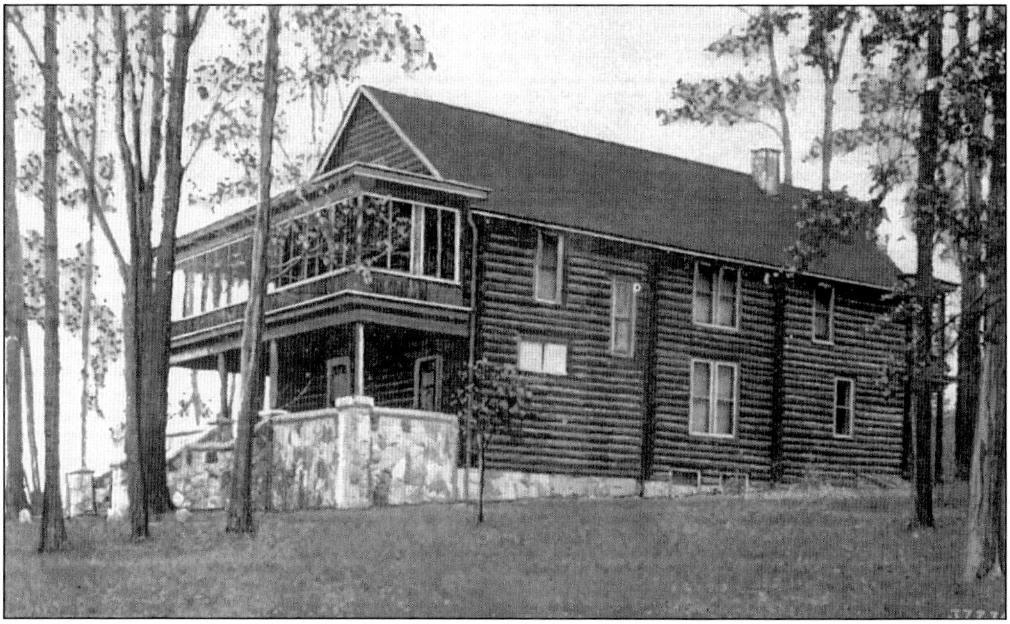

"Limberlost Cabin" Former Home of Gene Stratton Porter, Sylvan Lake, Rome City, Indiana. This popular Indiana author had a nature garden at her cabin.

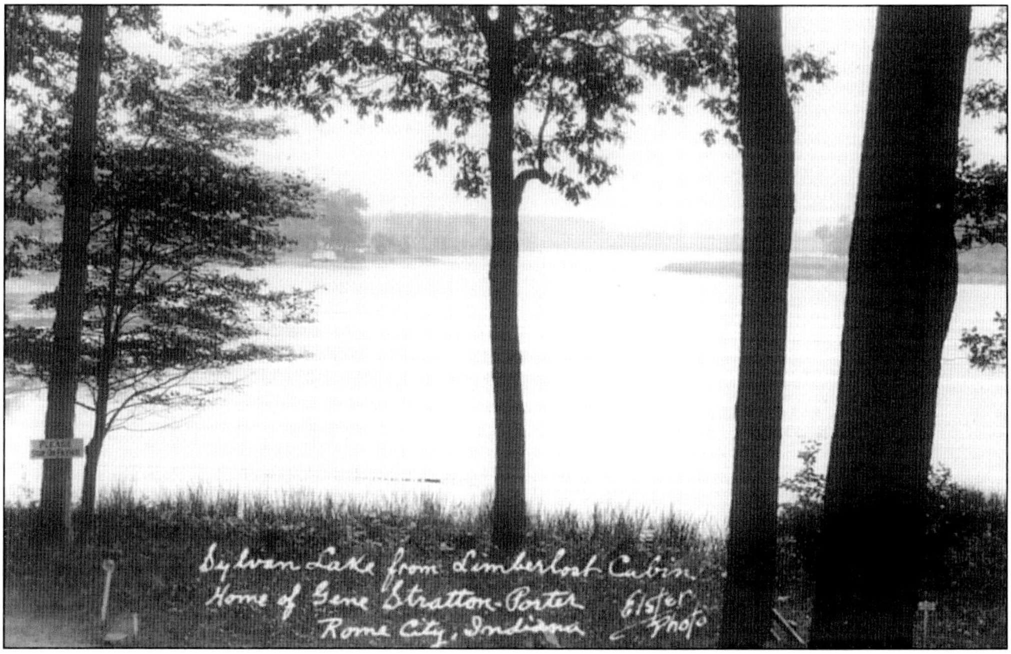

Sylvan Lake from Limberlost Cabin. This was the home of Gene Stratton Porter, Rome City, Indiana. The author had a great view of the lake.

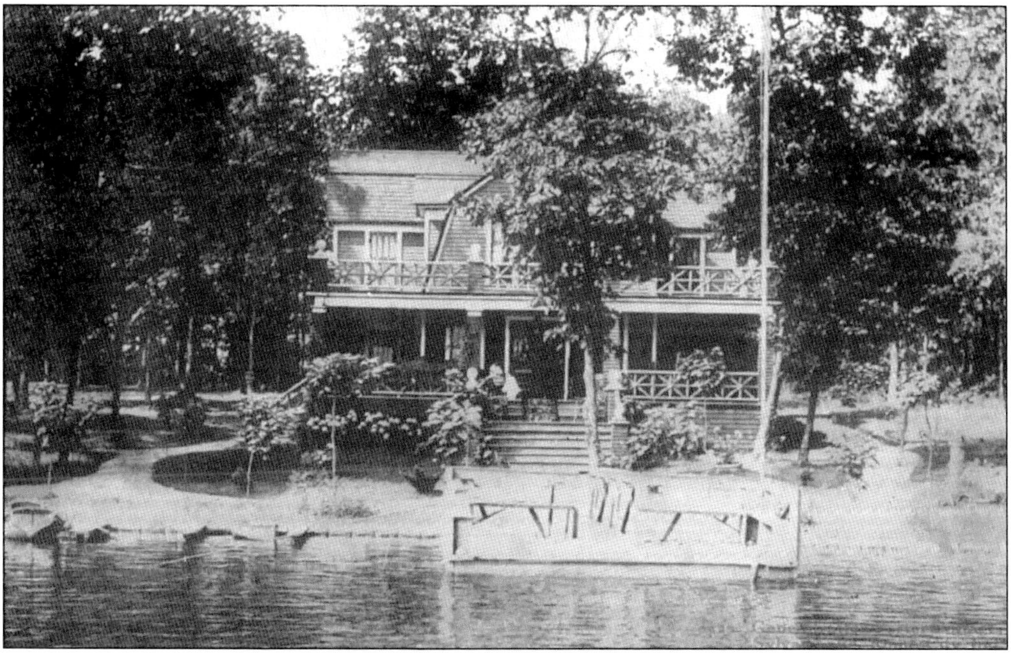

Gene Stratton Porter Cottage, Sylvan Lake, Rome City, Indiana. The cabin is located on the south side of the lake.

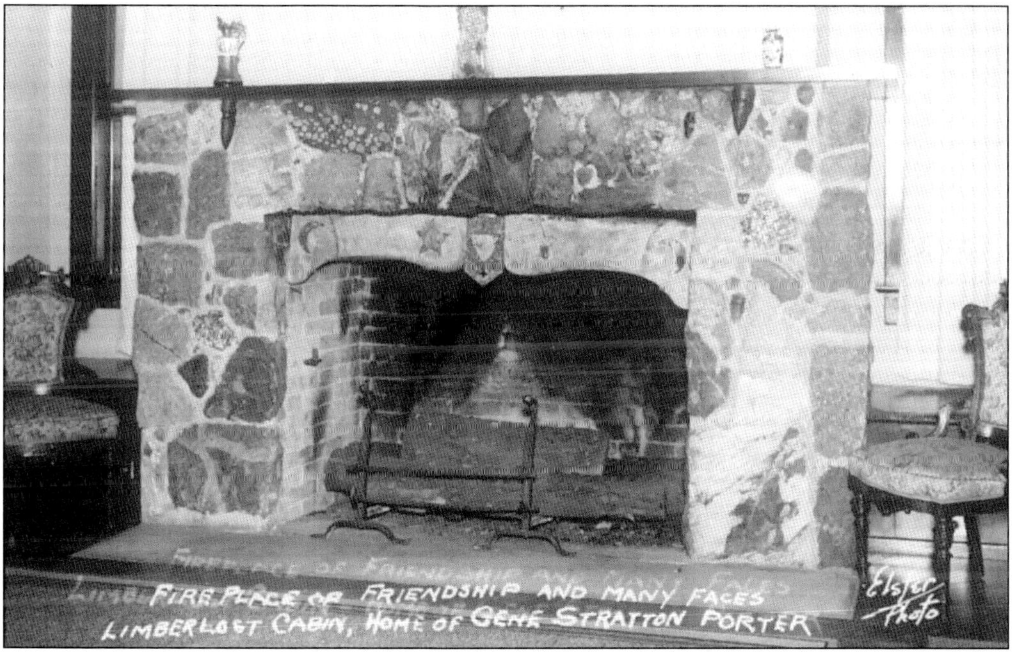

Fireplace of Friendship and Many Faces, Limberlost Cabin, Home of Gene Stratton Porter. The home is now an Indiana State Memorial and is open to the public.

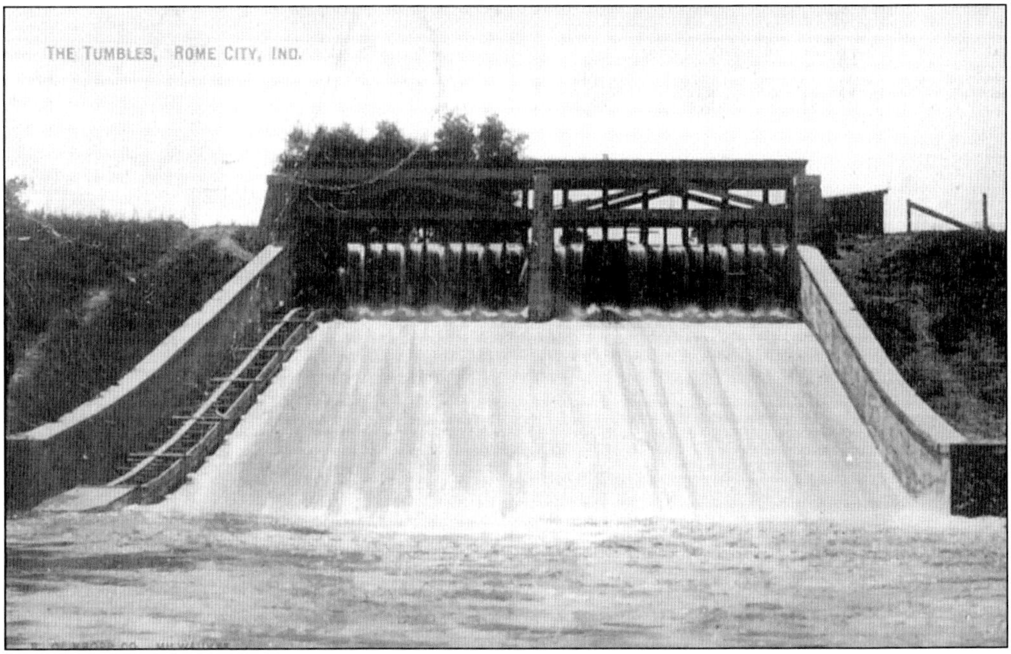

The Tumbles, Rome City, Indiana, c. 1908. This is a close-up view. The tumbles are the overflow from Sylvan Lake.

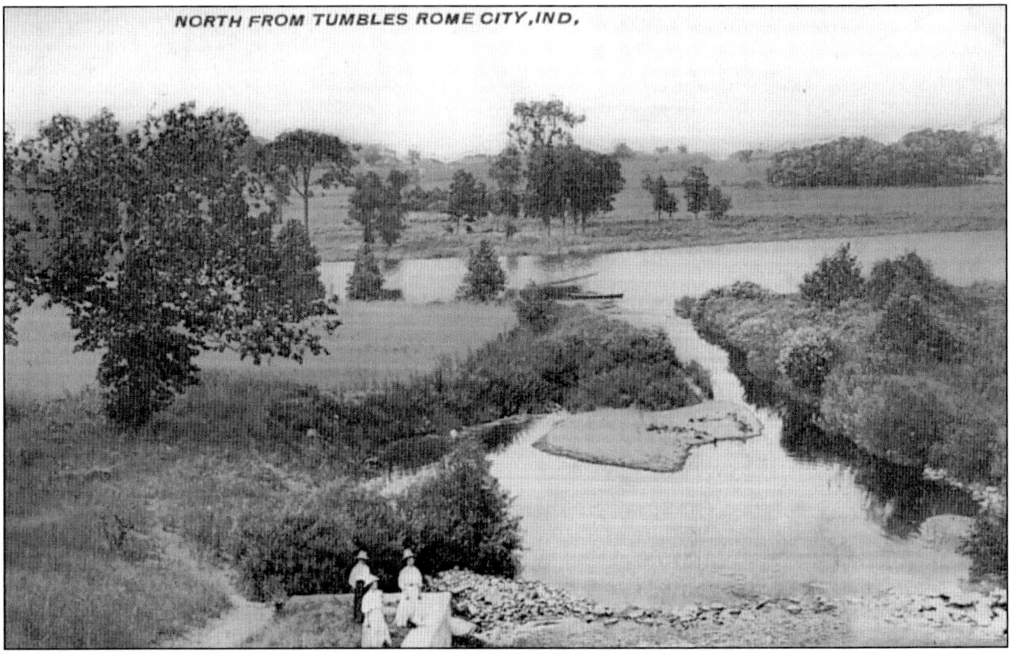

North From Tumbles Rome City, Indiana, c. 1910. The ponds created by the overflow from the lake are popular fishing spots. Kneipp Springs is in the distant background.

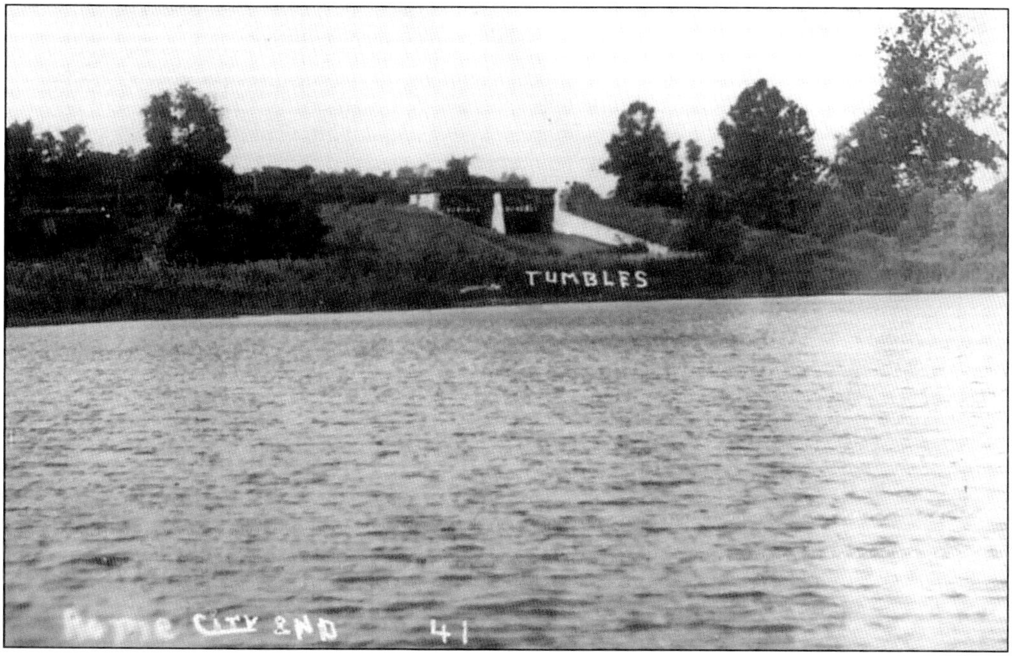

ROME CITY, INDIANA. The tumbles are in the background.

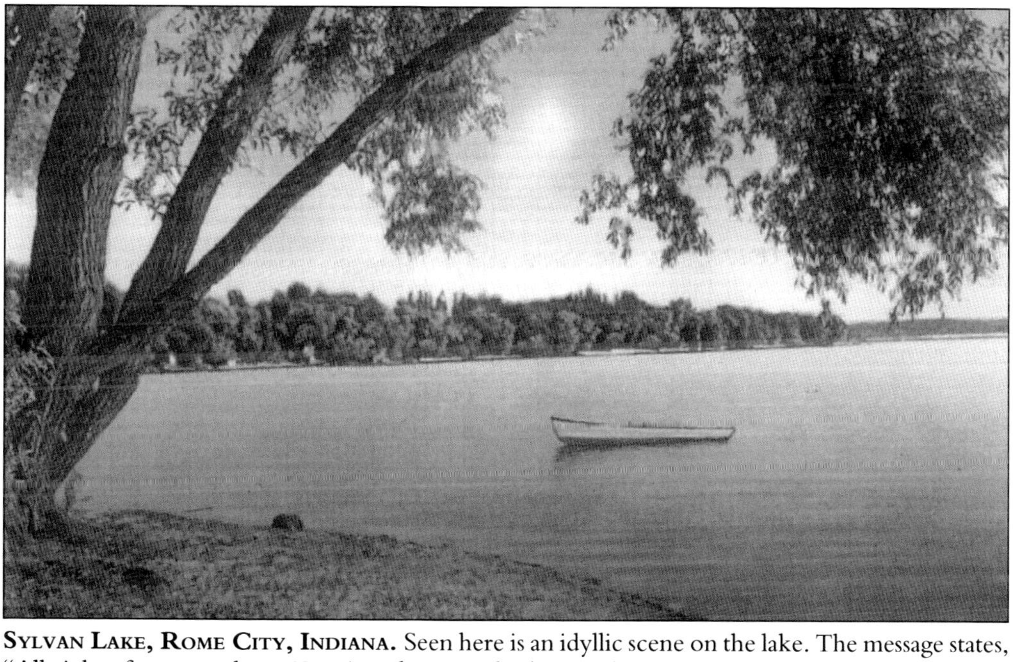

SYLVAN LAKE, ROME CITY, INDIANA. Seen here is an idyllic scene on the lake. The message states, "All eight of us are up here. Keeping plenty cool. I have to leave to go back to school. Avery's and the folks will be here the rest of the week. Vera and Russell will stay a day yet...Ruby."

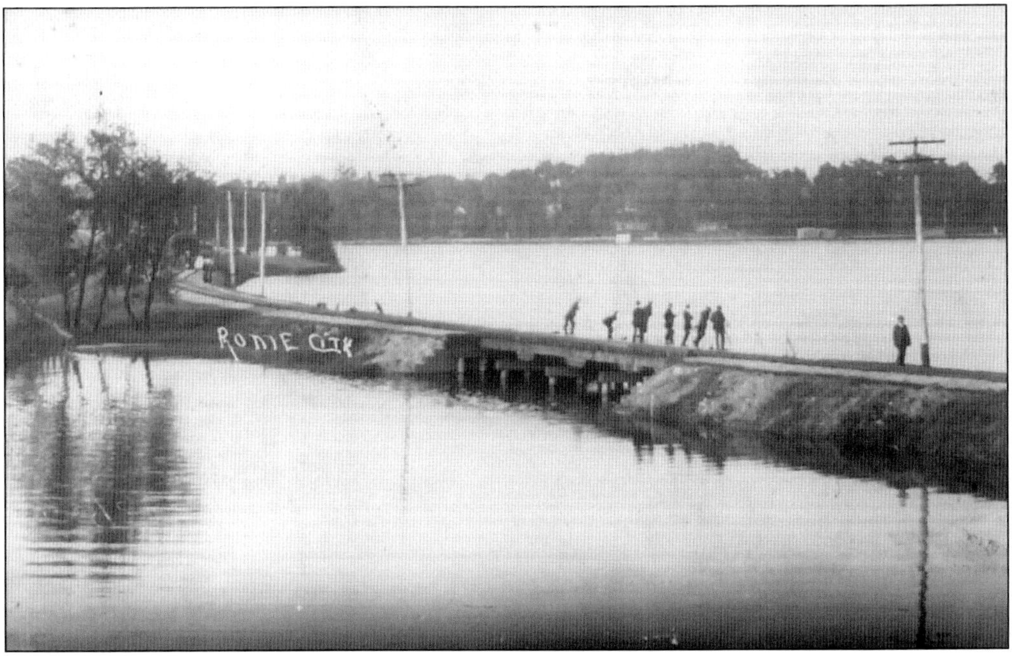

PLEASANT POINT, ROME CITY, INDIANA, *c.* 1910. Steam boat took sight-seeing trips around the lake.

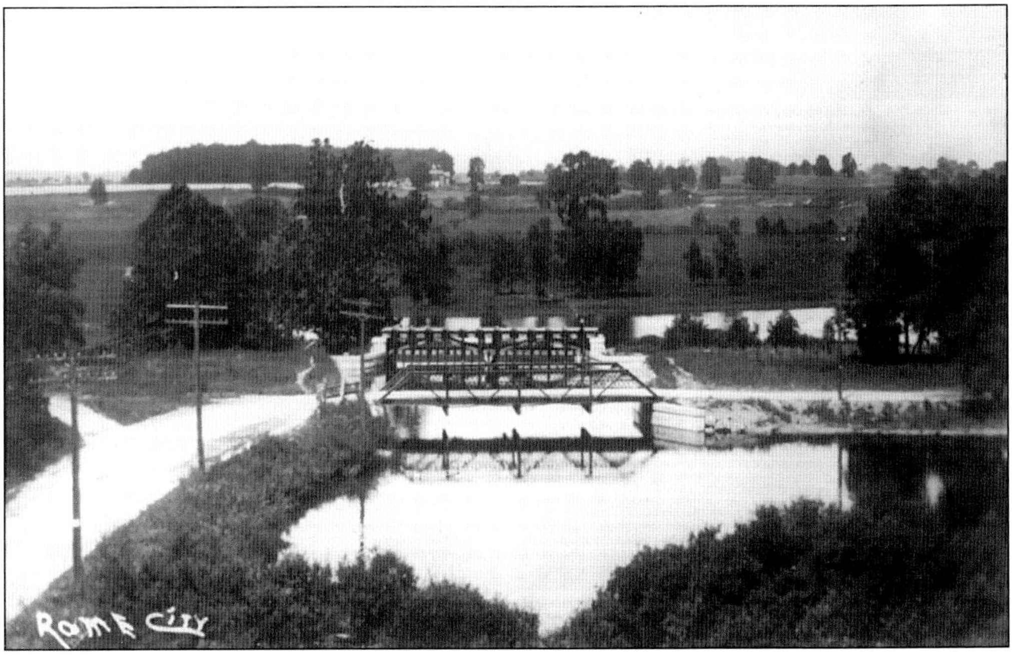

ROME CITY, INDIANA. The bridge is in the center.

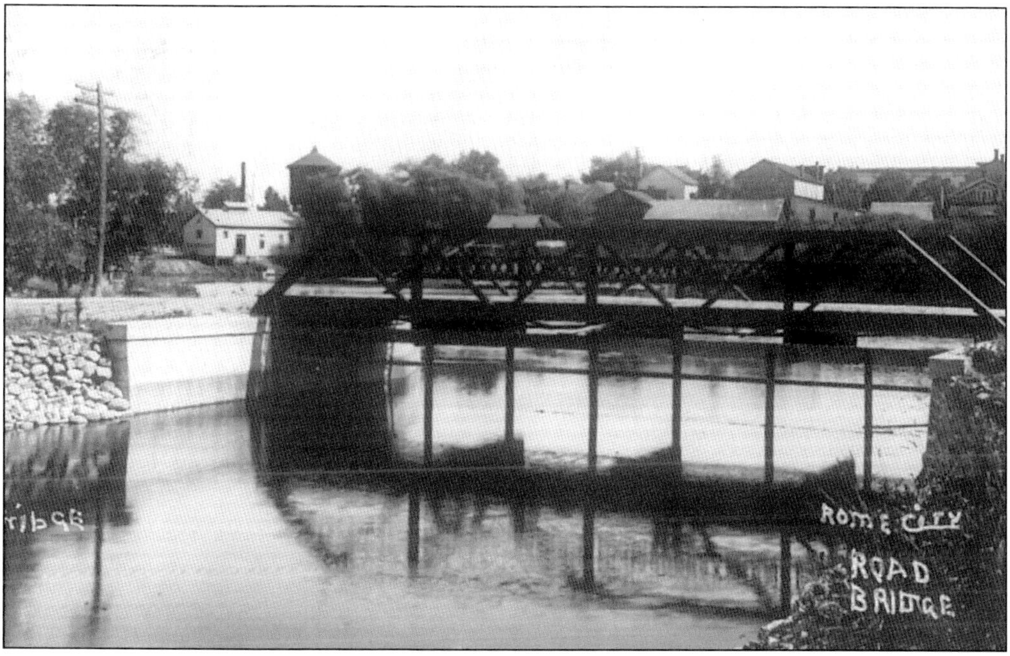

ROME CITY ROAD BRIDGE, *c.* 1910. The message states, "Coming home to-morrow to go to the dance? There is the biggest mob here this week, some mighty swell folks and some not so swell. There is a Mandolin Club, all dandy lookers and I want to tell you that I've been playing my cards for all I'm worth. They have been coming over to the store and playing for us evenings. Oh there's big doings. Flossie."

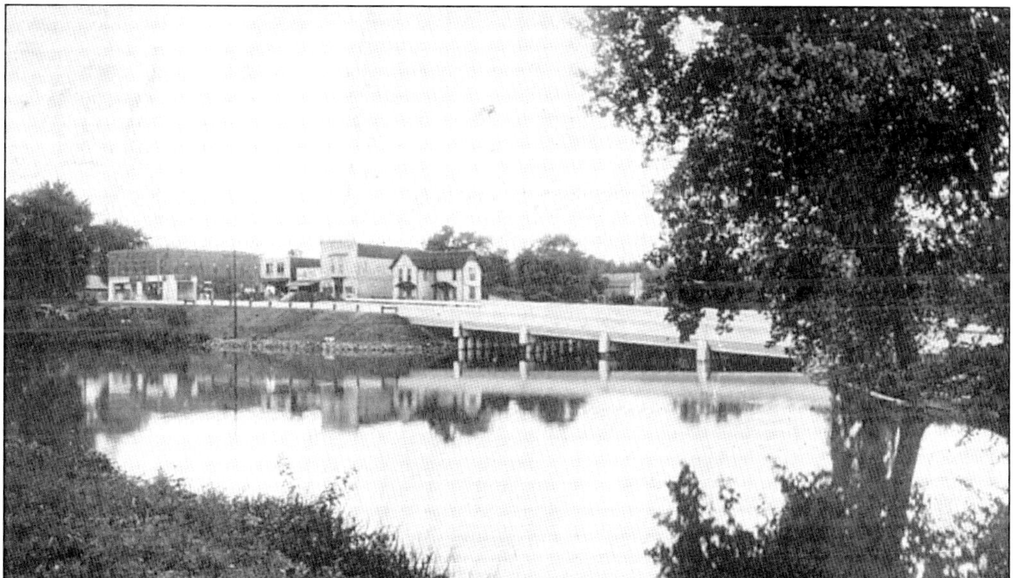

BRIDGE, ROUTE 9, ROME CITY, INDIANA, *c.* 1938. The "new" concrete bridge is shown with the town of Rome City in the background.

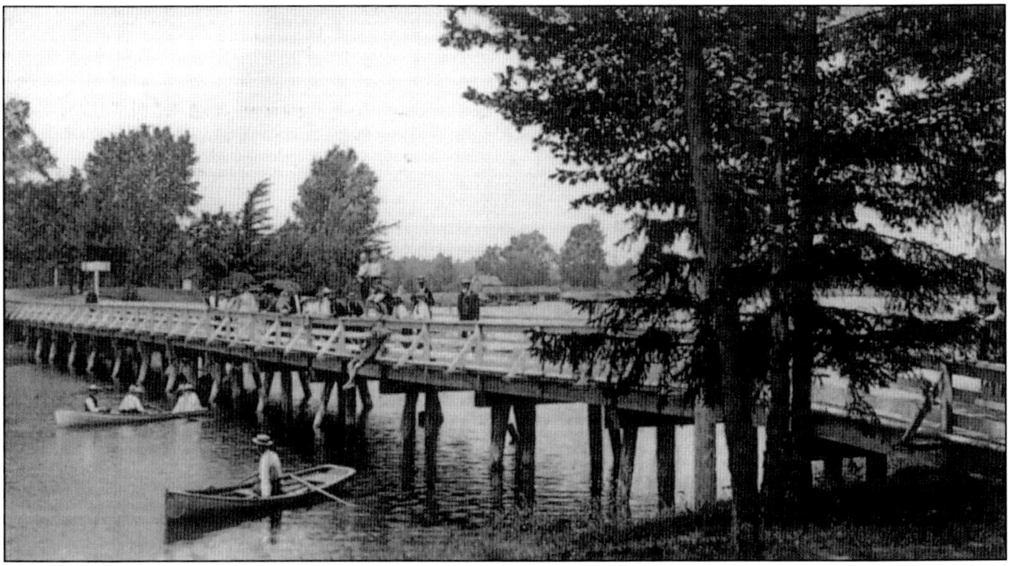

ISLAND PARK BRIDGE, ROME CITY, INDIANA, *c.* 1907. Ladies are carrying umbrellas as sunshades.

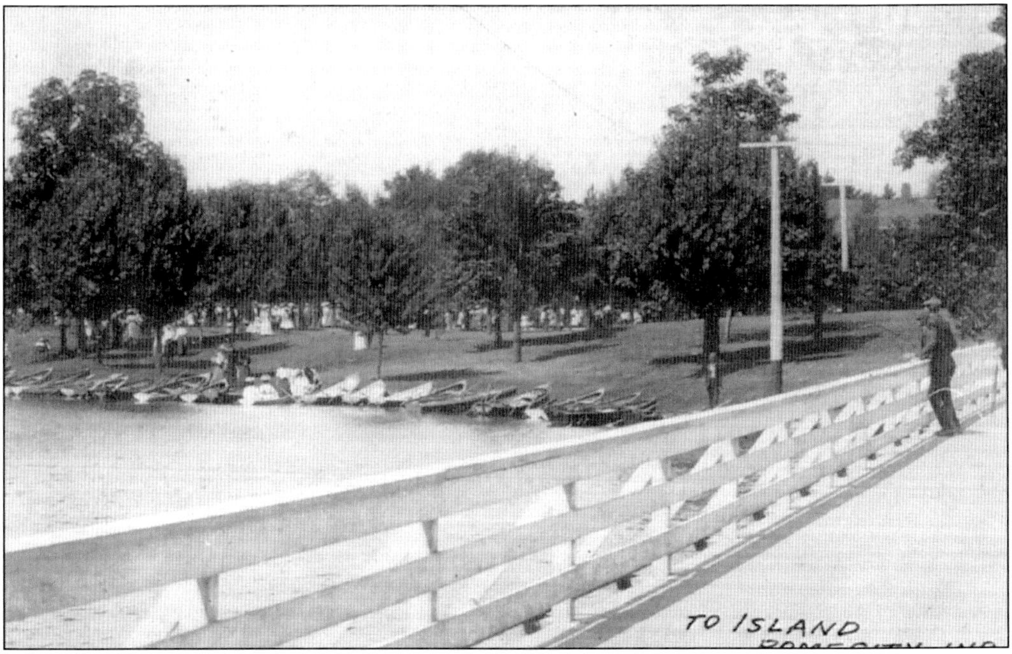

TO ISLAND, ROME CITY, INDIANA, *c.* 1909. Note the five ladies in their Sunday best boarding the boat in the center.

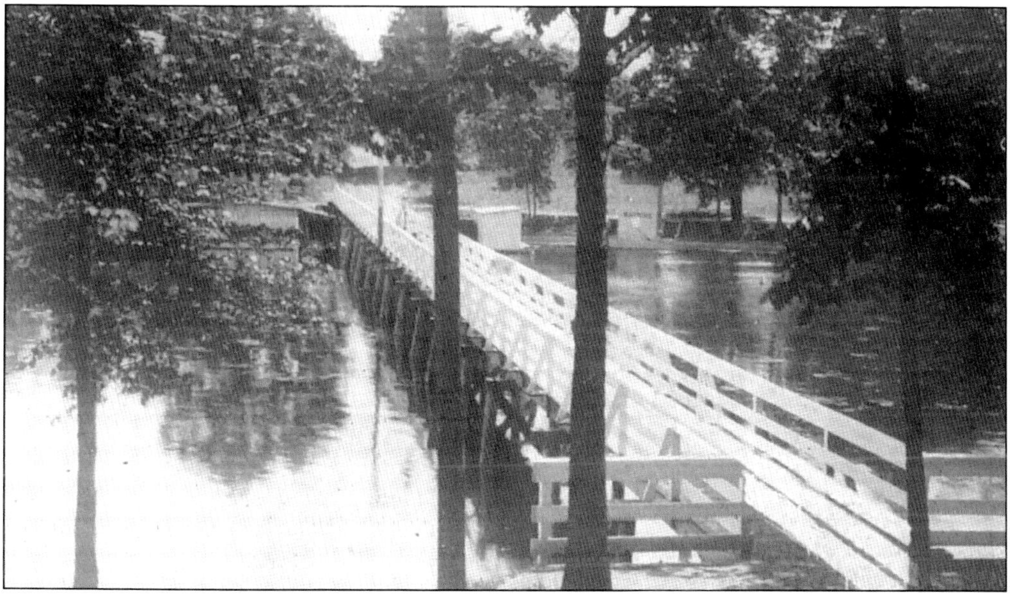

ROME CITY, INDIANA, *c.* 1921. The footbridge to the island was a popular subject of photographs.

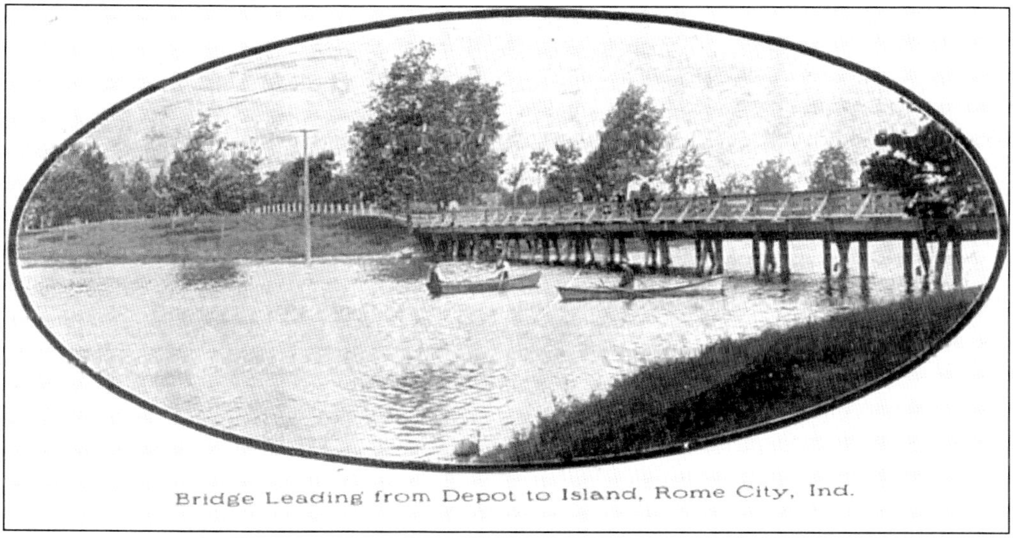

BRIDGE HEADING FROM DEPOT TO ISLAND, ROME CITY, INDIANA, *c.* 1907. The island was a popular place to visit.

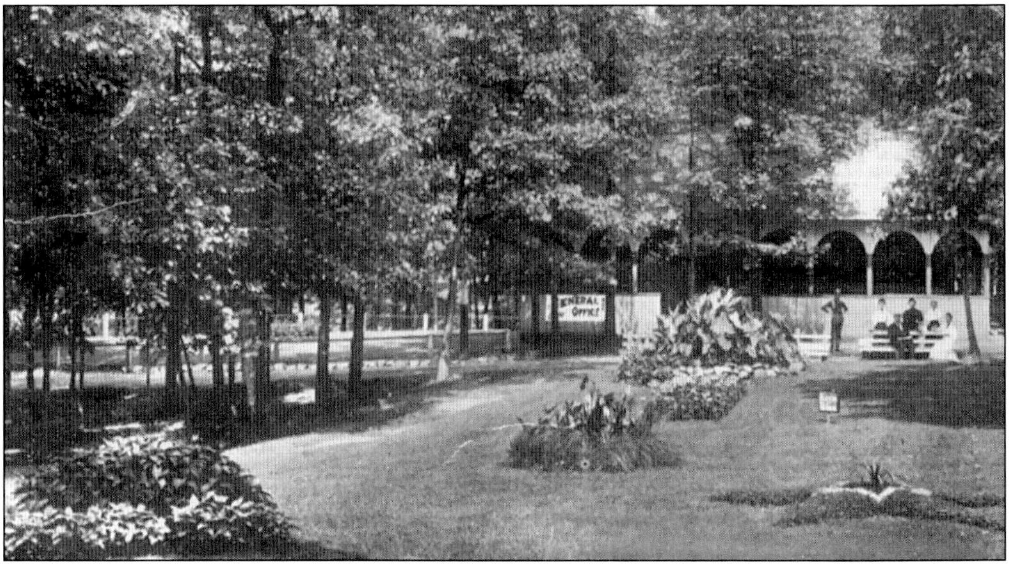

ON THE ISLAND, ROME CITY, INDIANA, *c.* 1907. The message states, "I am living high—nine steps."

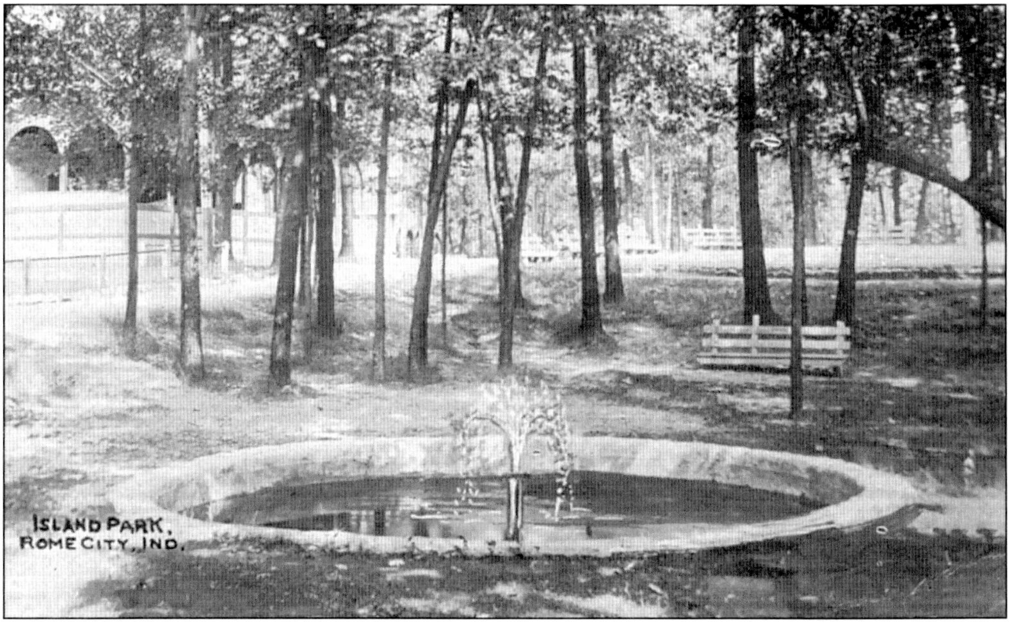

ISLAND PARK, ROME CITY, INDIANA. The island was landscaped and maintained as a park area.

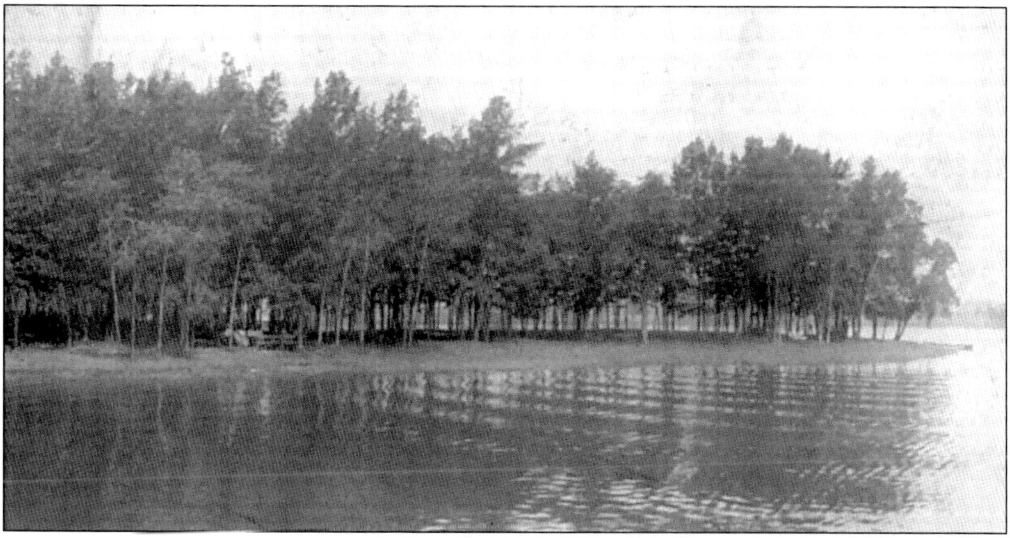

Island Park, Rome City, Indiana, *c.* 1908. This card is addressed to North Manchester and informs recipient, "I have a room engaged for you. Don't get off at Rome City but tell the conductor to leave you at the Sanitarium."

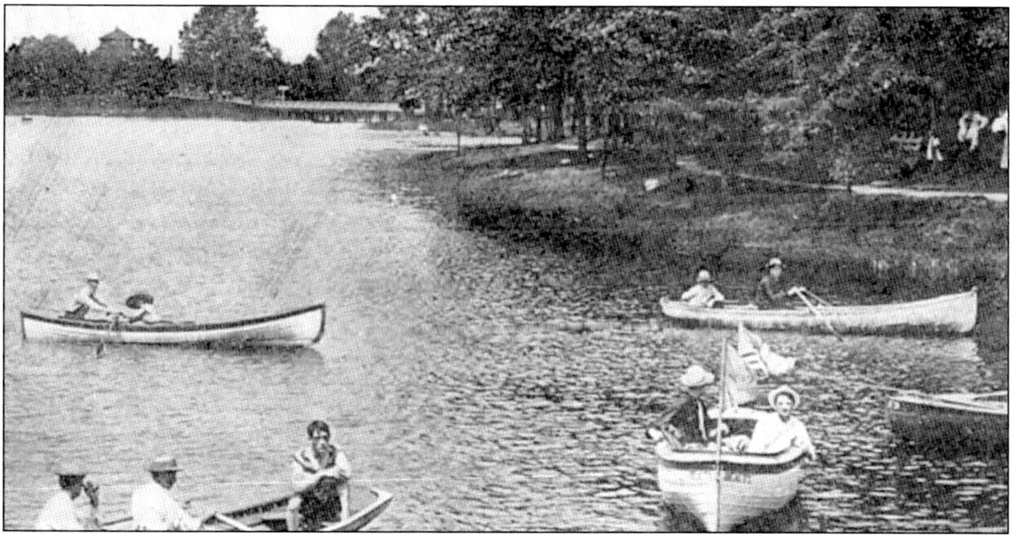

East End of Island, Rome City, Indiana. Boats were rented for trips around the lake.

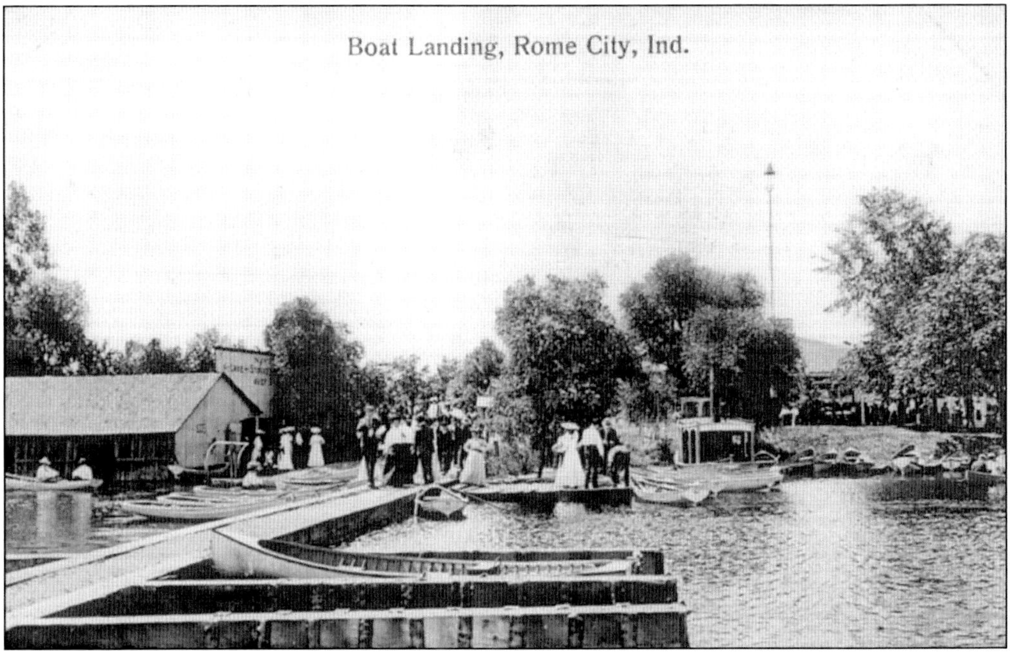

BOAT LANDING, ROME CITY, INDIANA. The guests are dressed very formally with the men in suits and ties and hats an the ladies in long dresses.

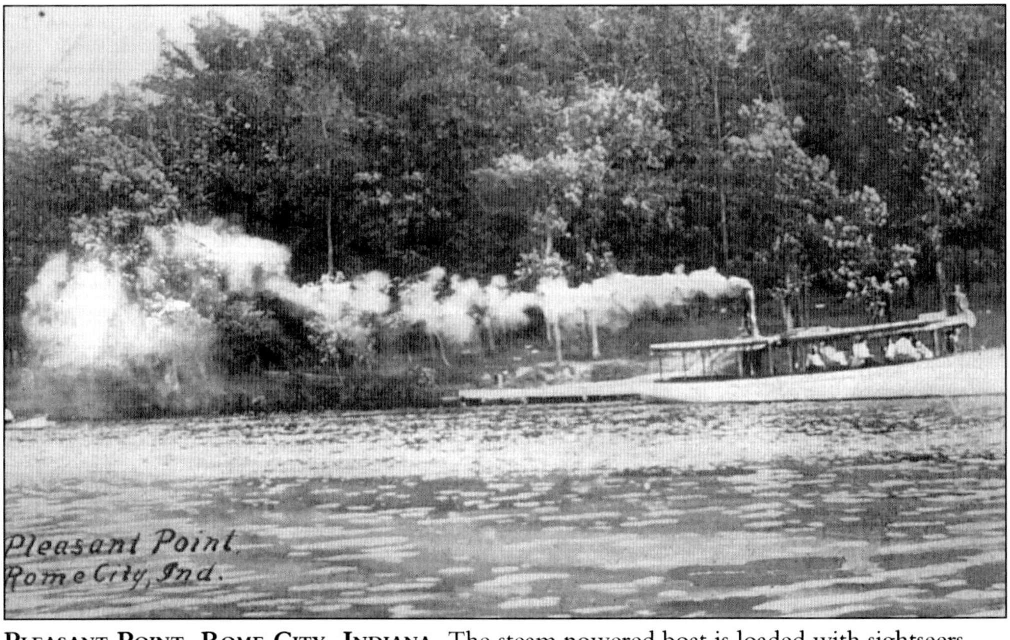

PLEASANT POINT, ROME CITY, INDIANA. The steam powered boat is loaded with sightseers.

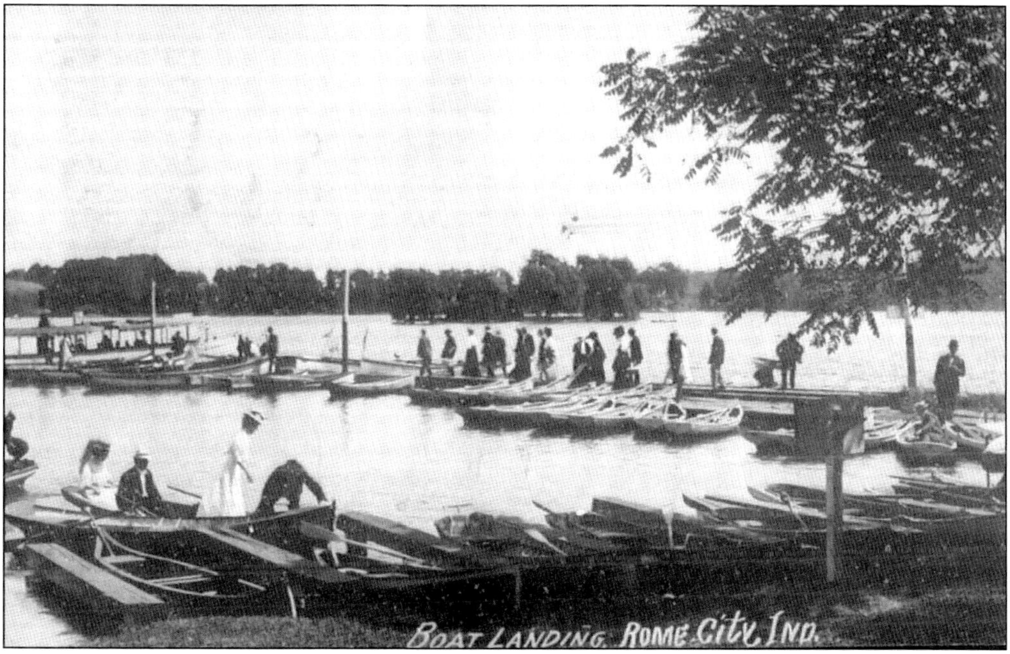

Boat Landing, Rome City, Indiana, c. 1909. Note steam boat at end of dock.

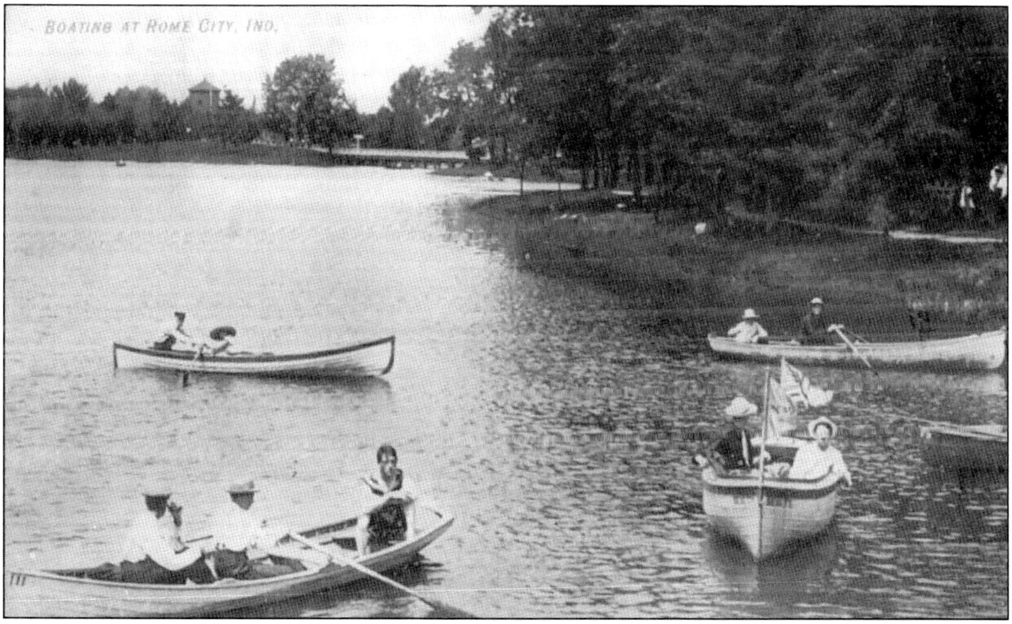

Boating at Rome City, Indianac c. 1908. The message states, "Am improving everyday. Think I will stay two months, this is a fine place."

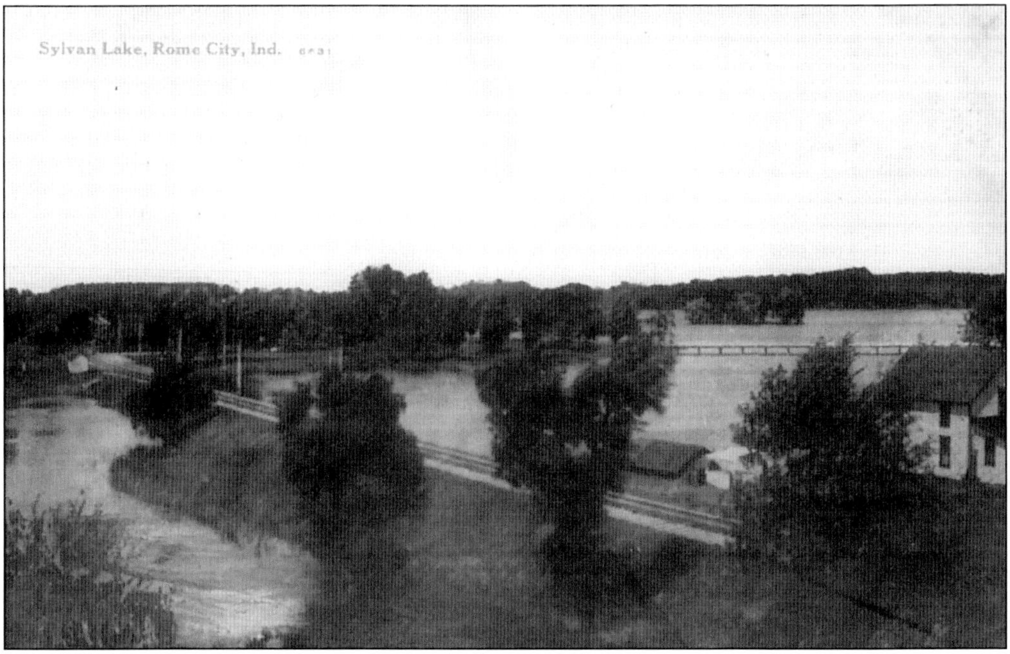

SYLVAN LAKE, ROME CITY, INDIANA, *c.* 1910. This picture shows the railroad.

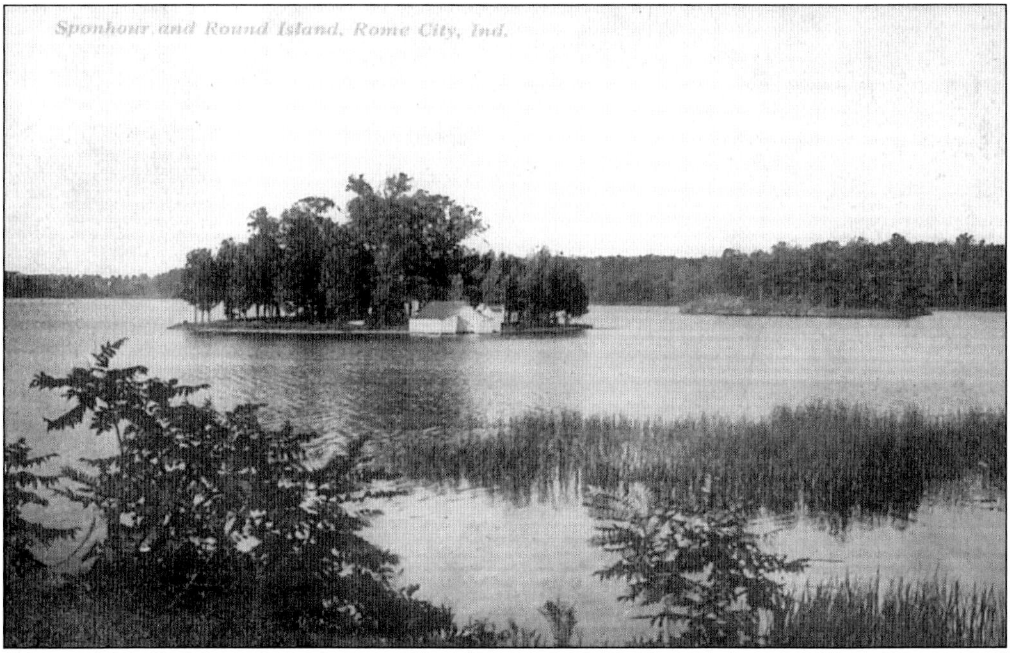

SPONHOUR AND ROUND ISLAND, ROME CITY, INDIANA, *c.* 1916. This card was addressed to Miss Nickols at Fort Wayne. There is only a big question mark in the message space.

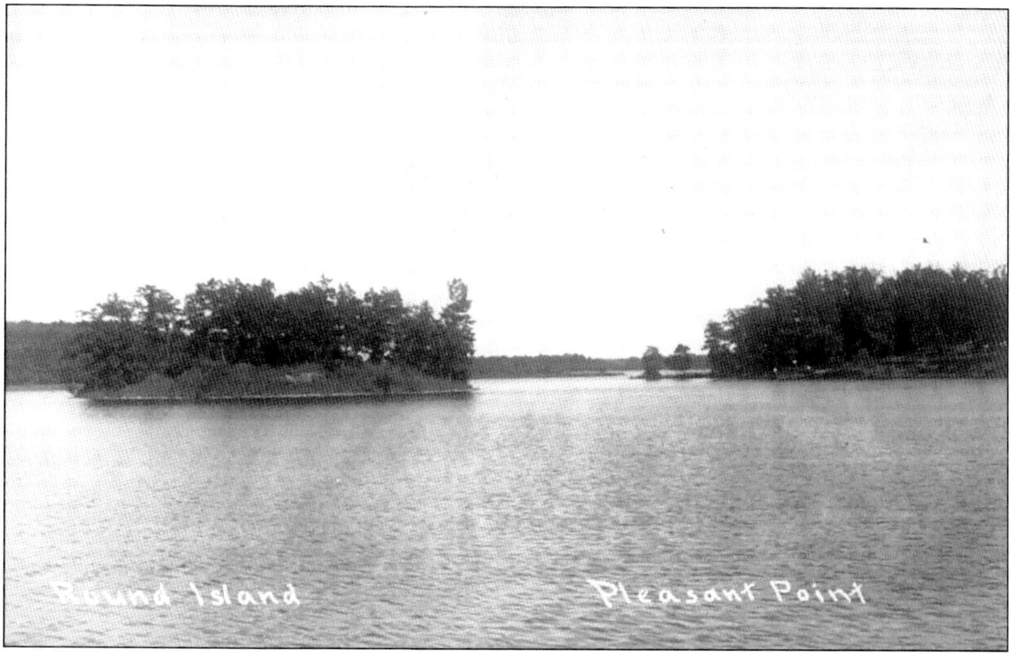

Round Island, Pleasant Point, *c.* 1907. There are several islands in the lake.

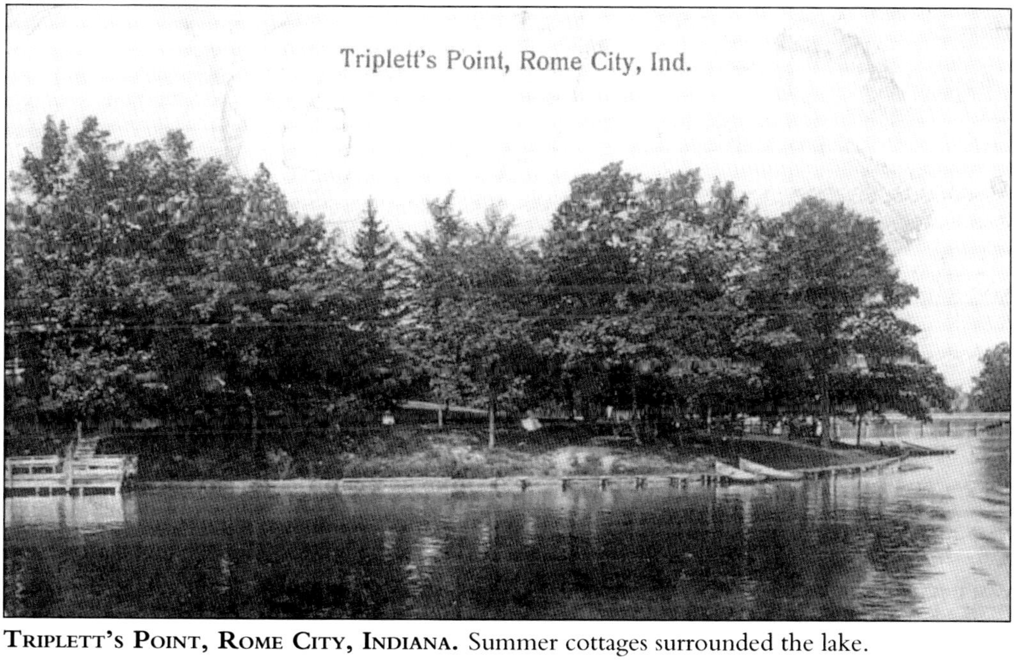

Triplett's Point, Rome City, Indiana. Summer cottages surrounded the lake.

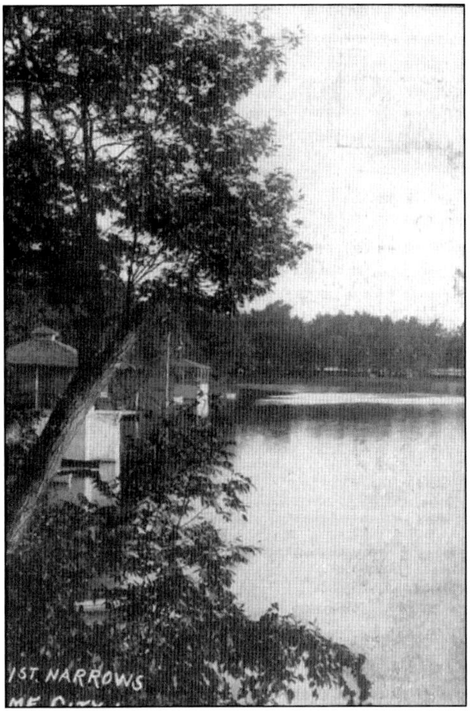

1st Narrows, Rome City, Indiana. The lake shore meanders creating several narrow areas.

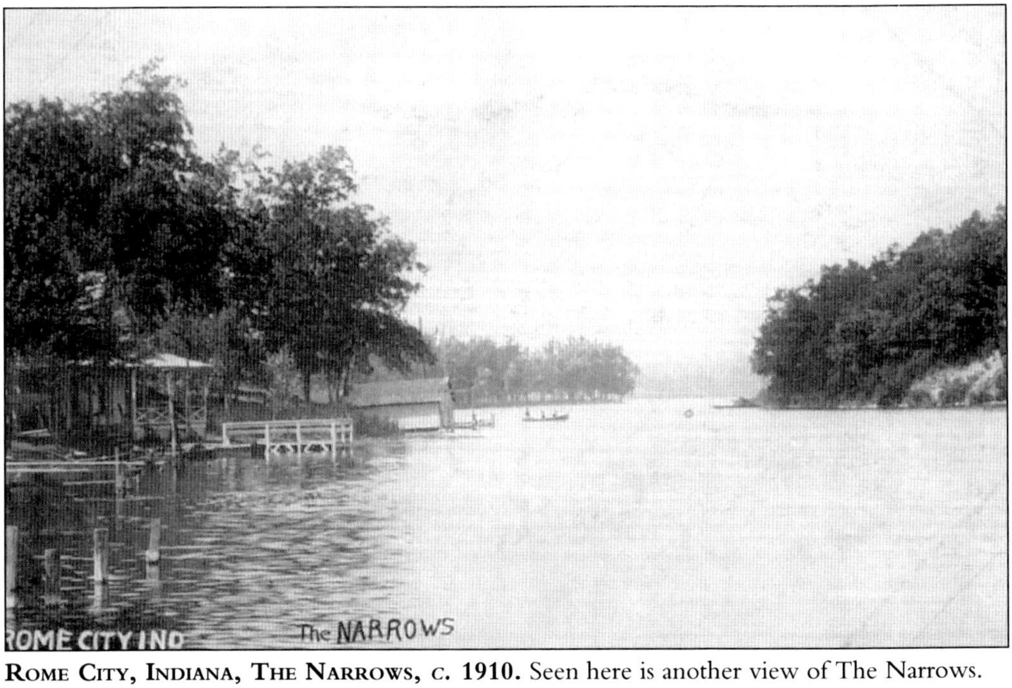

Rome City, Indiana, The Narrows, c. 1910. Seen here is another view of The Narrows.

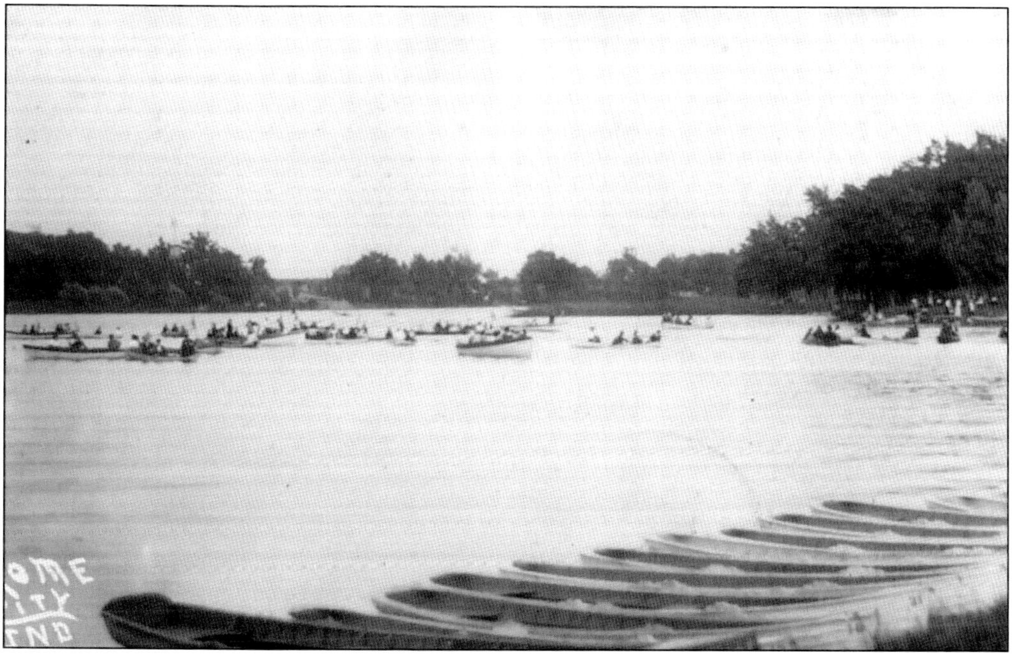

ROME CITY, INDIANA, *c.* 1909. Hundreds of boats were available for rent.

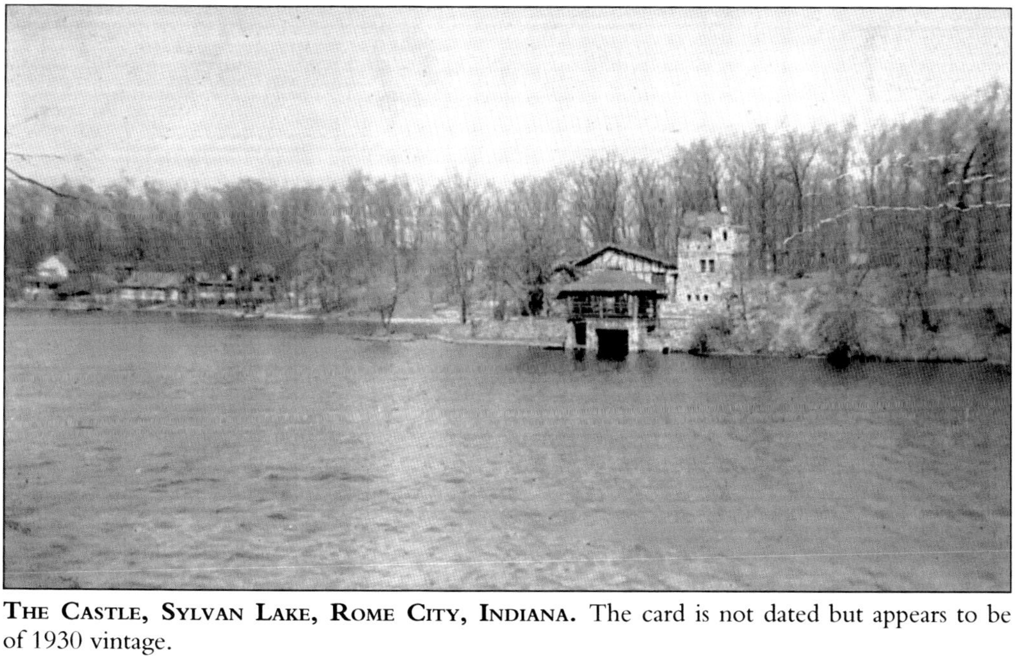

THE CASTLE, SYLVAN LAKE, ROME CITY, INDIANA. The card is not dated but appears to be of 1930 vintage.

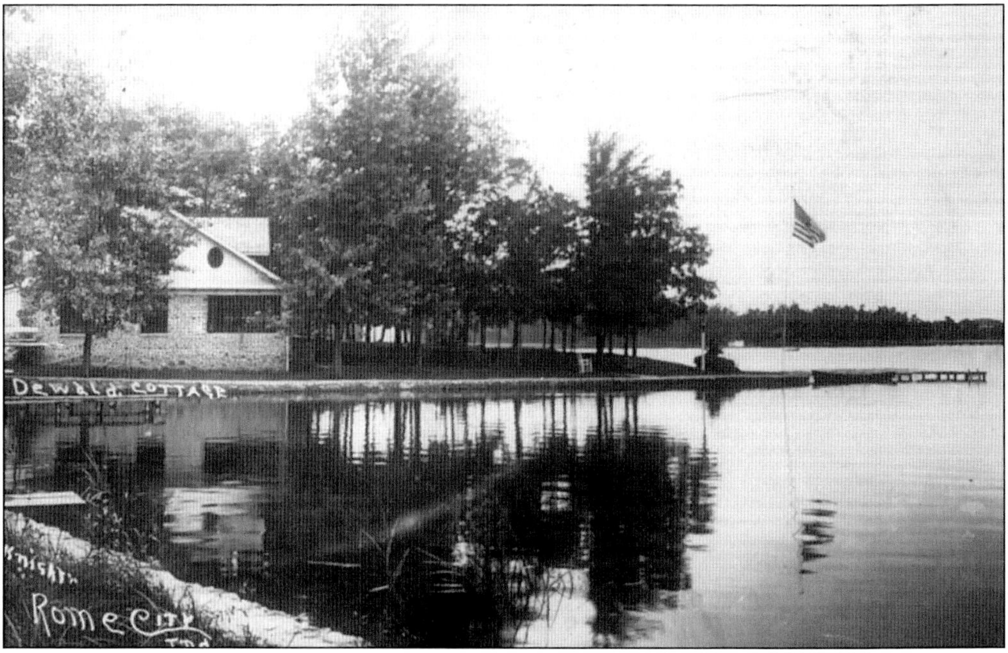

DEWALD COTTAGE, ROME CITY, INDIANA, C. 1910. Certain cottages with their elaborate seawalls, docks, and flag poles were landmarks around the lake.

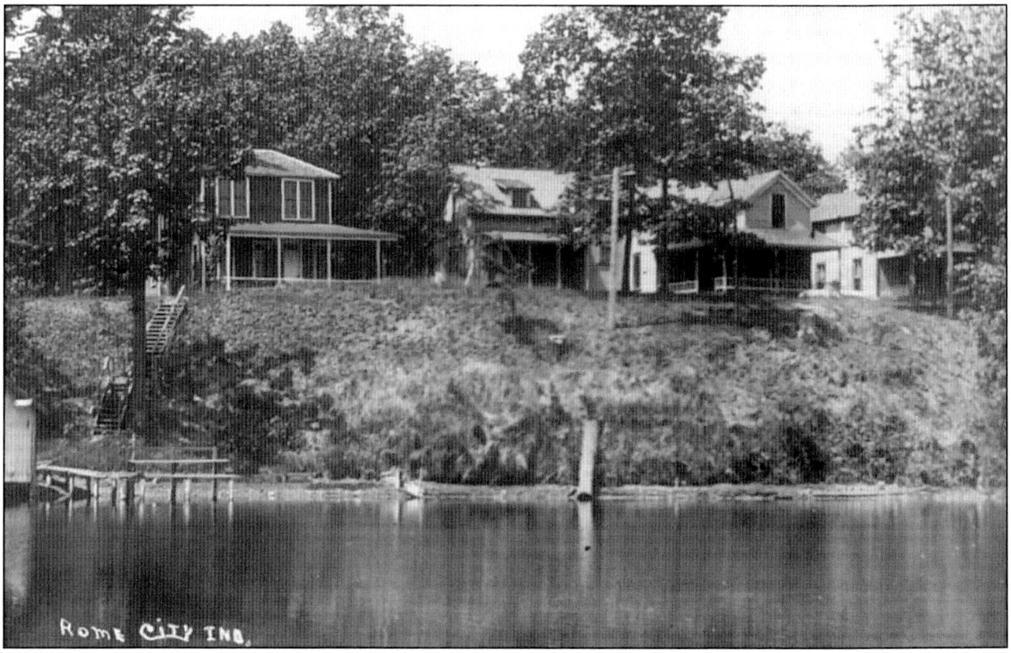

ROME CITY, INDIANA, C. 1910. These cottages on a bluff had a great view of the lake.

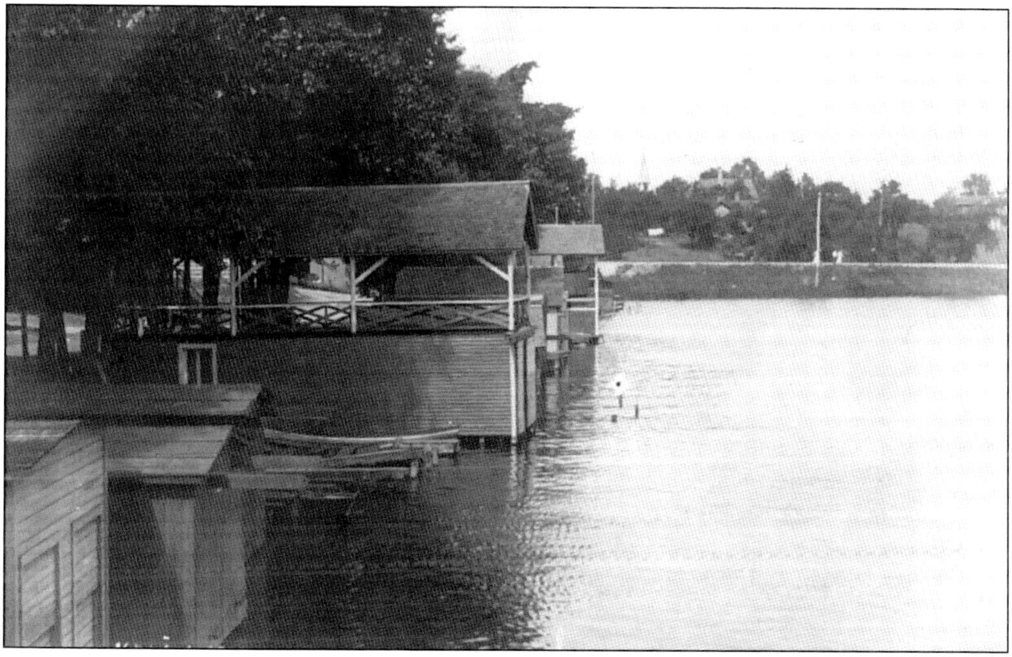

Boat Houses on Sylvan Lake, *c.* 1909. Most people had boat houses to protect their wooden boats when they were not in use. Some had hoists to lift the boat out of the water.

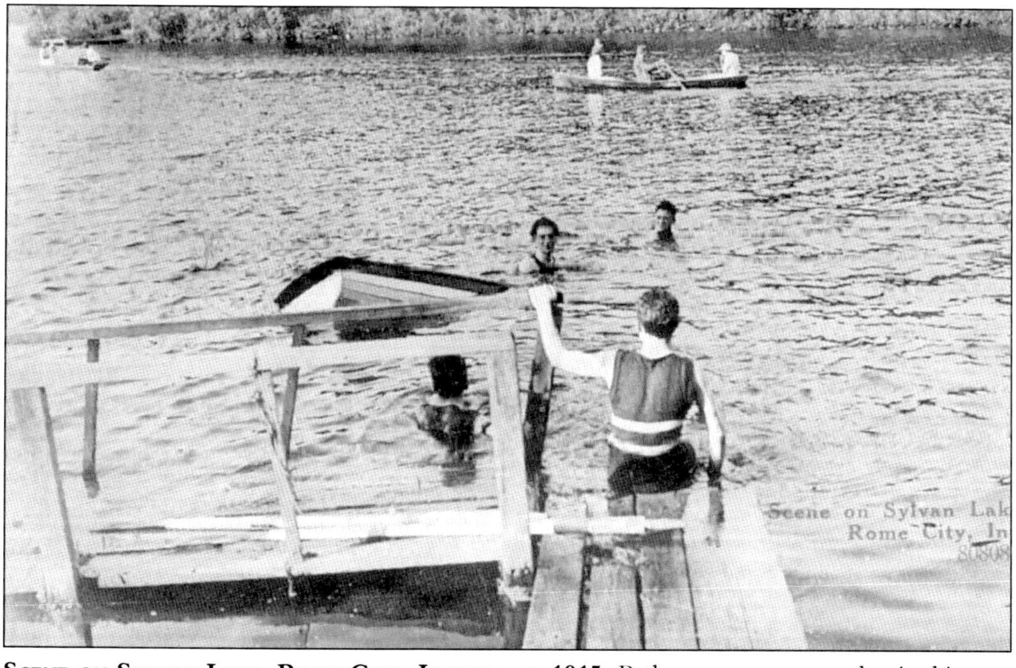

Scene on Sylvan Lake, Rome City, Indiana, *c.* 1915. Bathers were more modest in this era.

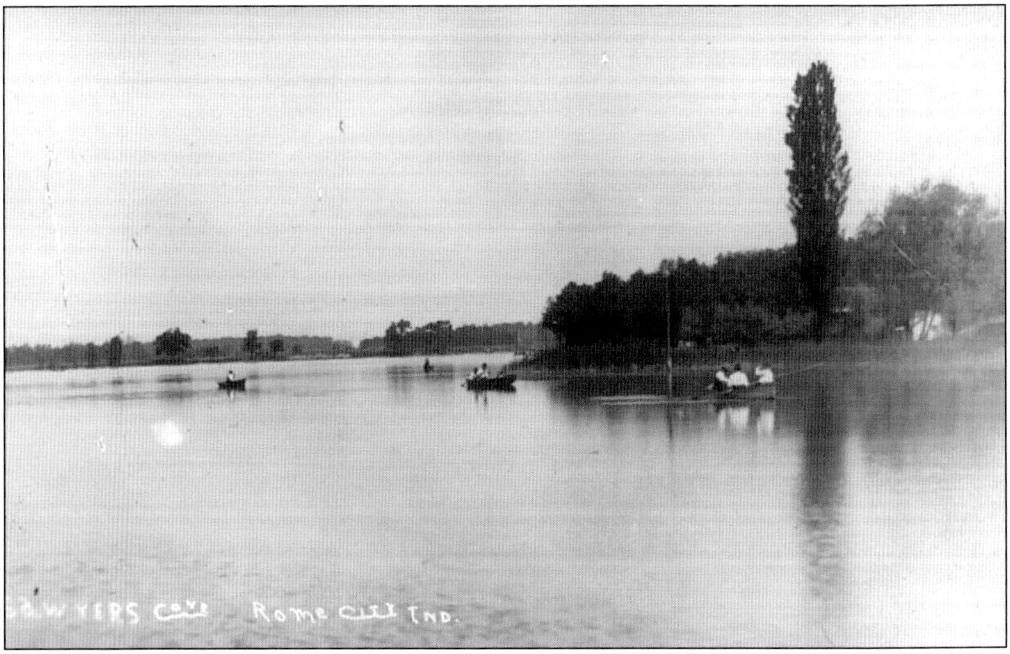

Sawyers Cove, Rome City, Indiana, *c.* 1910.

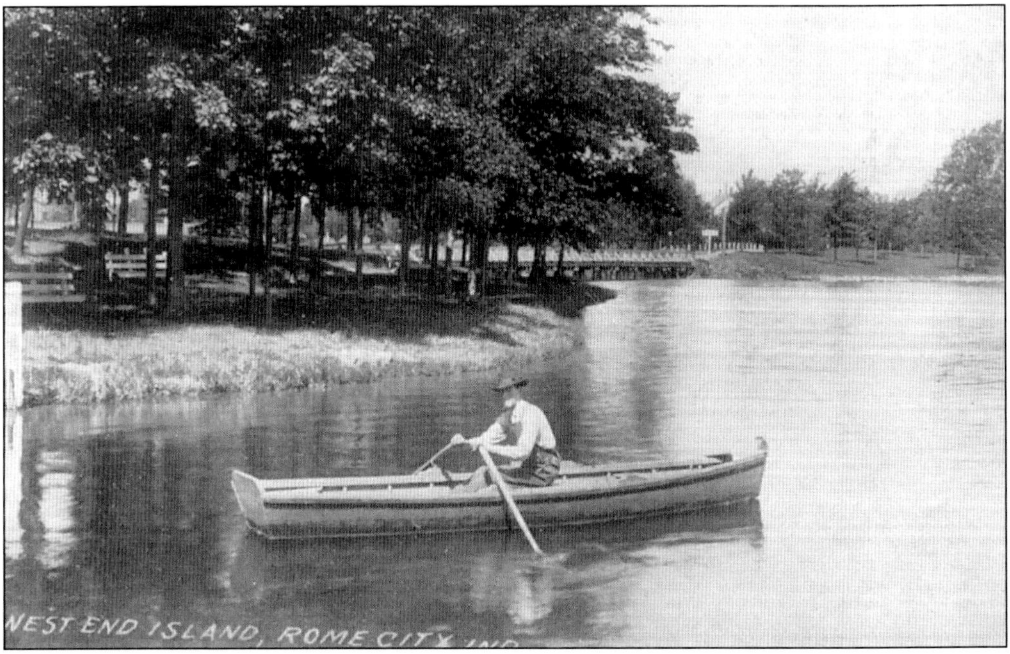

West End Island, Rome City, Indiana, *c.* 1909. The island was also know as "Big Island."

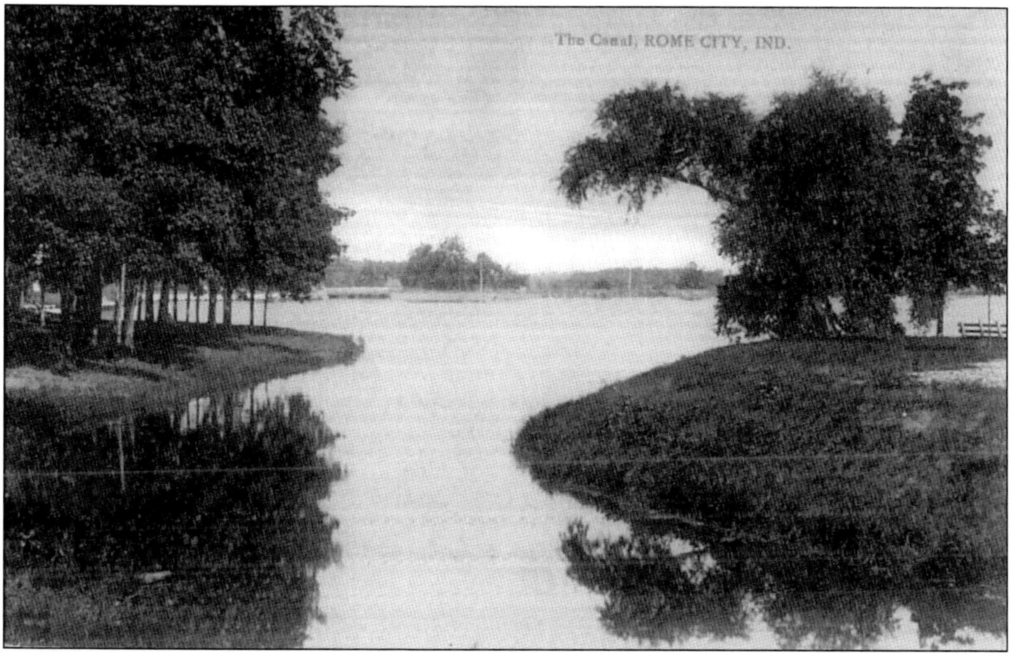

THE CANAL, ROME CITY, INDIANA, *c.* 1910. The canal was a popular place to go in a boat.

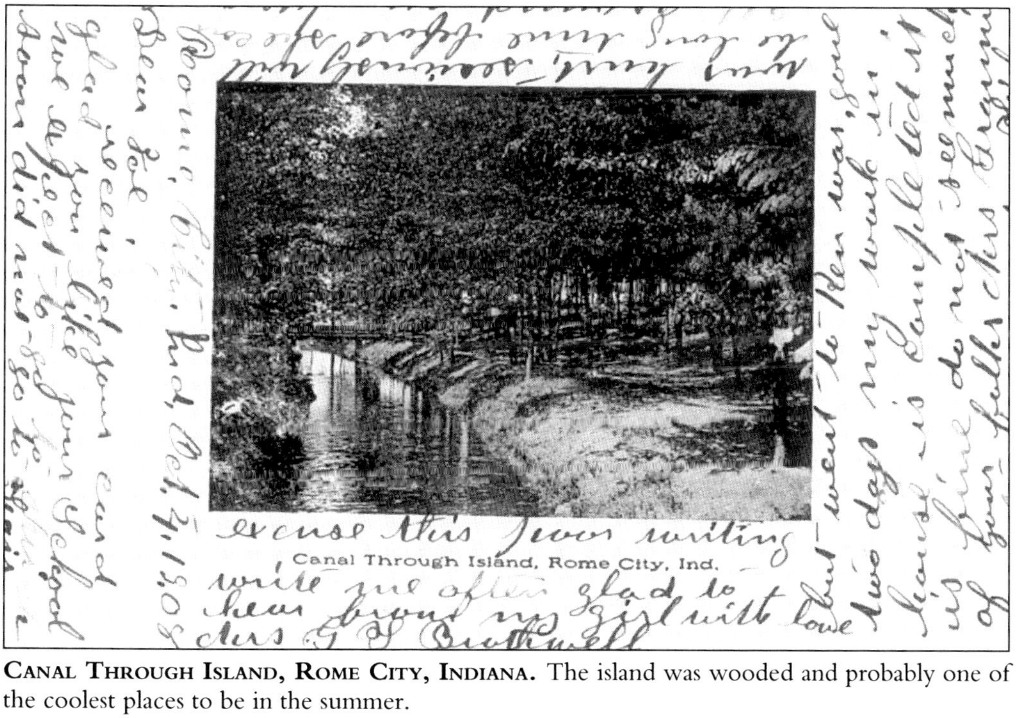

CANAL THROUGH ISLAND, ROME CITY, INDIANA. The island was wooded and probably one of the coolest places to be in the summer.

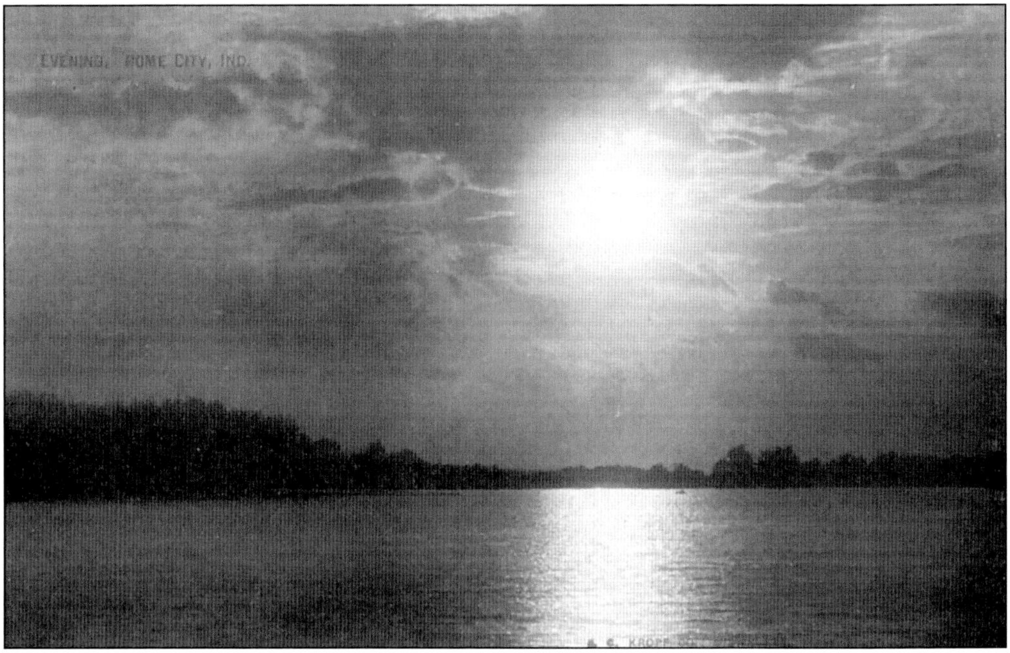

EVENING, ROME CITY, INDIANA. Seen here is a moonlight view.

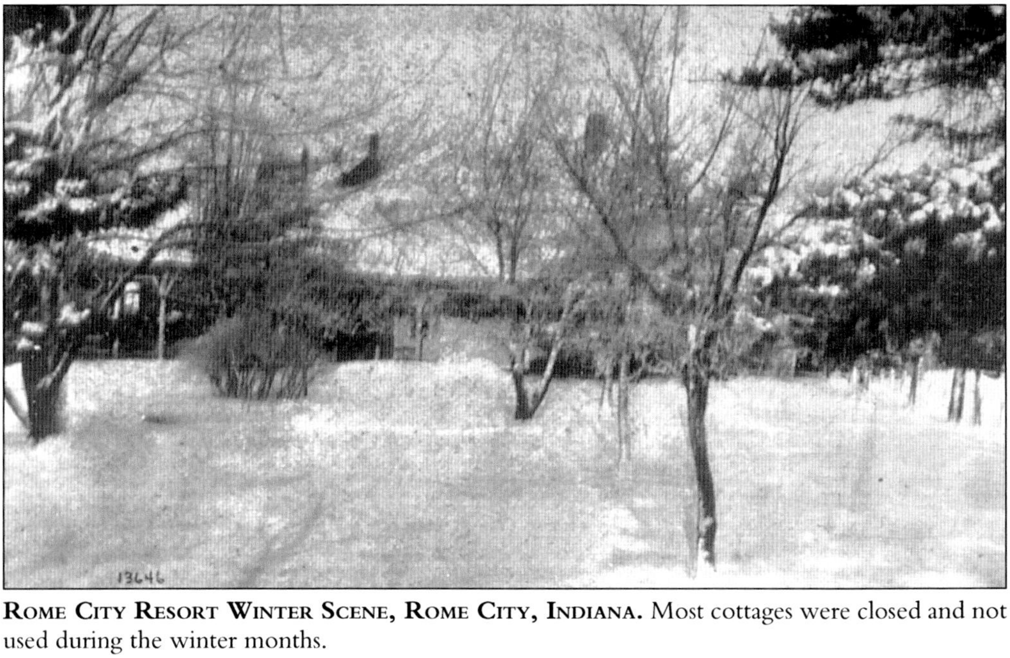

ROME CITY RESORT WINTER SCENE, ROME CITY, INDIANA. Most cottages were closed and not used during the winter months.

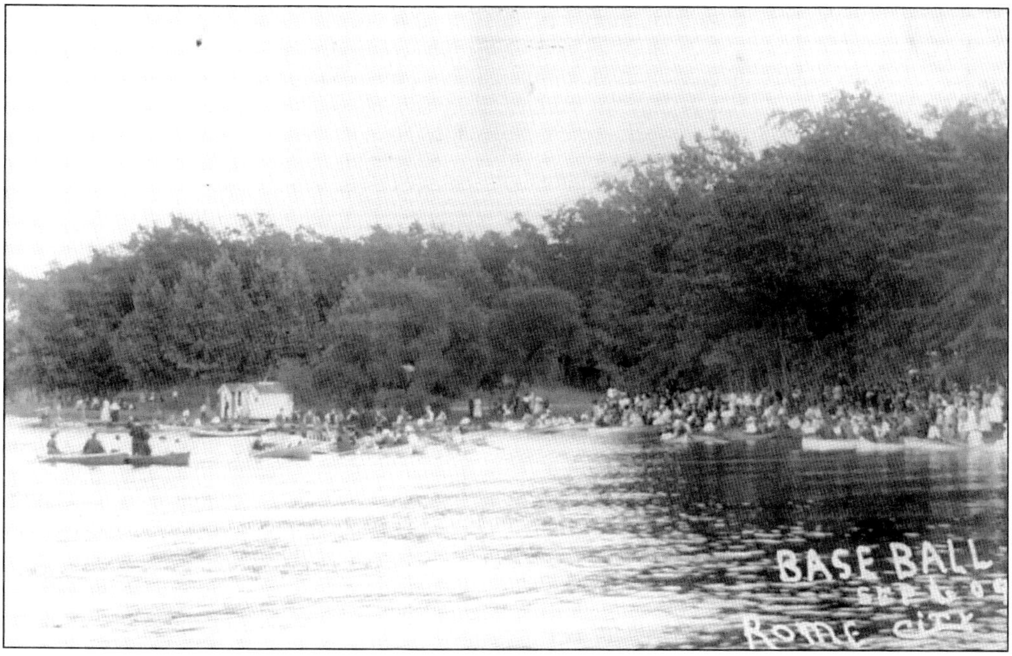

Baseball, September 6, 1909, Rome City, Indiana. A large crowd assembled for this event. Was this baseball played on the water?

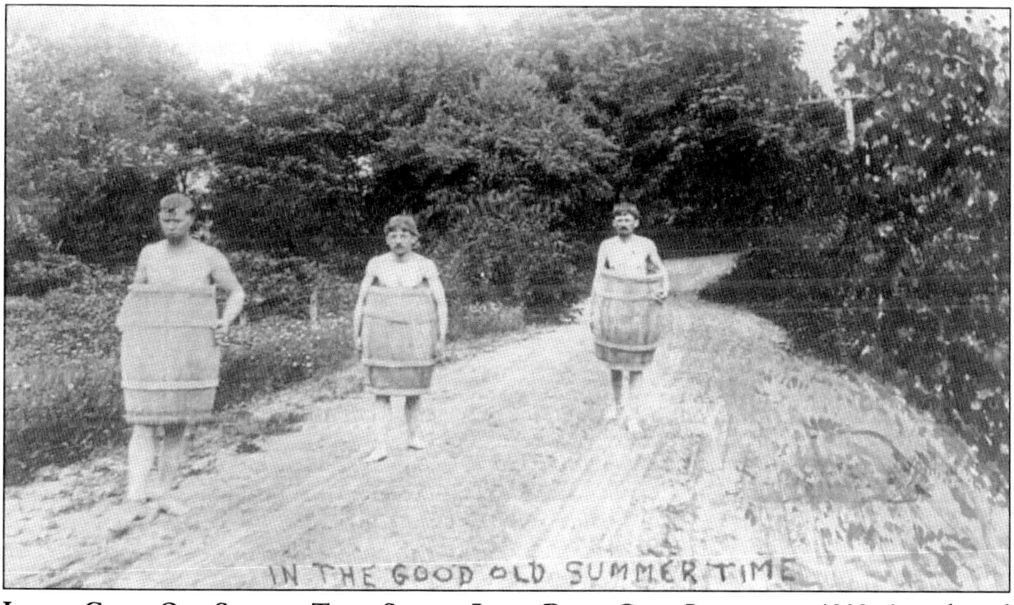

In the Good Old Summer Time, Sylvan Lake, Rome City, Indiana, *c.* 1909. A stock card with a local imprint.

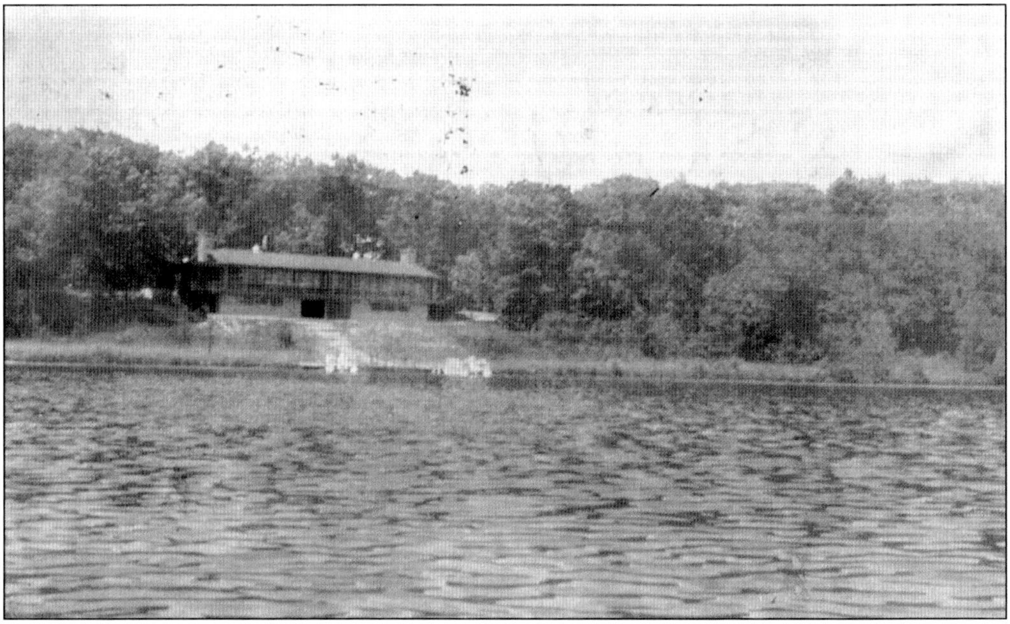

Silver Beaver Lodge, Camp Big Island, Rome City, Indiana. In later years the "Big Island" was used as a Boy Scout Camp.

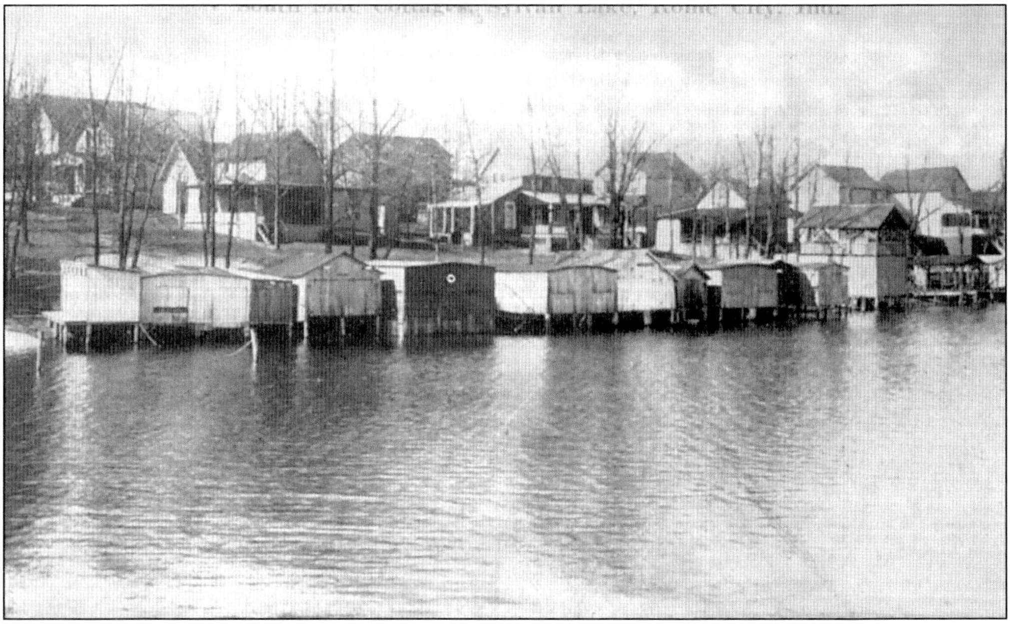

South Side Cottages, Sylvan Lake, Rome City, Indiana. The ramshackle boat houses tended to spoil the view of the lake.

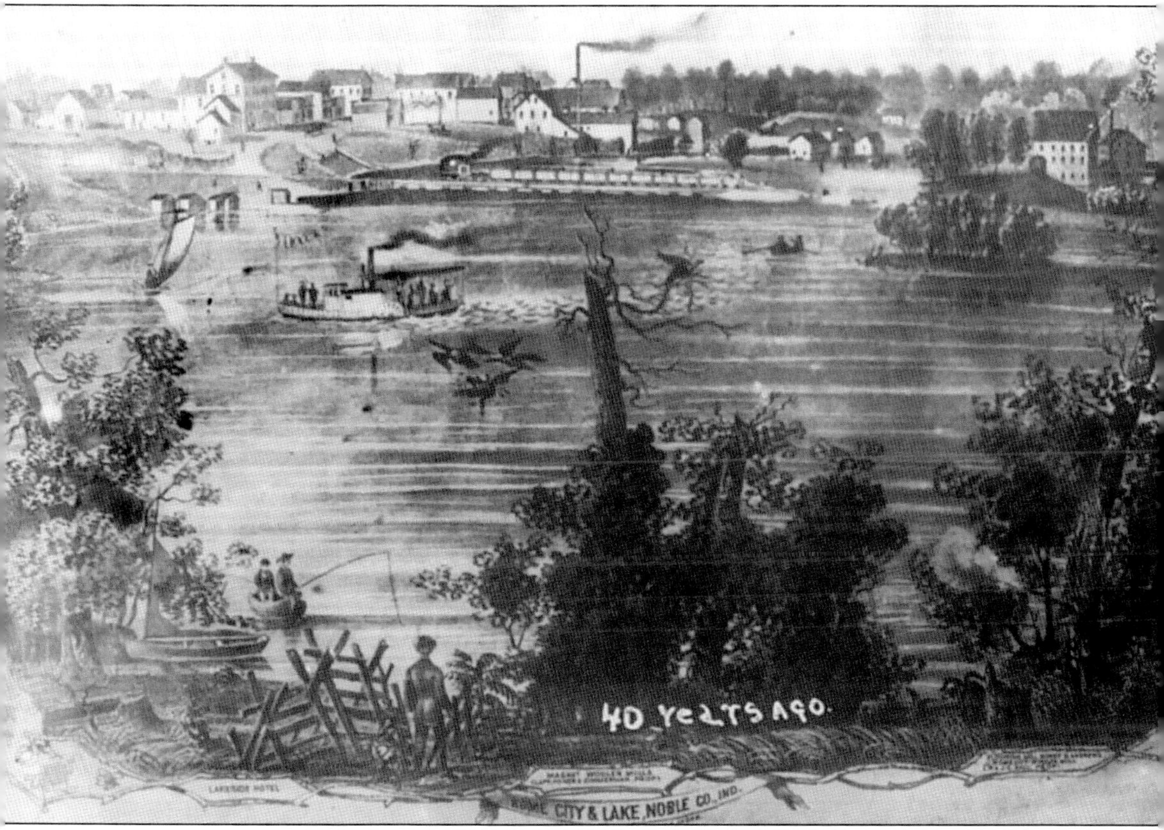

ROME CITY & LAKE, NOBLE COUNTY, INDIANA, *c.* 1880. This is a composite lithograph from the Noble County Atlas showing the village and lake.

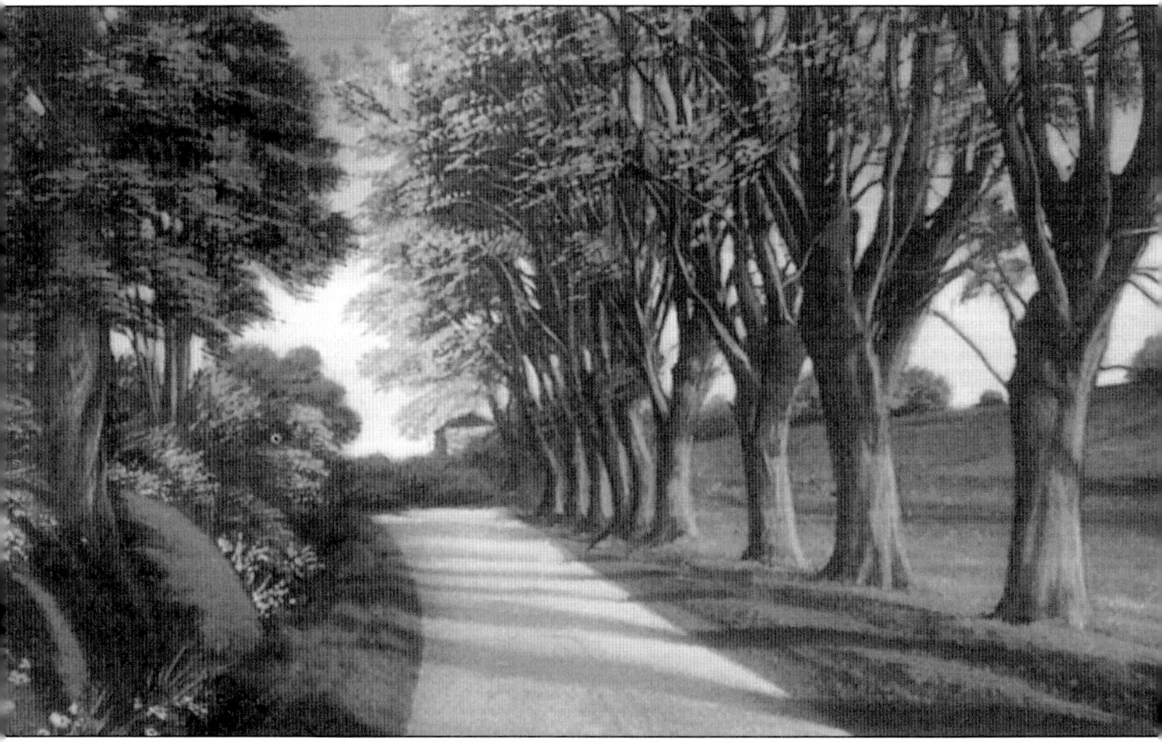

Greetings from Rome City, Indiana. This was a painting of an idyllic scene that could be imprinted with the name of any town.

Eight

SWAN

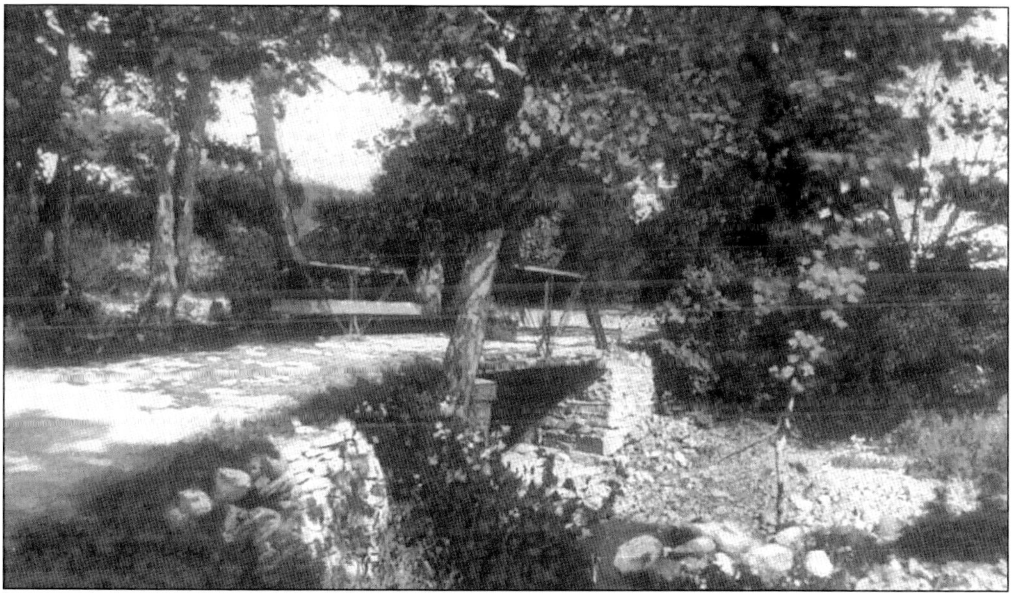

SCENE NEAR SWAN, INDIANA, *c.* 1917. This is probably not a scene near Swan, Indiana. It appears to be a stock card which was used for many localities.

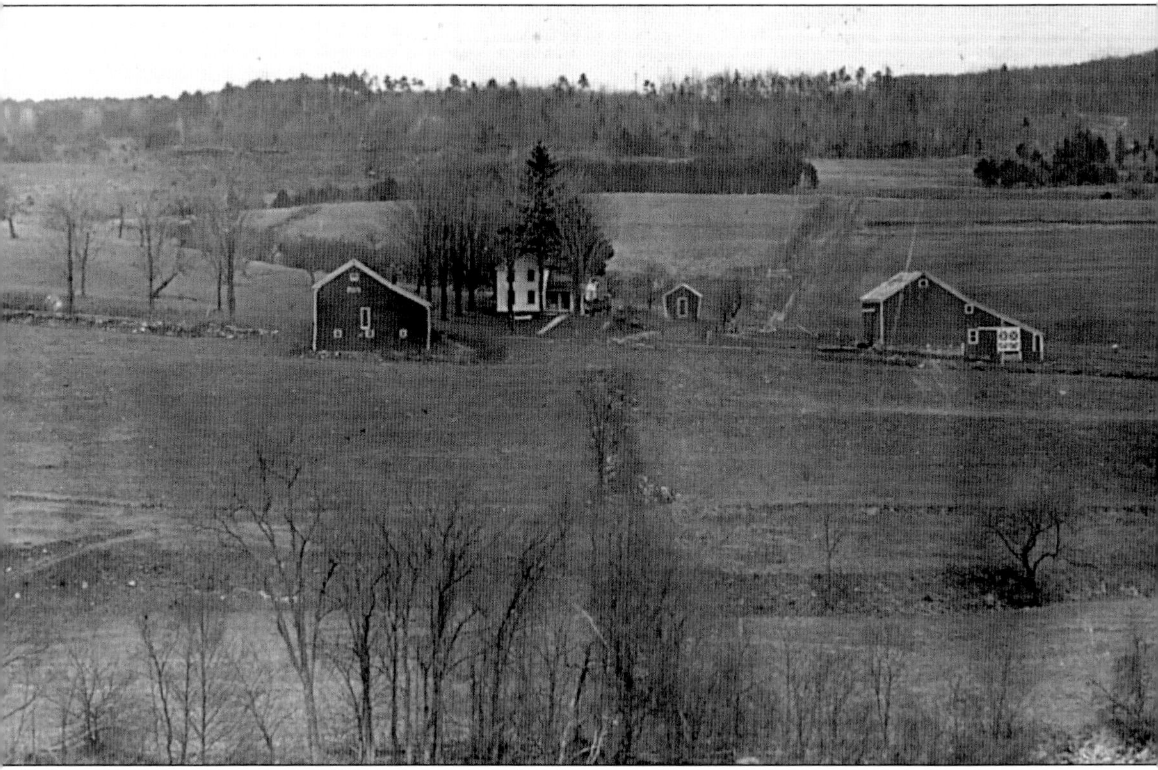

UNTITLED. Seen here is a farm scene in Noble County. The 95-acre farm was for sale for $5,000.

Nine

Wolcottville

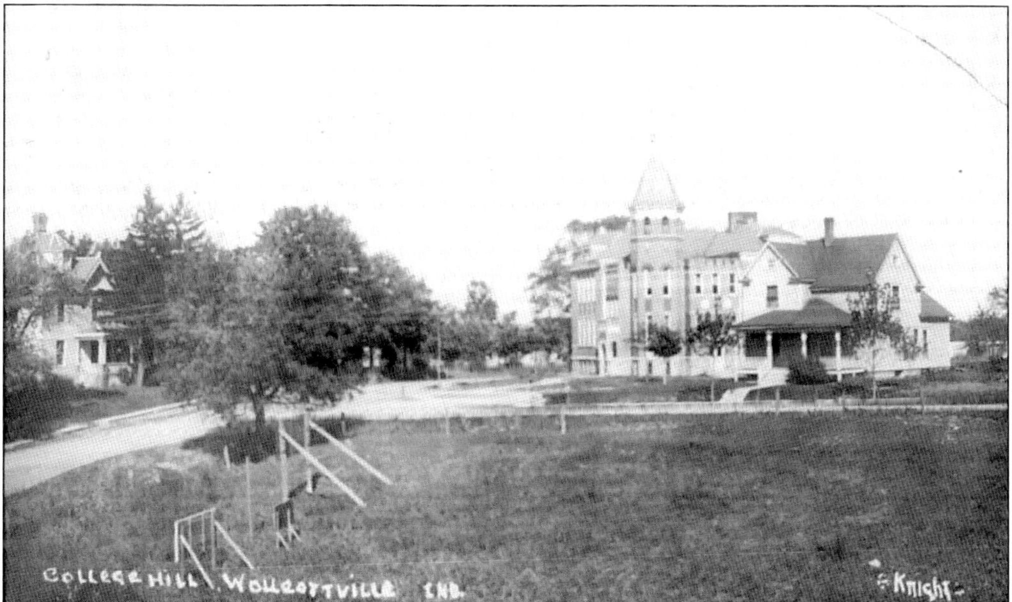

College Hill, Wolcottville, Indiana. The "College" was a landmark in Wolcottville.

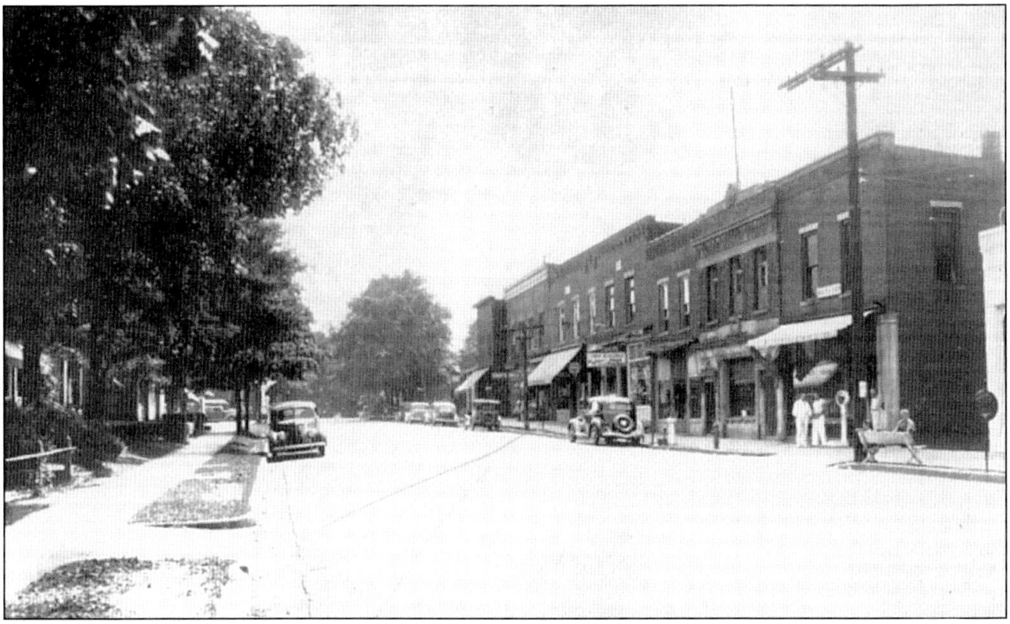

MAIN STREET, WOLCOTTVILLE, INDIANA, *c.* 1940. Seen here is a typical small town Main Street.

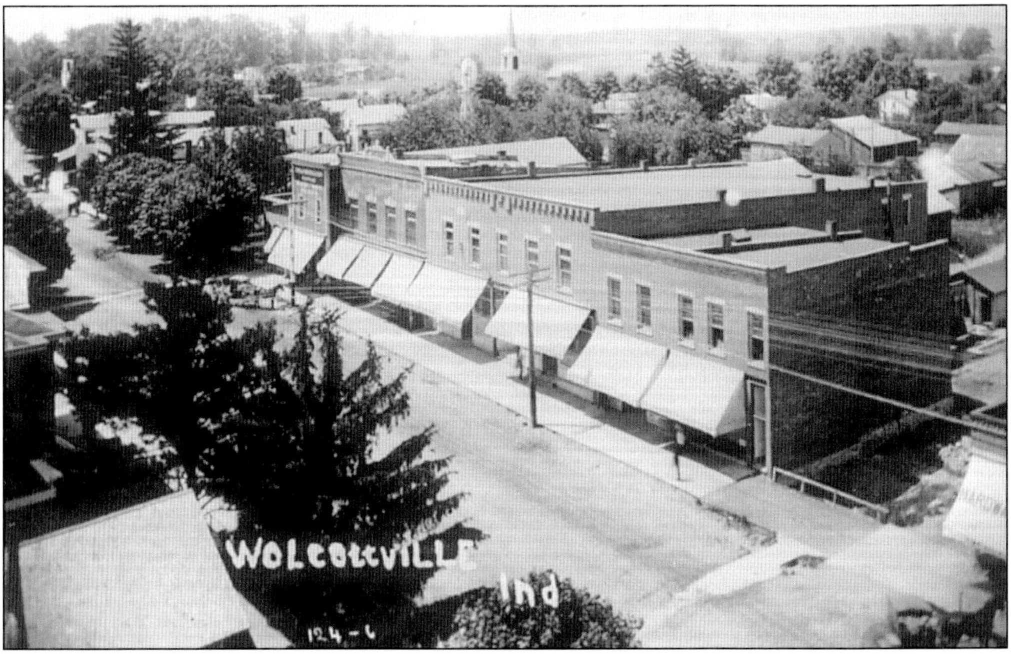

WOLCOTTVILLE, INDIANA, *c.* 1910. Note the windmill in center background.

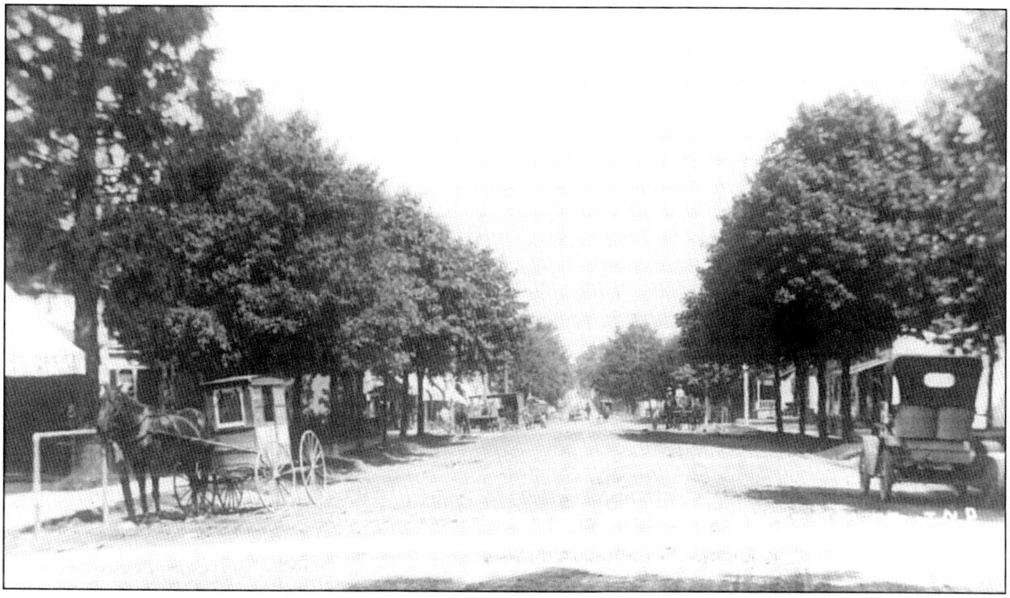

MAIN STREET, WOLCOTTVILLE, INDIANA. There was only one automobile among all the horsedrawn vehicles.

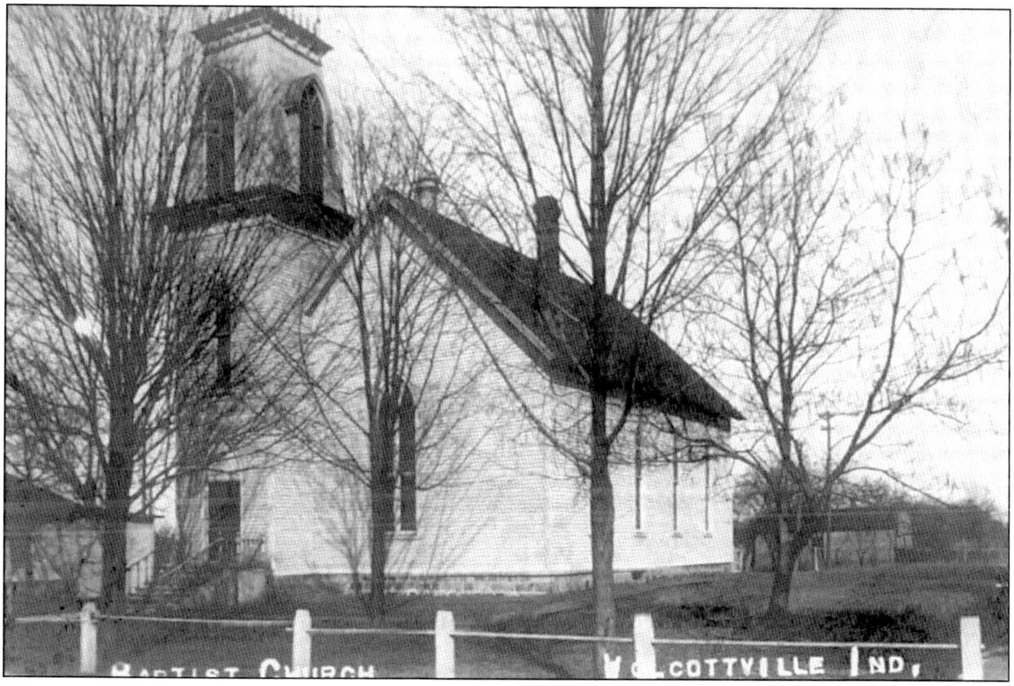

BAPTIST CHURCH, WOLCOTTVILLE, INDIANA, *c.* 1907. The message states, "Dear mother, You never will let Henry and I go away together again will you. Henry beat me fishing yesterday so had to stay to get a head. We are coming home Sat. noon sure. Feel fine and having a good time. We walked over here to buy a purchase for Henry since he decided to stay. We are going fishing this afternoon, I had to get some cream for my rare-bud to thrive upon. Hope you all success at your social. But had to stay. Bertha."

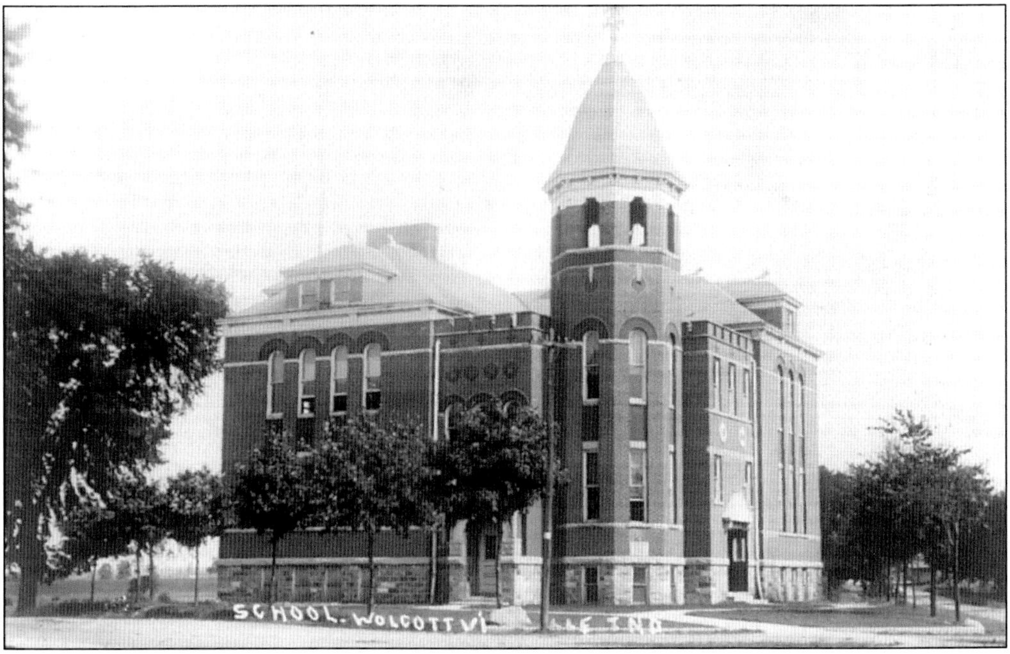

SCHOOL, WOLCOTTVILLE, INDIANA. The bell tower housed a large cast bell to call the children to school and from recess.

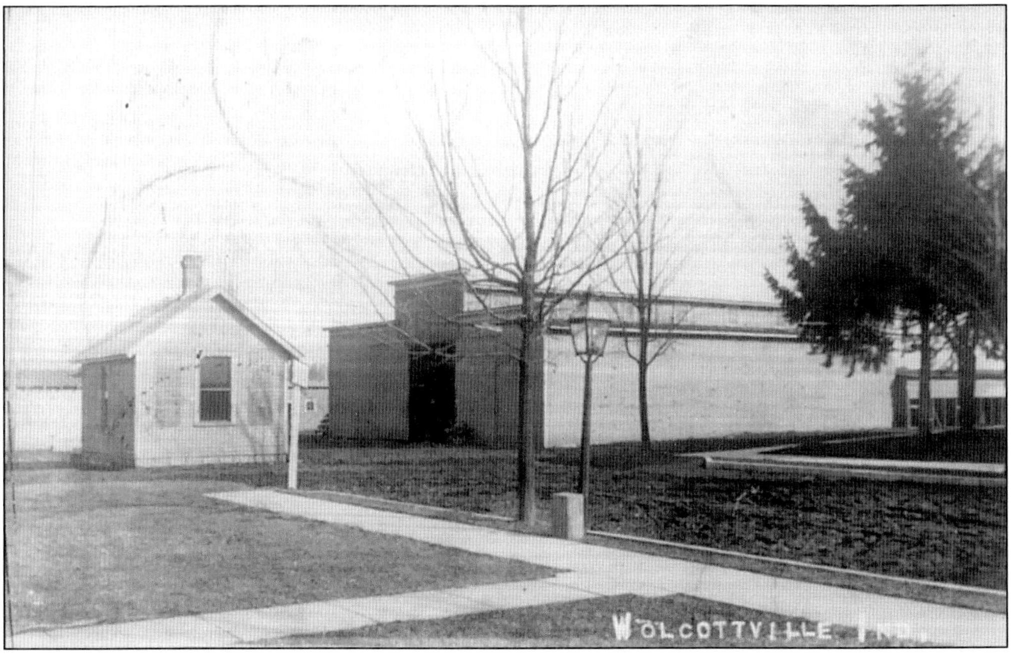

WOLCOTTVILLE, INDIANA, *c.* 1907. The message states, "Dear Mother, All is well am having a good time. Why dont I hear from you? Your son, Ed."

Ten

Wolf Lake

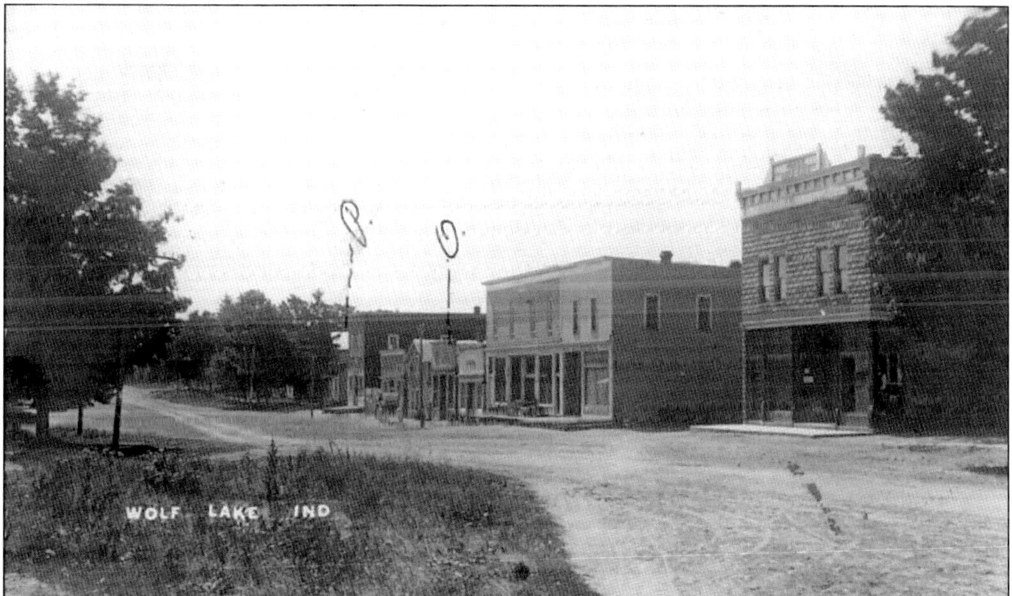

Wolf, Lake, Indiana. The sidewalk in front of the stores are made from rough sawn boards.

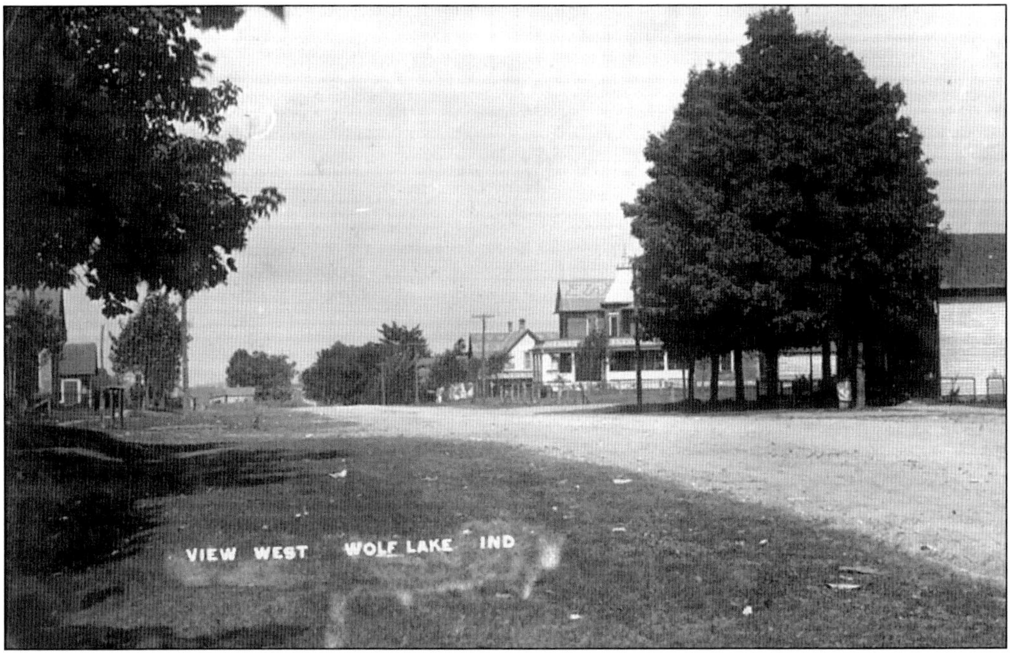

View West, Wolf Lake, Indiana. The large houses were a source of pride for the owners.

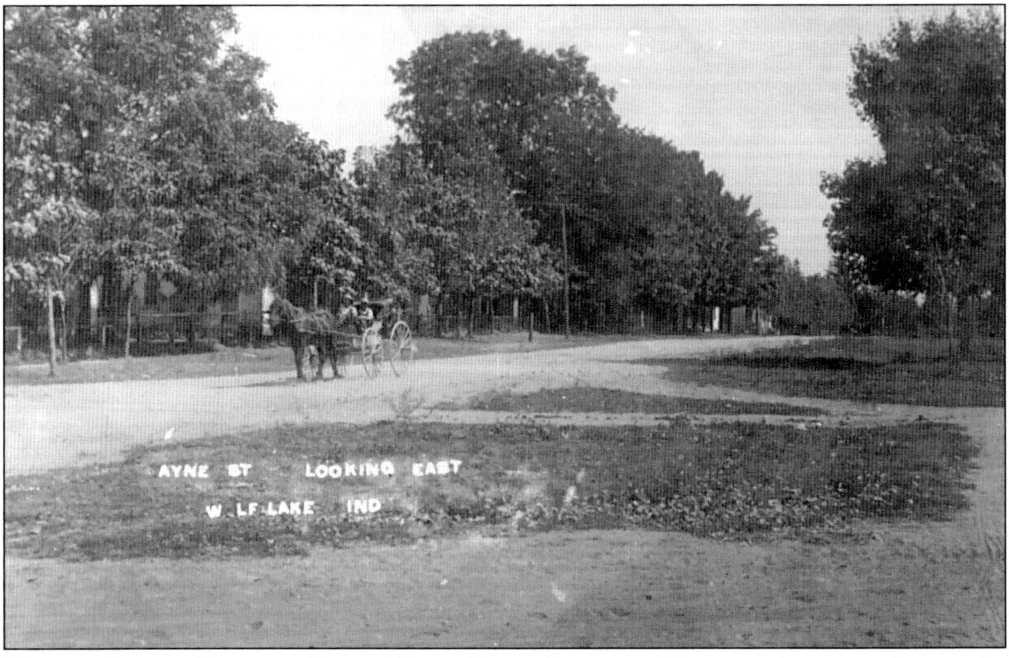

Wayne, Street Looking East, Wolf Lake, Indiana. Most travel was on foot or by horse drawn vehicles.

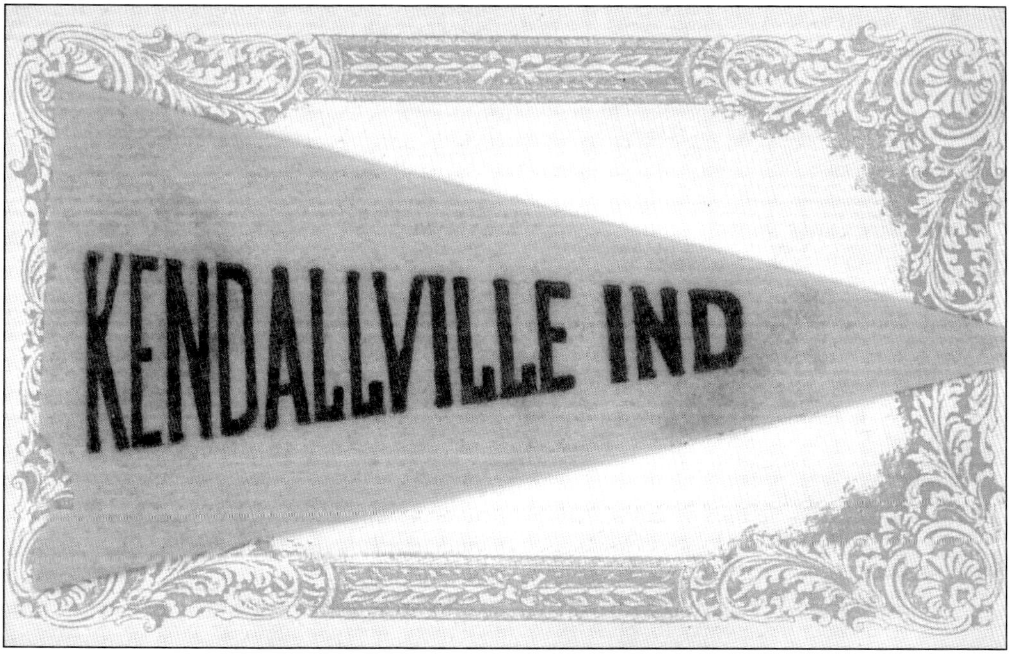

KENDALLVILLE, INDIANA. This is a real felt pennant glued to the postcard.

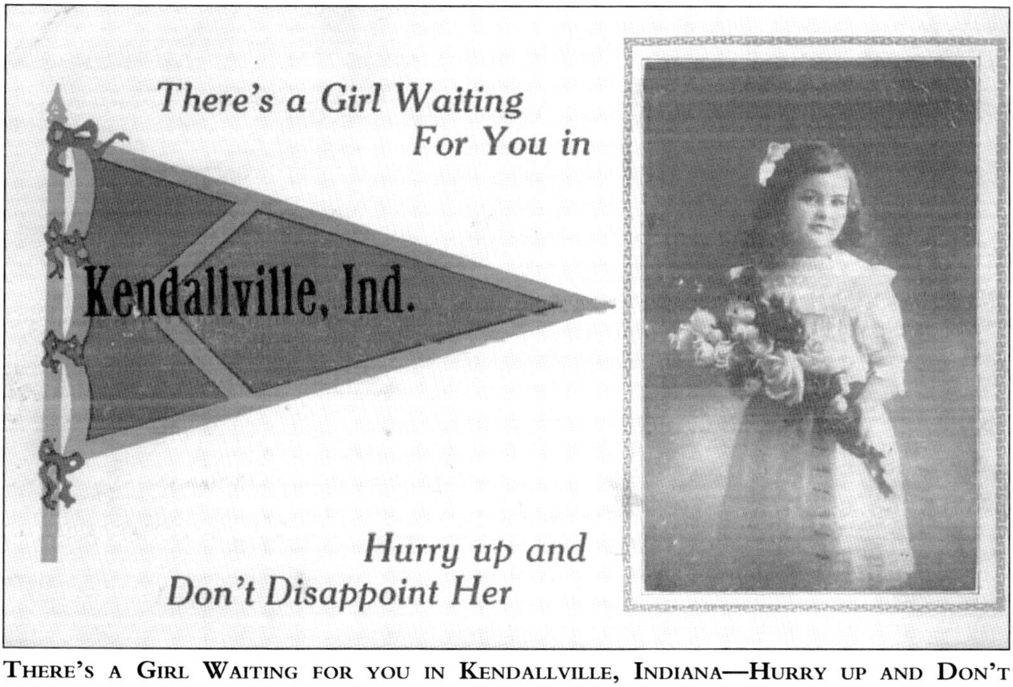

THERE'S A GIRL WAITING FOR YOU IN KENDALLVILLE, INDIANA—HURRY UP AND DON'T DISAPPOINT HER. Dated 1913, the message states, "Kind Friend—In a Hurry—My address is Ninnia Van Lear, Kendallville." Perhaps the message on the front was intended for the addressee—Chas Kline, Ashley, Indiana.

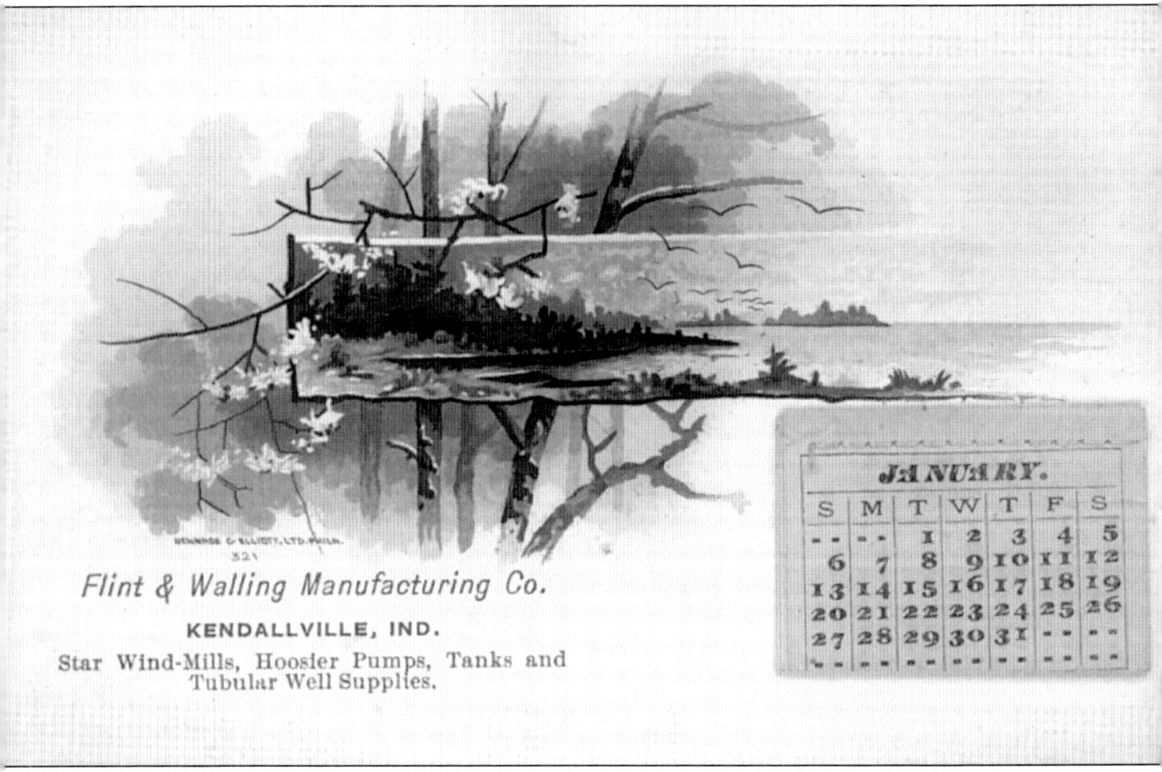

FLINT AND WALLING MANUFACTURING COMPANY. Merchants sent miniature calendars to customers.